The Boston College Church in the 21st Century Series

Patricia De Leeuw and James F. Keenan, S.J.,
General Editors

Titles in this series include:

Sexuality and the U.S. Catholic Church: Crisis and Renewal

Priests for the 21st Century

Inculturation and the Church in North America

Take Heart: Catholic Writers on Hope in Our Time

The Church in the 21st Century Center at Boston College seeks to be a catalyst and resource for the renewal of the Catholic Church in the United States by engaging critical issues facing the Catholic community. Drawing from both the Boston College community and others, its activities currently are focused on four challenges: handing on and sharing the Catholic faith, especially with younger Catholics; fostering relationships built on mutual trust and support among lay men and women, vowed religious, deacons, priests, and bishops; developing an approach to sexuality mindful of human experience and reflective of Catholic tradition; and advancing contemporary reflection on the Catholic intellectual tradition.

Apse Mosaic, depicting the Cross as the Tree of Life,
S. Clemente, Rome, Italy.
Photo credit: Scala/Art Resource, NY.

HANDING ON THE FAITH

The Church's Mission and Challenge

ROBERT P. IMBELLI, EDITOR

A Herder & Herder Book
The Crossroad Publishing Company
New York

The Crossroad Publishing Company
16 Penn Plaza – 481 Eighth Avenue, Suite 1550
New York, NY 10001

Printed in the United States of America

The text of this book is set in 10.5/14 Sabon.

Library of Congress Cataloging-in-Publication Data

Handing on the faith : the church's mission and challenge / edited by Robert P. Imbelli.
    p. cm. – (Church in the 21st century ; v. 1)
  "A Herder & Herder book."
  Includes bibliographical references and index.
  ISBN-13: 978-0-8245-2409-8 (alk. paper)
  ISBN-10: 0-8245-2409-8 (alk. paper)
  1. Mission of the church. 2. Catholic Church – Doctrines. I. Imbelli,
Robert P. II. Title. III. Series.
BX1746.H36 2006
266′.2 – dc22

                                  2006021808

1 2 3 4 5 6 7 8 9 10   12 11 10 09 08 07 06

In Memory of Pope John Paul II
Who, by Word and Witness,
Spent himself, Handing on the Faith

Contents

Part Three
COMMUNICATING THE FAITH

Beginning the Conversation

ROBERT P. IMBELLI

W HEN PRESIDENT William P. Leahy, S.J., launched "The Church
in the 21st Century Initiative,"[1] he identified, as one of its key
concerns, "handing on the faith to future generations." This challenge
is, of course, central to the mission of a Catholic university and crucial
to the very survival of the Church.

As an initial contribution to this ongoing endeavor, I had the privilege of organizing and hosting a conference that met at Boston College
for two days of conversation and spirited exchange: September 17–18,
2004. Some of the features that characterized the conference bear mentioning. First, it was limited to nineteen participants who came having
read papers prepared and distributed beforehand. The aim was to use
the time together to promote a conversation that allowed positions to be
engaged in a serious and sustained fashion. Two of the group, Paul Baumann and John Garvey, served as facilitators, focusing the conversation,
suggesting connections, probing implications. This formal conversation
then continued over meals and more informal discussions.

Second, though a majority of the participants came from colleges and
universities, bringing academic competence in theology, sociology, history, and religious education, we were eager to have several bishops as
full participants in the conversation to test insights and proposals from
the vantage of their pastoral experience and concern. Thus, in a small
but significant way, we sought to model fruitful and mutually beneficial
collaboration between bishops and academicians. Indeed, the conviction
underlying the conversation, as it does the entire enterprise of the Church
in the 21st Century, is the inseparable connection between the pastoral
and the theological.

Finally, the respectful conversations of the two days, the appreciative and discerning exchange of words, were placed in the context of a mutual listening to the Word. Each of the two days began with an adapted form of the Liturgy of the Hours; and the conference concluded with the celebration of the Eucharist. Dialogue began and culminated in doxology.[2] As a powerful reminder of the importance of image and the aesthetic in handing on the faith, a replica of the great twelfth-century mosaic of the Cross of Christ as the tree of life, fecundating the new creation (from the Church of San Clemente in Rome), was displayed prominently in our conference room. It serves as the frontispiece of this volume.

Though the actual conference was limited to the invited participants, integral to it was a public presentation, a keynote address by the Most Reverend Sean P. O'Malley, O.F.M. Cap., Archbishop of Boston. Archbishop (now Cardinal) O'Malley's talk, entitled "Passing on the Faith," was delivered at St. John the Evangelist Church in Wellesley, Massachusetts, on Friday evening, September 17, 2004. His address manifested both in its substance and in its parish context the intimate union of the pastoral and the theological.[3]

No conversation exists in a vacuum. Environment, both physical and human, plays a distinct role in its success. For their generosity in providing hospitality in a most congenial setting, sincere gratitude to William P. Leahy, S.J., President of Boston College; to Robert Newton, Special Assistant to the President; to Rose Mary Donahue, Assistant to the President; and to Dawn Overstreet, Assistant Director of the Church in the 21st Century Center. For their attention to the many details of support and logistics during the days of the conference, Michon Matthiesen, Randall Rosenberg, and Peter Fritz, graduate students in the Theology Department, deserve special thanks. Finally, Kevin Vander Schel, a graduate student in the Theology Department, provided invaluable assistance in the preparation of the manuscript.

September 3, 2006
Feast of St. Gregory the Great

Authors and Participants

R. Scott Appleby, Professor of History, University of Notre Dame

Reverend Robert Barron, Professor of Theology, University of St. Mary of the Lake

Paul Baumann, Editor, *Commonweal* Magazine

John Cavadini, Chair, Department of Theology, University of Notre Dame

Most Reverend Blase Cupich, Bishop of Rapid City, South Dakota

William Dinges, Associate Professor of Religious Studies, Catholic University of America

John Garvey, Esq., Dean, Boston College Law School

Paul J. Griffiths, Schmitt Chair of Catholic Studies, University of Illinois at Chicago

Thomas Groome, Director, Institute of Religious Education and Pastoral Ministry, Boston College

Reverend Michael Himes, Professor of Theology, Boston College

Reverend Robert Imbelli, Associate Professor of Theology, Boston College

Luke Timothy Johnson, Robert W. Woodruff Distinguished Professor of New Testament and Christian Origins, Candler School of Theology, Emory University

Sister Mary Johnson, SNDdeN, Professor of Sociology and Religious Studies, Emmanuel College

Most Reverend Gerard Kicanas, Bishop of Tucson, Arizona

Jeremy Langford, Director of Publications and Public Relations, Chicago Province of the Society of Jesus

Most Reverend Ricardo Ramírez, C.S.B., Bishop of Las Cruces, New Mexico

Christopher Ruddy, Assistant Professor of Theology, University of St. Thomas in St. Paul

Deborah Ruddy, Assistant Professor of Catholic Studies and Director of the Program in Catholic Social Teaching and Catholic Education, University of St. Thomas in St. Paul

Terrence Tilley, Chair, Department of Theology, Fordham University

Robert Louis Wilken, William R. Keenan Jr. Professor of the History of Christianity, University of Virginia at Charlottesville

Introduction

Discernment, Newness, Transformation

Musings Inspired by a Conference

ROBERT P. IMBELLI

I N APPROACHING SO VAST and crucial a topic as "Handing on the Faith," it seemed helpful to distinguish three inseparable aspects of the one gift and task we face. What is the concrete context in which this vital ecclesial ministry transpires? What is the substance of the faith, the promise of the hope that we seek to transmit? What are apt modes and models of communication for this all-embracing challenge? Hence "context," "content," and "communication" organized our labors and focused our reflection.

However, it quickly became clear that to each of the areas we brought explicit or, more often, implicit suppositions regarding the other two. The richness of the conversation stemmed from the different "readings" of each of the three areas on the part of the participants. Certainly, many of the readings bore a "family resemblance" among themselves. Others, though divergent, were clearly complementary. Finally, to the surprise of no one, a few were divergent. John Cavadini in the "After-word" has sought to capture some of this harmony and disharmony in his personal post-conference reflections. The two days together were only intended to begin a conversation that we hope this book will continue to promote.

In this "Introduction" I ponder some of the issues engaged, considering them under the headings "discernment," "newness," and "transformation." I hope, thereby, to offer some vantage upon ecclesial tradition and cultural formation as they interact in the hearts and minds of each of us.

Discernment

I urge you, brothers and sisters, by the mercies of God, to offer your
bodies as a living sacrifice, holy and pleasing to God, your spiritual
worship. Do not conform yourself to this age, but be transformed
by the renewal of your mind, that you may discern what is the will
of God, what is good and pleasing and perfect. (Rom 12:1, 2)[1]

Although the contemporary cultural and societal context of the United
States is indeed diverse and multiform, are there overarching influences,
orientations, sensibilities that characterize the context in which the Gospel must be proclaimed and the ecclesial catechumenate unfold? In
our conversations the term "cultural catechumenate" quickly became
the preferred designation to indicate the power and pervasiveness of
this cultural influence, fueled by market capitalism and propagated by
advertising. The participants differed somewhat in their assessment of
the complex economic and intellectual situation: some inclined to a
more critical, others to a more appreciative reading of "the signs of the
times."

Whatever the final judgment on this score, Paul Griffiths's acute analysis of culture's role in *the shaping of desire* and thus of our very selves
provides a very helpful heuristic, both for considering the culture and for
guiding Christian formation. One crucial need, in my view, is to restore
the ancient practice of discernment of spirits to the very forefront of
preaching and catechesis today. In the post-Vatican II era of renewed
appreciation for the role and responsibility of the laity, it is imperative
for the entire people of God to mature in its task of becoming skilled
diagnosticians in matters of the Spirit.

It is, certainly, true that the Catholic tradition has steadfastly affirmed
that God's image in the human is not eradicated by sin. Hence there
is a native optimism to Catholicism — native, but not naïve! For that
same tradition also displays a critical realism regarding the effects of
sin in us, both personal and institutional. Sin desensitizes and deforms
conscience; darkening the mind by self-serving illusions, binding the will
by self-gratifying addictions.

Brian Daley, S.J., drawing upon the rich heritage of the Ignatian tradition of spiritual discernment, puts it well, in words equally applicable
to individuals and communities.

Granted that the human heart does instinctively reach out for the God it glimpses behind the beauty and goodness of the world, still the heart is all too easily led to settle for substitutes: for causes, for the latest psychological or pseudo-religious fad, for religious experience in itself, rather than to seeking God in all his majestic, demanding otherness. Our spiritual instinct, our spiritual yearning, needs always to be subjected to careful discernment, to be tested by the norms of faith, if we are to be confident that what we are seeking, and what we are offering to each other, is not simply another image of ourselves, but is the God who is ultimately real.[2]

Long before postmodern scholarship advocated the exercise of a "hermeneutics of suspicion," the great masters of the Christian spiritual tradition spoke of the need to direct a hermeneutics of suspicion, in the first instance, towards oneself. They recognized the deep-seated propensity in each of us to self-deception and the ongoing call of the Gospel to *metanoia*, conversion.[3]

In retrospect, the theme of "conversion," so central to the proclamation and practice of the New Testament, should have played a more prominent role in our deliberations. Perhaps it was taken for granted. Yet the widespread appeal in contemporary North American culture to "experience," often construed in that excessively individualistic sense that William Dinges documents, gives one pause. Presumably, if conversion is the narrow gate that opens upon the Christian Way, "my experience" too will need radical re-orientation, my "world of meaning and value" (to borrow a phrase of Bernard Lonergan, S.J.) will require the sort of "consciousness raising" that the very word *metanoia* enshrines. The transformed experience that is the fruit of conversion finds summary expression in the letters of Paul as well as in the Gospel narratives by the exultant exclamation: "I once was blind, but now I see!"[4]

If the practice of discernment is thus central to Christian life and to the handing on of Christian faith, the urgent issue that arises is: what are the criteria for discernment, what is the measure of authentic experience? The very wellspring of Christian discernment of spirits is Paul's First Letter to the Corinthians. Paul writes: "I tell you that nobody speaking by the spirit of God says, 'Jesus be accursed.' And no one can say, 'Jesus is Lord,' except by the Holy Spirit" (1 Cor 12:3). Two millennia later, the inaugural statement of the Catholic Common Ground Initiative, "Called to Be Catholic: Church in a Time of Peril," faithfully echoes the claim. "Jesus Christ, present in Scripture and sacrament, is central to all that we do; he must always be the measure and not what is measured."[5]

Newness

> Blessed be the God and Father of our Lord Jesus Christ, who in his great mercy gave us a new birth to a living hope through the resurrection of Jesus Christ from the dead. (1 Pt 1:3)

St. Irenaeus, Bishop of Lyons at the end of the second century, has often been called "the first great Catholic theologian." Born in Asia Minor, he witnesses to the Tradition of the undivided Church, both East and West. In opposition to the followers of Marcion who claimed that the Old Testament derived from a different God than the God and Father of the Lord Jesus Christ, he defended the integral unity of both Old and New Testaments, whose source was the one God, Creator and Redeemer. When asked, what then was the "newness" that Christ brought, he responded in a way that recapitulates the conviction of the orthodox Tradition: "Christ brought all newness by bringing Himself."[6] The new covenant is the very person of Jesus Christ. And Christ's newness renews all creation, bearing new life.

As Irenaeus intimates, Christianity is not ultimately a "religion of the book," but a religion of the person, the living Lord Jesus Christ. In this regard it distinguishes itself decisively from both Judaism and Islam. Much of Pope John Paul II's magisterium bears this Irenaean imprint. In his splendid "Apostolic Letter" written on the occasion of the new millennium, John Paul wrote:

> We shall not be saved by a formula, but by a Person, and the assurance which he gives us: I am with you! It is not therefore a matter of inventing a "new program." The program already exists: it is the plan found in the Gospel and the living Tradition, it is the same as ever. Ultimately, it has its center in Christ himself, who is to be known, loved, and imitated, so that in him we may live the life of the Trinity and with him transform history until its fulfillment in the heavenly Jerusalem. This is a program which does not change with shifts of times and cultures, even though it takes account of

time and culture for the sake of true dialogue and effective communication. This program for all times is our program for the Third Millennium.[7]

Handing on the faith, then, is not primarily a handing on of "doctrines" (though these are important), nor even a handing on of practices (though these are indispensable). It is, above all, evoking and fostering an encounter with the living person Jesus Christ. If "witnessing" is key to this, as those who participated in the conference are agreed, then it must be in the manner of John the Baptist who points away from self to the Bridegroom.

In a work that has become a contemporary classic Ronald Rolheiser has expressed this central point with verve and cogency.

> What Jesus wants of us is that we undergo his presence so as to enter into a community of life and celebration with him.... Within Christian spirituality, long before we speak of anything else (church, dogmas, commandments, even admonitions to love and justice), we must speak about Jesus, the person and the energy that undergirds everything else. After all everything else is merely a branch. Jesus is the vine, the blood, the pulse, and the heart.[8]

Neither Rolheiser nor the Catholic Tradition would countenance reducing this realization to a privatized "Jesus and me" spirituality. This would contradict Catholicism's profound corporate and communal essence. The living Jesus is always head of the body, the Church. And living Jesus is always living a profoundly ecclesial existence.[9] But even as Catholicism never separates the risen Lord from his ecclesial and sacramental body, so it never reduces the Lord to the community. Jesus always stands over against the Church as its Source of new life in the Spirit and, because of this, as its Judge.[10]

It has become a truism to contrast pre-Vatican II and post-Vatican II understandings of Tradition. The former, allegedly, focused upon tradition as the handing down of content, the so-called deposit of faith; whereas the latter, ostensibly, focuses on the process of handing down. The first can be designated by the Latin word *tradita*: those things handed down; the second by the Latin word *traditio*: the activity of handing down. A moment's reflection shows that handing on the faith demands both: both content and process. The Gospel has determinate content:

it is not some amorphous good news. Its manner of communication is manifold: it can range from earthy parable to metaphysical exploration.

But the burden of this reflection on the "newness" of the Gospel is that there is a reality deeper than, though inseparable from, tradition either as *tradita* or as *traditio*. Let me offer a third Latin word to indicate this reality: *Traditus.* The Lord Jesus himself is *the One handed over.* He is the Gift that the Father "hands over" to the world. He continues to give himself for our salvation, to hand himself into our hands. The Church arises and is daily sustained by this Tradition: Christ's Eucharistic gift of himself. The very title of Pope John Paul II's last encyclical, the final testament of his spiritual conviction and theological vision, expresses this succinctly: *Ecclesia de Eucharistia.*[11] The Church's very being daily derives from the Eucharistic sacrifice of its crucified and risen Lord.

The Church has nothing to offer the world, nothing to give, but Jesus Christ. This is the Church's awesome blessing and responsibility. It can only faithfully communicate Christ by the witness of its own new life received from him. Thus the truly credible communicators of the faith are the saints whose transformed lives most clearly manifest the newness Christ has realized and enabled. As St. Francis of Assisi reportedly instructed his friars: "Go and preach the Gospel. If necessary, use words!"

Transformation

> Now the Lord is the Spirit, and where the Spirit of the Lord is, there is freedom. All of us, gazing with unveiled face on the glory of the Lord, are being transformed into the same image from glory to glory, as from the Lord who is the Spirit. (2 Cor 3:17–18)

A subject mentioned but not given sustained attention at the conference is that of the Rite of Christian Initiation of Adults, the RCIA, which has become so important a part of Catholic life and pastoral practice since Vatican II. The RCIA is, arguably, one of the most important reforms or, better, recoveries, achieved by the Council. While the baptism of children remains, statistically, the "normal" practice of the Catholic Church in the United States, the initiation of adults is the "normative" practice. If we would see what becoming a Catholic Christian signifies and entails, then the RCIA is where to look. It provides precious guidelines for handing on the faith.

Integral to the RCIA is the period of preparation for the rites of initiation known as the "catechumenate." This extended period, which may last for two years or more, offers some hope of countering the potent catechumenate of the culture, by liberating desire from its idolatrous distortions. In the provocative phrase of Aidan Kavanagh, it promotes "conversion therapy."[12] It does so by engaging the catechumen in a holistic process that engages affections and actions, heart, mind, and body.

Unlike the private "instructions in the faith" of the pre-Vatican II era, the catechumenate is rooted in the local Christian community and in its liturgical life. Participation in the community's worship through the Liturgy of the Word is central to the catechumenate. And the various stages in the process toward full initiation are liturgically and ritually celebrated.

Accompanying the candidate through his or her catechumenal journey is a sponsor who serves as mentor, guide, and support. Thus a form of apprenticeship in the new Christian Way takes shape, a precursor to the continued importance in mature Christian living of a spiritual guide. In addition to formal catechesis the candidate is involved in the social outreach of the community, its concern for the poor and needy in its midst. Moreover, there is nothing automatic about the process; discernment is key: both the community's discernment of the candidate's aptness and readiness, and the candidate's discernment as to whether she or he is prepared for total commitment to God, through Christ, in the Spirit.

The culmination of the catechumenate is the "awe-inspiring rites of initiation" themselves, most properly celebrated at the Easter Vigil, the keystone of the arch of the liturgical year. Here the candidate is plunged sacramentally into the life-giving death and resurrection of the Lord. To achieve its full symbolic significance this baptism should be by immersion. In this form, the spiritual reality of death to sin and new life to God finds physical resonance in the darkness and loss of breath of descent under the waters, and then being raised again into light and air.

The RCIA refers to "initiation" rather than simply "baptism," because here baptism is completed by confirmation or anointing and is consummated in the Eucharistic celebration where the newly baptized and the entire community are nourished by the very body and blood of the Redeemer and Lord and made one in him. Thus the celebration is the fullest sacramental expression of the reality signified: the death of the old self and the birth of a new self renewed in Christ.

As is well known, the last stage of the journey of the RCIA is called "mystagogia." During the period between Easter and Pentecost those newly initiated come together to ponder further what has transpired in them, to enter further into the Mystery of new life in Christ, its meaning and implications.

But, in another and deeper sense, this last "stage" is never-ending and is not restricted to the new initiates. Christian life is an ongoing mystagogia: an ongoing immersion into the inexhaustible Mystery of Christ. For conversion and new birth are but the beginning of new life, of ongoing transformation in Christ "from glory to glory." No writing in the New Testament is more aware of the challenge of continued growth in Christ than the Letter to the Ephesians. Indeed, Ephesians makes "spiritual growth" a defining mark of the Church and the Christian.

> And Christ gave some as apostles, others as prophets, others as evangelists, others as pastors and teachers, to equip the holy ones for the work of ministry, for building up of the body of Christ, until we all attain to the unity of faith and knowledge of the Son of God, to mature manhood, to the measure of the stature of the fullness of Christ, so that we may no longer be children, tossed to and fro, swept along by every wind of teaching arising from human trickery, from cunning and deceitful scheming. Rather, speaking the truth in love, we will foster the growth of all into him who is the head, Christ, from whom the whole body, joined and held together by every supporting ligament, with the proper functioning of each part, brings about the body's growth, as it builds itself up in love. (Eph 4:11–16)[13]

Handing on the faith necessarily includes handing on this hope of final transformation. And Ephesians reveals how catholic, how comprehensive, is Christian hope. For it embraces not only personal transformation, but communal and even cosmic transformation as well. In a culture where hope is often reduced to material expectation, the sheer scope of Christian hope can liberate imagination and energy on behalf of human dignity, social justice, and environmental stewardship — even as we await the blessed fulfillment of hope: the coming of our Savior, Jesus Christ.

"Discernment," "newness," "transformation": these are but verbal markings, pointing haltingly to the Mystery: Christ in us, "the hope of glory" (Col 1:27). In the perennial task of handing on the faith nothing is more needed than that parents and pastors, catechists and communities rekindle in themselves the flame of the Christic imagination.[14] In undertaking this joyful labor we can take as teachers and guides the anonymous artists who created the great San Clemente mosaic of the Cross as Tree of Life. It sustained them in an age of crisis and upheaval. It will surely sustain us.

Part One

THE CONTEMPORARY NORTH AMERICAN CONTEXT

Chapter 1

Religious Education in Its Societal and Ecclesial Context

Mary Johnson, SNDdeN

RELIGIOUS EDUCATION in the Catholic tradition today is conducted amid great societal and ecclesial diversity in a nation and Church marked by deep wounds. Our learning and teaching take place within the societal context of a post-9/11 nation, and in the ecclesial context of a post-1/6 Church. September 11, 2001, and January 6, 2002, mark days when the sun set on a different nation and a different Church.

This paper will focus on societal and ecclesial factors which contextualize the mission of Catholic religious education in a diverse and wounded nation and Church. It will provide, in broad strokes, a panoramic view of key demographic variables from recent data from the U.S. Census Bureau in order to understand the challenges facing the nation.[1] These data are national in scope. Regional differentiation demands that all of us locate our local reality within this wider picture. The paper will then focus on issues within the Church that challenge us profoundly as educators. And, finally, no contextualization of Church factors would be complete without an honest critique of how religious education has been perceived to have been done in the recent past in order to talk about what needs to be done better in the present and the future. That will occupy the last part of this paper.

The Societal Context

The following sociological factors are selected from my undergraduate Introduction to Sociology course at Emmanuel College. I often tell my students that this overview is like flying from Boston to Los Angeles.

It provides breadth but we have to get off the plane in order to find the depth. Similarly, while this overview will illuminate issues national, sometimes international, in scope, the question of how each is addressed in religious education programs depends in large measure on local and diocesan responses.

While we learn and teach in a global community, we will focus here on demographic variables that pertain to the United States, a complex society of over 290 million members. The Catholic Church is a large and complex organization within that national society that, in large measure, demographically mirrors the society. It is in the midst of this society that we theologize and then transmit the fruits of our theologizing to new, and sometimes not so new, generations in our religious education programs.

Our overview will focus on the variables of age, race and ethnicity, social class, and religion in order to illuminate some of the challenges that confront educators and to highlight some of the possibilities for theologizing and catechizing.

Age

First, let us examine issues related to age. The United States ranks fifteenth in the world in life expectancy. Today, life expectancy at birth is 77.3 years. Hong Kong ranks first in the world for life expectancy at 82.8 years. Japan, Australia, Canada, and several Western European nations follow Hong Kong. Much attention is paid to the factors that may enhance life expectancy, diet being one. Attention is also paid to issues related to life span, the maximum length of life possible. While there is disagreement as to the maximum, it is at least 122 years. Documentation of the age at death of Jeanne Louise Calment in France in 1997 substantiates that figure. Verifications are pending for the age at death of several Eastern Europeans which point to longer life spans.

Longer life expectancy has led social scientists to the usage of a new term: the "graying" of America. This refers to the increasing percentage of older people in the population. Today, 13 percent of the population is over age sixty-five as compared with 4 percent in 1900. There are 7 million more elderly people in the population than there are teenagers. Demographers and policymakers warn of the need for the society to build an infrastructure to support the elderly and their caregivers as more people live into their eighties, nineties, and hundreds and become frail elders, with a variety of physical, social, psychological, and spiritual needs. As one who has provided care for elderly relatives over the last several years, I can attest from personal experience that the society is far from attaining that goal.

From the point of view of the Gospel, however, to what does the aging of America call us? How is it a blessing? What does it tell us about the fullness of human life? What does it mean for the old, for the young, and for everyone in between? What does the age distribution of the society demand of the Church?

Race and Ethnicity

The United States is becoming increasingly racially and ethnically diverse, with the youngest generations being the most diverse, and therefore, by virtue of their socialization, the most accustomed to diversity. The approximate percentages of the population by race and ethnicity are: Americans of European descent — 68 percent; Latinos — 13 percent; African Americans — 12 percent; Asian Americans — 4 percent; Native Americans — 1 percent; and Americans who claim two or more races — 1 percent. About one-third of the population consists of people of color.

The largest groupings of Americans of European origin are German, Irish, English, and Italian. These account for approximately 40 percent of the total European American population.

Sixty-six percent of Latinos trace their ancestry to Mexico; 15 percent to Central and South America; 9 percent to Puerto Rico; 4 percent to Cuba; and 6 percent to other origins.

Twenty-four percent of Asian Americans trace their ancestry to China; 18 percent to the Philippines; 16 percent to India; 11 percent to Vietnam; 11 percent to Korea; 8 percent to Japan; and 13 percent to other origins.

Discussion about racism in the society has to take seriously the fact that institutionalized racism continues to plague the structures of reality in the United States. And the relationship of race to social class continues to be a significant one.

For religious educators, what does the changing color of the face of the United States mean for the content of religious education programs? What does racial and ethnic diversity reveal to us about God? What does the existence of individual and institutionalized racism demand of the Church?

Social Class

Today we are living in the midst of a society deeply divided along class lines, but deeply wedded to the myth of a classless society. The chasm between the rich and poor has widened greatly over the last twenty years, bringing with it a myriad of social problems due to economic inequality.

Currently the top 20 percent of the population controls 80 percent of the wealth (assets of land, stocks and bonds, etc.). The next 20 percent controls 15 percent of the wealth and the remaining 60 percent divide the remaining 5 percent of the wealth, with most people owning nothing.

There are many schemas used to describe social class. Some social scientists who study stratification use household income to rank the American population by class. One such schema follows:

The upper-upper class is made up of 1 percent of all households. Their annual income is above $1,000,000.

The lower-upper class comprises 12.4 percent of all households. Their annual income falls between $100,000 and $999,999.

The upper-middle class is made up of 22.5 percent of all households. Their annual income is between $57,500 and $99,999.

The average middle class is made up of 18.8 percent of all households. Their annual income is between $37,500 and $57,499.

The lower-middle (or working) class comprises 22.7 percent of households and has an annual income between $20,000 and $37,499.

The lower class is made up of 22.6 percent of all households. Their annual household income is between $0 and $19,999.

This analysis of household income demonstrates that two-thirds of the society is average middle class or below — a far cry from the media characterization that a majority of Americans are in the upper-middle class.

The study of stratification demands a complex analysis, but suffice it to say that many dimensions of the issue of economic inequality are particularly troubling. One such issue is that of the "working poor," an oxymoronic term but, unfortunately, true. They are often hidden, even in tables that analyze social class. Countless social scientists and journalists have documented the lives of men and women who work many hours per week for the minimum wage or less, with little or no benefits and who, with their families, barely survive.

What is the Gospel message to the rich, to the poor, and to those in-between? How is Christ proclaimed across class lines in the United States? Who is Christ to each of these classes? Where is the Church in a society deeply divided by class?

Religion

In addition to the age, racial, ethnic, and social class diversity described above, the United States is also marked by tremendous religious diversity. That religious diversity can be analyzed through the lens of age, race, ethnicity, and class, too.

Because of the religious pluralism in what social scientists call the "religious economy" of the United States, there is no one dominant religious body. Catholicism is the largest religious body and has been so since 1850. It currently comprises approximately 25 percent of the population (65 million people). All Protestant denominations together constitute approximately 50 percent of the population, and although some commentators say Protestantism still has a hegemonic hold on American culture, Protestantism is marked by great internal diversity as well.

The Southern Baptist Convention is the largest Protestant denomination with about 20 percent of the population as members. After Catholicism, Southern Baptists are the largest single religious body in the United States; Episcopalians and Presbyterians are relatively small denominations, comprising 2 percent and 3 percent, respectively, of the total population.

These particular denominations in America make interesting case studies of the analysis of religion, social class, and race. While the Episcopal Church and Presbyterian Church are relatively small in membership, the majority of those members come from the middle and upper classes. On the other hand, the majority of Southern Baptists come from the lower and working classes. The membership of the Southern Baptist Convention is also made up of a larger proportion of people of color than are the Episcopalian or Presbyterian churches.

Observers of religion pay particular attention to Protestant evangelicals as distinct from what is termed "mainline" or "liberal" Protestantism, especially during national elections. Scholars also trace patterns of what is called "religious switching." This phenomenon can be traced across religious lines but is a pattern found most often across denominational lines within Protestantism. Scholars often trace complex patterns of switching. Sometimes members switch to a denomination of a higher social class as they move into the professions. On the other hand, there are also examples of people assuming a born-again status as part of their religious identity, thus necessitating their switching to a denomination that comprises members from a social class that is lower than the denomination of origin.

But Christianity, while numerically the largest religious entity in the United States, is far from the only religious story. Like so much of the American narrative that needs to look to the world stage as backdrop, American religious pluralism must be analyzed in reference to global religious pluralism. The five major world religions are Judaism, Christianity, Islam, Hinduism, and Buddhism.

There are approximately 14 million Jews in the world, with Judaism the predominant religion in Israel. The Jewish population in the United States is more than 5 million — about the same number as in Israel. American Jewish diversity is manifest in four denominations: Orthodox, Conservative, Reform, and Reconstructionist. The roots of American Jewish diversity lie outside the United States and are centuries old. The majority of American Jews are in the middle and upper classes. A contemporary challenge facing Judaism in this country is the high rate of intermarriage. Recent media accounts detail efforts on the part of some Jewish communities to serve as dating services to bring young Jewish adults together with the hope that they may marry.

While Judaism came to the United States in a significant way in the waves of immigration from Eastern Europe in the last quarter of the nineteenth century and after World War II, recent immigrants to the United States have brought the other world religions, along with many other religious traditions, with them. First, I consider Islam.

Islam and Catholicism are the two largest religions in the world, each with about 1 billion members. Therefore, each is demographically significant in a world of 6 billion-plus people. While Christianity is the largest world religion with approximately 1.9 billion adherents, Islam is second. Christianity is predominant; that is, in approximately 114 nations of the globe more than half the people in each nation adhere to it. Those nations are located in North and South America, Europe, southern Africa, and

Oceania. Islam is predominant in 39 nations located in the Middle East, central and northern Africa, and regions of Asia.

Demographers note that less than 1 percent of the U.S. population is Muslim, but Islamic scholars contend that even before 9/11, Muslims were reticent to state their religious identification to survey researchers for fear of reprisal. Therefore some scholars argue that the number of Muslims may, in fact, equal or even exceed the number of Jews in the United States, who represent 2 percent of the total population. Mosques are becoming more visible on the American religious landscape with a diversity of members by social class and ethnic origin. While some members are from the upper classes, many are from the lower and middle classes.

Hinduism is the world's third largest religion, with approximately 760 million adherents, about 13 percent of the world's population. Hinduism is predominant in three nations; India has the largest number of adherents. Hindus comprise less than 1 percent of the U.S. population.

Buddhism is the world's fourth largest religion. It has approximately 350 million adherents, about 6 percent of the world's population. It is the predominant religion in eight Asian nations. In the United States, less than 1 percent of the population is Buddhist, of which Asian immigrants or the children or grandchildren of immigrants make up the majority. Interestingly, though, religious switching figures here, too. Some white, middle-class Americans born into the Christian tradition have switched to Buddhism. This is primarily a West Coast phenomenon. Also, scholars note an interest in the weaving of Buddhist prayer practices within some Christian traditions in a new syncretism.

A new line of thinking has developed, too, in the analysis of world religions by demographers. Sikhism is sometimes called the fifth major organized religion because it has 20 million adherents. They are located in the state of Punjab in India. This is another case of the need for robust analytical power in the analysis of religion. While the 20 million Punjab Sikhs demographically outnumber the 14 million Jews in the world they do not hold, at this moment in history, the same place in the global sphere of influence as Judaism does in its historical and contemporary contexts and as the root of Christianity and Islam. So it is clear that a new debate will revolve around the question of what constitutes the definition of a major world religion: is it numbers, or influence, or both, or a combination of factors we have not witnessed yet in world history?

Religious diversity will increase in the United States in the years ahead. What does that mean for Catholic religious educators? What does that mean for education in a new ecumenical and interfaith national and international society? Who is Christ today? What does God look like? Is our image of God too small? How shall we teach people to pray? What does it mean to be Catholic amidst this diversity?

The Ecclesial Context

Young Adult Catholics

While the above gives us a broad sweep of key demographic variables that illuminate the sociological diversity that is the United States today, we need to deepen our analysis by locating our Catholic reality within that wider national view. To that end, we turn now to findings from our national study of young adult Catholics,[2] and we focus on a key generation of 20 million people whose experiences of Church and society can shed light on issues that need attention by religious educators, and members of the Church more broadly, in the years ahead.

In addition to the external societal issues that are described above, it is essential that we also be mindful of the internal ecclesial issues that impact the ministry of religious education. Those issues have to do with structural and attitudinal realities of young adults in the Church.

In our study we interviewed by telephone a national sample of Catholics who had been confirmed during adolescence and were at the time of interview between the ages of 20 and 39. We collected two samples, one of Latinos and one of non-Latinos (European Americans, African Americans, and Asians). Latinos are the fastest-growing and largest ethnic group in the Church in the United States. We also collected data from dozens of individual face-to-face intensive interviews and focus group interviews across the country.

What follows are data from the telephone interviews that can be generalized to the population of confirmed young adult Catholics, the majority of that generation. We begin with the number of years of religious education. When we asked our two samples — the Latinos and non-Latinos — if they had attended religious education classes in junior high and high school, 74 percent of the Latinos and 68 percent of the non-Latinos said yes. When asked if they had attended for four or more years, 59 percent of the Latinos and 73 percent of the non-Latinos answered affirmatively.

When we asked about Catholic school attendance, we received the following responses: Regarding elementary school, 50 percent of the non-Latinos had attended Catholic elementary school, as did 35 percent of the Latinos. On the secondary level, 28 percent of the non-Latinos and 15 percent of the Latinos attended Catholic high school, most of them for four years.

Smaller percentages attended Catholic college or university. Of everyone who had at least some amount of college education, 14 percent of the non-Latinos and 10 percent of the Latinos attended an institution of Catholic higher education.

We also asked about other kinds of religious programs which socialize young people in the faith. When we asked about involvement in Catholic youth ministry or youth programs while in high school, we were told the following: 16 percent of the non-Latinos said that they were often involved in them and 28 percent said they were involved occasionally. Of the Latinos, 20 percent were often involved and 22 percent were involved occasionally.

We asked those who attended college for any length of time about involvement in campus ministry or Newman Center activities. Fourteen percent of the non-Latinos and 8 percent of the Latinos had participated in such groups.

Finally, we tested for effects of Catholic education. We found that Catholic elementary school, high school, and college produced higher levels of knowledge and understanding of the Second Vatican Council. But beyond that, we could not discern any specific effects of education in Catholic schools or religious education programs.

We asked about other ecclesial issues that certainly contextualize the efforts of religious educators. They are issues that are alive in both the Church and society. (Recall that we asked these questions in the late 1990s, before the crisis in the Church moved to become national and international in its scope in January 2002.) The issues we will focus on here are gender, authority of the laity, and social justice.

First, we treat gender. Young adult Catholics have been socialized during a time of greater gender equality than was known in recent previous generations. At the same time, there are efforts to broaden the role of women in every social institution, religion included. One of the most startling findings of the study, and one that has far-reaching implications for religious education for younger people is that, of the non-Latino young adults who had married at the time of our study, 50 percent married someone who was not a Catholic. One of several implications of this finding is that many young adults and their children have been and will be ministered to by women clergy of other faith traditions. So the increasing presence of women in significant roles in politics, media, health care, business, and religion in the United States has been a strong socializing force in the lives of many young adults in the last couple of decades.

We posed the following statements to measure attitudes about gender:

- It is important that the Catholic Church put more women in positions of leadership and authority. Seventy-five percent of both the Latinos and non-Latinos agreed.

- The Catholic Church should allow women greater participation in all ministries. Eighty-seven percent of both the Latinos and non-Latinos agreed.

The findings reveal a strong and favorable attitude toward greater participation of women in ministry, authority, and leadership in the Church, which is consistent across ethnic groupings in our study.

Second, we discuss the laity. Since the crisis in the Church began to unfold in 2002, there have been calls for greater lay involvement in the Church. Voice of the Faithful is the most obvious example of the organized laity as it calls for support of the abused, support of priests of integrity, and for structural change in the Church. Voice of the Faithful and other lay reform groups study the documents of the Second Vatican Council and more recent decrees in order to better assume their role within the structures of the Church.

We put forward several statements and questions to ascertain the attitudes of the young adults toward the laity:

- Lay people are just as important a part of the Church as priests are. Ninety-one percent of Latinos and 88 percent of non-Latinos agreed.

- The Catholic Church should facilitate discussion and debate by the laity on doctrinal issues such as divorce, remarriage, and human sexuality. Seventy-nine percent of Latinos and 80 percent of non-Latinos agreed.

◆ Do you favor or oppose more lay involvement in Church affairs at the local parish level, on matters that do not involve questions of faith and morals? Of the Latinos, 59 percent were in favor, 16 percent were opposed, and 25 percent were unsure. Of the non-Latinos, 71 percent were in favor, 10 were opposed, and 19 percent were unsure.

The findings indicate that the notion that the priesthood is a higher state than the lay state is not accepted by the vast majority of young adults. It is also clear that the Church is being called by a large majority of young adults to discuss and debate doctrinal issues that have caused great pain in the lives of some young adults and in their families and that pertain to dimensions of human sexuality, divorce, and remarriage. Both of these findings indicate no difference between ethnic groupings.

The last finding points to a difference in attitude between Latinos and non-Latinos regarding local parish life, with more non-Latinos than Latinos favoring more lay involvement in Church affairs at the local level. It should be noted that a majority of both groups favor lay involvement. The difference, and the fairly large number in both groups who indicated that they were unsure, may be due to the lack of exposure to models of lay involvement in the local area. As the priest shortage escalates in the next few years due to the retirement, illnesses, and deaths of the generation of priests formed during the Second Vatican Council, a broader experience of lay involvement in parish life will be normative for more Catholics, even in urban areas which had large numbers of priests in the past.

Finally, let us consider social justice issues. These statements point to the complexity of young adult Catholic thinking with regard to the implementation of the social mission of the Church. We posed the following statements:

◆ The Church should stick to religion and not be involved in economic or political issues. Fifty-two percent of Latinos and 54 percent of non-Latinos agreed.

◆ I take seriously the pronouncements of the Pope on social, political, and moral issues. Sixty-five percent of Latinos and 59 percent of non-Latinos agreed.

◆ Catholics have a duty to try to end racism. Ninety percent of the Latinos and 86 percent of the non-Latinos agreed.

- Catholics have a duty to try to close the gap between the rich and the poor. Eighty-three percent of Latinos and 76 percent of non-Latinos agreed.

- Catholics have a duty to try to live more simply in order to preserve the environment. Eighty percent of Latinos and 73 percent of non-Latinos agreed.

These findings point to a few dimensions of a critical issue for Catholicism.

The first finding points to a key polarity: half of the young adult Catholics believe that the Church should stay out of economic and political issues and the other half feel that they should not. A somewhat higher percentage states that it takes seriously the Pope's pronouncements on social, political, and moral issues. And a large percentage say that Catholics have a duty to end racism, close the gap between the rich and the poor, and live more simply for the sake of the environment. On the whole, Catholics are supportive of a progressive social agenda, through acts of charity and through work for social justice. It is how and why the Church interfaces with the state that are the tension points for some Catholics. Further research is needed on this timely, complex, and crucial topic.

Religious Education

Religious education is also part of the ecclesial context that must be examined here. In our in-depth interviews with young adult Catholics across the nation the following phrases were used to characterize their experience of their own religious education:

- The pedagogy was horrible.

- Teachers aren't prepared.

- Too rote, too mechanical.

- Nothing in depth, just Jesus is love.

- We got "God loves you" but not much else.

- No content; touchy-feely.

- Insufficient.

- Silly.

+ I was confirmed and had no idea of what was going on.
+ A baby-sitting session.
+ More social than anything else.
+ By and large, my religious education was abysmal.
+ Emphasis was on social issues.
+ We played biblical Trivial Pursuit.

We heard these comments, and others like them, spoken by young adult Catholics, then in their 20s and 30s, in the late 1990s all around the United States. Sometimes they were said with humor, sometimes with anger. I found the critique of religious education to be one of the most powerful findings for me in all of the research we conducted because of its profound generational consequences for the mission of the Church and for the faith life of individual Catholics.

All kinds of challenges are contained therein. First among them is that many of the teachers of religious education today come from the generation that feels it received such poor quality religious education themselves. The response of the Church to their need for pedagogy is critical for the passing on of the faith to their children. The young adults remain a key bridge to the future and because of their generational size and generational place their experience cannot be taken lightly.

It remains to be seen by other survey researchers twenty years hence what the perception of the next generation, the children of today, will be regarding their religious education. Today, we have impressionistic evidence of religious education efforts in particular parishes or dioceses, but we cannot generalize from these experiences to the national level. It would serve the Church well to do the kind of evaluation research and assessment that is needed to determine the efficacy of religious education efforts on a wide scale.

In order to accomplish that, a fundamental premise must be that if we intend to ask a question, we must be willing to hear the answer. This can be difficult, especially if one is concerned about something that is valued deeply. And it can be difficult if the responses are challenging to the status quo. In our focus groups and individual interviews we heard many challenging statements. In particular, I remember meeting a young man years before we conducted this research who summed up his religious education with this sentence: "I needed meat and the Church gave me

Twinkies." Years later I heard variations of that theme over and over again as I heard hundreds of people describe the meaninglessness of arts and crafts activities, the lack of content in their class work, the poor quality of the teaching, the lack of connection to the deep structures of the faith.

Some could go on after the joking to express satisfaction with one or more dimensions of their religious education but others could not. Some expressed anger after they joked about their experience. Anger, as one young woman said, at being set up by the Church. Three examples of this follow. One woman said that she went to a public university with a very active Campus Crusade for Christ and was embarrassed in front of her evangelical friends by her lack of knowledge of the Scriptures. She wanted to know why a course in the Bible was not part of her religious education.

Another young woman talked about her workplace and the religious diversity that was present there. She said that she is embarrassed when she is asked questions about her faith and she cannot answer them. She said that a lot of her time in religious education was spent in cutting out pictures from magazines and gluing them to cardboard in order to make collages. I believe that the image of the collage is the metaphor for the religious education of many in this generation: a one-dimensional piece with a mish-mash of color and shape with no structure, no depth, and no meaning.

A young man who married a woman from another faith tradition is embarrassed in front of his in-laws when they can articulate their tradition so easily. He is hard put to answer some of the fundamental questions they ask him about the symbols of the Catholic Church, about the liturgical seasons, about the saints.

This is the sociological diversity I talked about earlier — the places that many young Catholics will spend their lives — a public university, an ecumenical and interfaith workplace, a marriage to a spouse of another faith tradition or no faith tradition.

We concluded our book with ten recommendations to the Church regarding ministry to young adults including the Church making a "preferential option" for young adults; promoting a distinct Catholic identity; building Catholic identity in a positive way; enhancing the liturgical context; building better community; offering better marriage preparation; supporting more recruitment to the priesthood, religious life, and lay

ministry; teaching about spirituality, prayer, and meditation; support-
ing young adult Catholic initiatives; and, providing better young adult
religious education. On this last point, I quote our recommendation
verbatim:

> There is a critical need for credible and relevant adult religious
> education. As one young adult observed, "The Church settles for
> less than the best." This is especially true in three areas: Bible study,
> Vatican II theology, and the Church's social teachings.
>
> Disputation over Vatican II's meaning and implementation is
> an undercurrent in the contemporary Church. It is still a source
> of polarization and division among Catholics. Yet many young
> adult Catholics know little about the Council, its deliberations,
> documents and theology, and what is known is piecemeal and
> superficial. A respondent's comment that, "My understanding of
> the Vatican Council was it made the Latin Mass become non-Latin
> and...changed some of the words in prayers," is emblematic of
> the situation. This is a serious lacuna in Catholic life today — as is
> the general lack of knowledge regarding Catholic social teachings
> since Vatican II.
>
> The three areas — Bible, Vatican II, and social teachings — need
> to be addressed with programs that are intellectually edifying and
> challenging, action-oriented, community building, and helpful for
> integrating young Catholics into parish life. Many young adult
> Catholics are eager for instruction in their faith and will prove
> receptive to initiatives.
>
> The problem of Catholic young adult religious education tran-
> scends the issues of content and development of curriculum; it is
> also one of pedagogy. Greater attention needs to be given to the
> training of teachers and those involved in young adult education.
> Resources should be directed to these ends, along with the devel-
> opment of youth groups, community service projects, and retreat
> programs which implement these teachings.

Those words were published in 2001. Today, in a Church that continues to bleed from multiple wounds, and in a world yearning for
justice, peace, and reconciliation, the mission of religious education in
the Church seems to be even more necessary for the spreading of the

Gospel. How shall we respond? I believe that there should be three principles to which we are committed:

First, we need a commitment to excellence. The word "mediocre" was used again and again in regard to religious education. When asked if they had ever heard of the Second Vatican Council only 29 percent of the Latinos and 54 percent of the non-Latinos said yes. When those who said yes were asked if they had ever read about or discussed any of the ideas of the Second Vatican Council, only half said yes. We cannot accept this kind of systemic failure.

Second, we must have a willingness to be critiqued by this generation of young adults. Some men and women who are professionals in their fields in this generation consider themselves to be religious illiterates. Others in a variety of jobs and lifestyles say that when they faced struggle and sorrow, they had not been given a lot of help in their faith development. Are we willing to listen non-defensively to a perhaps painful critique in order for new ideas, new creativity, new vision, new energy to be unleashed by people who experienced religious education in this generation, who hope for a more substantive and meaningful religious education for their children, and who echo one respondent who does not see substantive change on the local level and says, "We can do better than this"? Denial can run deep and efforts to minimize these findings, or to say that they are not as widespread as they are, or that everything is fine now, will only delay the needed reform for tens of millions of young adult and young Catholics in this country.

Third, we must make a commitment to broadening and deepening what is working well and renewing efforts to change what is not. In our study, there were points of strength that were articulated by respondents: retreats, community service, and the witness of individual teachers. Can we learn retrospectively from what people hold dear now, from what they continue to be inspired by, from what continues to sustain them, from what moved them to further reflection or action, from what kept them in relationship with God and with the Church?

So much hinges, individually and institutionally, on the transmission of the faith. Families have a profound responsibility for this mission but are not always up to the task.

A great responsibility rests on the pedagogy and content of religious education. Continued involvement in the life of the Church can flow from it. One college senior discussed the consequences:

It was too vague. I would hesitate to call it teaching or learning. I don't think much was taught, and I certainly don't think much was learned from my perspective. I think my lack of knowledge is what made me disinterested in the Catholic Church.

Let me conclude this paper with a personal word. I was thirty-nine years of age when I began the research project on young adults. So I was a member, albeit at the tail end, of the generation I was studying. The stories I heard brought my own experiences of religious education back to me, sometimes on a daily basis. In my memory I could recall my classmates and me making collages year after year. I still do not know why we made them. But as one who was fortunate to receive more meat than Twinkies in her post-Vatican II religious education, I would say that second to my family, those teachers who gave me my religious education made all the difference in my life. Their meat gave me life-giving sustenance. For the sake of a changing world and a changing Church and in a society with such a deep spiritual hunger, I hope that when the next generation of Catholics is surveyed that they can say the same.

Chapter 2

Faith, Hope, and
(Excessive) Individualism

WILLIAM D. DINGES

MY PRESENTATION in this chapter is straightforward. I will address a dynamic of American society rife with promise and peril for the transmission of faith. It is a relatively easy target, and one about which much has already been written. This is the dynamic of individualism (or, perhaps I should say "excessive" individualism) that is at the core of the American ethos, and that is now an increasingly significant element of American Catholic identity.

The genesis (and apotheosis) of American individualism is varied and complex, but stems in large part from the genius of Protestantism and its hegemonic influence in shaping what Robert Bellah has called the American "cultural code." Individualism has deep roots in Protestant theological sources, notably in the emphasis on the sacredness of individual conscience and, in more extreme expressions, in a near "divinization of the Self."[1]

Beyond the influences of Protestantism, postmodern cultural patterns also accentuate individualism, especially among the more affluent social classes that include growing numbers of American Catholics.

"Identity" in the postmodern context has increasingly become a self-constructed project. In the context of pluralism and the radical openness of social life, the synthesis of global culture, and the eclectic mixing and diversity of various "authorities," achievement and autonomy become primary determinants of identity. Ascribed statuses and inherited relations wane in significance. Anthony Giddens, for example, notes that in the highly pluralistic, multicultural, and fragmented milieus of postmodernity, the self is a more deliberative and reflexive project.

Individuals try to negotiate and sustain a coherent, yet continuously revived biographical narrative within a context of multiple choices filtered through various abstractions and social systems.[2]

Charles Taylor has also explored the shift toward a more radical individualism with its ethic of authenticity and moral and spiritual instrumentalism, most recently in his reexamination of the thought of William James. According to Taylor, the impact of individualism on religion means that there is no "necessary embedding of our link to the sacred in any particular broader framework, whether 'church' or 'state.'" Today it is simply axiomatic that one should never conform to some external authority that doesn't seem comprehensive as a form of spiritual life, or that does not ring true to the dictates of one's own inner sense of self.[3]

Within this identity-as-self-construction paradigm with its more psychological and dynamic conception of the self, religion readily transforms into a "private affair," one segment of identity work in which the individual selects a world of meaning and significance from a variety of choices.[4] As Thomas Luckmann observed some time ago, one of the most revolutionary traits of (post) modern society is that personal identity becomes essentially, a "private phenomenon." These choices, however, receive little or no support from the primary institutions of society.[5] In addition, the role of traditional patterns of authority is seriously attenuated as vertical authority yields to horizontal authority and as these patterns — including those of religious authority — are perceived as only *one form* of authority among others, that is, parts of the indefinite pluralism of expertise in the postmodern context.[6]

A related dynamic that accentuates individualism and that weds religion to the free market is that of "cultural commodification." By cultural commodification I mean the totality of social, cultural, and psychological factors surrounding the objectification and consumption of religious symbols, narratives, practices, and spiritual wares.[7]

Consumer capitalism's cultural impact on religion is profound. One of its most significant effects is in moving the locus of the sacred from traditional religious institutions into the realm of the marketplace, thereby transforming religion into another "cultural resource" for individual consumption.[8] This dynamic of commodification, which divorces religious symbols and practices from traditional community contexts, readily facilitates the construction of an individualized religious identity.

Some of the tendencies toward religious commodification come from within religion itself. In the American culture of religious voluntarism, it is hardly surprising that matters of the soul must be "sold," or that church "shopping" is pervasive. The problem, however, runs much deeper than one of denominational marketing imperatives.

In the postmodern context, it is increasingly difficult for religious traditions to control their meaning systems. Religious symbols and practices, like aesthetic ones, are highly vulnerable to cooptation, bricolage, and mass commodification. Unlike many commercial institutions that employ the full power of civil law to protect the integrity of their corporate symbols, religious institutions exercise little normative control over theirs.[9] Religious symbols are readily dislodged from their historic connection with a theological tradition, a moral ethic, a disciplined community, or with a distinct religious identity. They become fragmented into the commercial and pop culture milieus where they are easily vulgarized, stripped of depth, and reduced to decorative functions, or to patterns of entertainment and "life-style" enhancement. Significantly, this dislodging occurs in a social context in which individuals are encouraged to pursue an "affluence ethic" devoted to consuming a greater variety of things[10] and where, as Vincent Miller observes, they are also deprived of communal and traditional sources of identity while simultaneously being enticed by the mass media to invest in commodity-based self-enhancements.[11] Buy "this" and you can become "that."

The issue I am raising here is not whether or not religious symbols sustain power to evoke the sacred. They can and do — sometimes in surprising and creative ways, especially among the young.[12] It is rather that these symbols are increasingly promoted as yet another consumer product and transformed into yet another venue for the exercise of the self-justifying virtue of "choice." They are abstracted from their interrelationship with other symbols, beliefs, and practices that determine their meaning and function in their traditional context. They become more fluid and ambiguous.[13] As such, they are less helpful as group signifiers, less compelling in shaping individual lives, and less capable of challenging the status quo. Divorced from group- and culture-specific contexts, religious symbols are easily conformed to the values and practices of the dominant culture. They can be deployed in the service of virtually any interest-group or ideal and are especially vulnerable to cooptation by the entertainment and therapeutic domains.[14] Religious institutions, in turn, increasingly compete with therapists, popular writers, academics, and talk-show hosts and entertainers for the meaning and interpretation of their spiritual traditions.[15]

Religious Individualism in America

Religious individualism in America has many hybrids and has been labeled various things — the privatization of religion, religious disestablishment, the new voluntarism, do-it-yourself-religiosity, Sheilaism, personal religion, post-denominationalism, and so forth.[16] Studies inaugurated by Robert Bellah and colleagues in *Habits of the Heart* (1985), along with the work by Robert Wuthnow in *Acts of Compassion* (1991) and in subsequent research on small groups[17] have focused attention on the negative relationship between individualism and commitment in American life — as do Robert Putnam's well-known probings in this regard.[18] This research on disengagement in the civic sphere points to a parallel displacement of communal and tradition-centered beliefs and practices by more privatized and individualist ones in the religious sphere. Privatized religiosity — which easily accommodates the utilitarian and expressive individualism of American culture — makes it difficult to articulate and sustain religious commitments. Specifically, religious individualism has been linked with autonomy in the moral realm; with the diminution or rejection of ecclesial authority; with more direct access to the sacred; with a higher priority for personal spiritual fulfillment; and with a privatized spirituality only loosely connected with established traditions.[19] In short, with what Wuthnow calls "me-first" religion.[20]

What I want to emphasize here is not simply that religious individualism means that religious identity is more autonomous and deliberate today; it is that this individualism signals a loss of how religion is anchored in a sense of belonging. The issue is the decline in connectedness; a weakening or severing of the *social* basis of religion in family, marriage, ethnicity, and community; a decline in the perceived *necessity of communal or institutional structures as constituent of religious identity*. Outside of more fundamentalist-like enclaves, religious identity today is not only less bounded by doctrine or creed; it is also less nurtured and reinforced by community. This trend has serious implications for Catholicism.

I am not denying, of course, that religion in America has a social or institutional face. It obviously does. Denominational structures are the primary expression of religion's social presence. A higher percentage of people are affiliated with a church today than at any other time in American history.[21] Excellent parishes and vital congregations — especially some of the "new immigrant" ones — can be found in many parts of the country.[22] The majority of Americans continue to experience religion in some type of social context. Nevertheless, a body of cumulative research points to a weakening of the social sources of religious identity, a process not entirely compensated for by the emergence of alternative "lifestyle enclaves." The number of Americans wholly uninvolved with a church has gradually increased as religious institutions have lost much of their monopoly over the quest for the sacred.[23] Other developments also mark these trends.

To begin with, the broader cultural *Gestalt* reflects a steady decline in the legitimacy of institutional authority *of any kind* — contributing to what Robert Wuthnow has described as a society of "loose connections." "Loose connections" are both cause and effect of "porous institutions" (including religious ones) that do not hold individuals very securely.[24] Thus the loss of legitimacy by religious institutions is part of the broader problem of widespread alienation from *all authoritative institutions* that has occurred in American society.[25] Second and more explicitly, an increasing number of Americans report their religious identity as a "personal religion" or "none." Religious "nones" now constitute about 14 percent of the adult population.[26] Gallup polls show that seven in ten Americans believe that one can be religious without going to church.[27] And over three-quarters of Americans believe that a person should come to his or her moral values independent of what the person's church, synagogue, or mosque may say.[28] Almost 40 percent of Americans have no connection with organized religion.[29]

A third and highly significant marker of the de-institutionalization of religion is its uncoupling from "spirituality." Significant numbers of Americans, especially baby boomers, see little necessary connection between being spiritual and being part of a historic tradition, or part of a disciplined community of faith.[30]

We live in an era of widespread religionless spirituality. The popular mantra is: "I'm spiritual, but not religious." Wuthnow has charted this uncoupling process, notably the replacement since the 1950s of "habitation spirituality" associated with formal institutions, by a "spirituality of seeking" associated with individual exploration.[31] In contemporary parlance, "religion" is often a dirty word laden with a host of negative connotations — institutionalism, bureaucracy, hierarchy, doctrines, dogmas, creeds, sexism, patriarchy, and boring rituals — and who wants any part of this?! (In the Catholic context, we now also have a heightened association of the term with sexual abuse, callousness, secrecy, and administrative malfeasance.) The default option for many individuals today is a vague and nonspecific "spirituality." The satisfaction of this "spirituality" fuels the "spiritual seeker" syndrome and finds widespread expression in the generic discourse of "faith journey" or "individual growth."[32]

The uncoupling of spirituality from religion is also reinforced by the mass media's not-so-subtle message that you don't need a religious community to engage "God issues." For all of the Religious Right's inveighing against America's "secular" media, many movies and television programs promote morality themes and treat spiritual and supernatural ones. They do so, however, in ways that avoid traditional religious venues. As *TV Guide* recently declared, "Transcendental television" is here — and we're not talking about Sally Fields as *The Flying Nun*. Shows such as *Joan of Arcadia, Tru Calling, Six Feet Under, Crossing Over,* and *Wonderfalls* expose viewers to themes of supernaturalism, spirituality, and "higher powers." They do this, however, in non-specific ways unassociated with traditional religion or with traditional religious communities.[33] (As even "God" responded in the first *Joan of Arcadia* episode to Joan's assertion that she was "not religious": "It's not about religion, Joan. It's about fulfilling your true nature.")[34] Given the power of the mass media in shaping the religious and cultural imagination, particularly among Gen X and Millennial youth, this is hardly an insignificant message.[35]

A fourth factor illustrating the trend toward religious individualism is that much of the "new religious consciousness" associated with the flowering of religious movements since the 1960s preaches individualism. Pragmatically, the focus of many of these movements, especially the quasi-therapeutic and self-help ones that arose in the wake of the "Age of Aquarius," has been on what they can do for the individual, and only secondarily on religion's social sources or connections, or on its benefits for the broader social environment.

Finally, I note that some of the most vibrant forms of religion in America today — the mega-church or seeker-church phenomenon, along with evangelicalism in general — accentuate religious individualism. These movements are *not* characterized by a strong institutional identity, or by a strong ecclesiology or theology of church. They emphasize *individual* spiritual empowerment and a subjectivist and therapeutic understanding of religious participation. As Sargeant, Miller, and others have pointed out,[36] while these churches have obvious institutional structures and dynamics, they appeal primarily because of their "consumer friendly" satisfaction of *individual* needs, not because of their communal or social ecclesiology.

Other scholars of contemporary religion echo themes of choice, autonomy, and individualism in American religious life. Religious identity, like other kinds of identity, recapitulates the motif of choice in both the democratic political process and in the consumer marketplace. Christian Smith observes:

> For moderns . . . the ultimate criterion of identity and lifestyle validity is individual choice. It is by choosing a product, a mate, a lifestyle, or an identity that one makes it one's very own, personal, special, and meaningful — not "merely" something one inherits or assumes.[37]

As the level of individualism has risen, many in the religious mainstream have come to believe that church going and church authority are optional. Nominal membership increasingly replaces active involvement, a development paralleling national civic trends.[38] Fewer Americans are spending time in church-related endeavors.[39] Religion is less perceived as an inherited phenomenon, or as a binding community of discipleship and obligation. Religious leaders and institutions, which traditionally provided the framework within which religious meaning was constructed, have become increasingly peripheral to the spirituality and "lived religion" of private personal enterprise.[40]

Alan Wolfe in his recent book, *The Transformation of American Religion: How We Actually Live Our Faith* (2003), reiterates the pervasiveness of this trend. Wolfe shows that even when people speak of their relationship to a church, it is not typically in terms of its rules and requirements and ecclesiastical structures per se, but in terms of their personal spiritual needs in this regard.[41]

Religious Individualism and Catholicism

Signs that growing numbers of American Catholics have embraced an individualist approach to faith and religious identity are obvious. It is long since passé to observe that many Catholics (on both the left *and* right of the ecclesial spectrum) make up their own minds about an array of beliefs and practices in the Church. Contemporary Catholic identity is fluid, porous, and indeterminate. The Church's authority structure and social cohesion have weakened. Historical and distinctive Catholic cultural patterns have declined or disappeared. Nor is this loosening of Catholic identity confined to the realm of popular religiosity — where institutional and normative authorities in the Church have always had weak and limited impact. Where Catholics embrace the tradition today, many do so selectively and by choice, rather than by necessity or conformity. Although new patterns of community are emerging within Catholicism (small faith communities; so-called "lay movements") the prevailing trend is toward weakened communal and institutional attachments and lower levels of commitment and participation.[42] As we observed in our study of young adult Catholics — and as the culture of commodified religion mandates — the tradition for many Catholics today is not so much a binding community of discipleship and obligation as a toolkit of sacred wares for selectively constructing a personal spiritual identity.[43] This is especially true of post-Vatican II Catholics, in spite of their preferences for remaining Catholic and their alleged adherence to "core" doctrines of the faith.[44] And, while younger Catholics may be attracted to or enamored by Catholic "stuff," or by Catholic-specific identity markers (spiritual traditions, the pope, rituals), this attraction does not necessarily translate into an embrace of the institutional Church and its structures of authority.[45] Other indicators are also relevant.

As noted, it is increasingly difficult for the hierarchy to force compliance behavior outside of the Church's own institutional infrastructure. Consider Mass attendance, a central expression of Catholic sacramentalism, ritualized solidarity, and an obvious public marker of Catholic identity.

In spite of official admonitions to the contrary ("obliged in conscience," "grievous sin"), significant numbers of Catholics disregard the
seriousness of missing Mass. Regular Sunday attendance runs only in
the 25 to 30 percent range.[46] Even more revealing, nearly 64 percent
of Catholics agree with the statement, "You can be a good Catholic
without going to Mass"[47] — a conviction that surely poses questions
about Catholic communal sensibilities, institutional attachment, and the
durability of a sacramental "Catholic imagination."

Studies also show that significant numbers of Catholics are only mar-
ginally or occasionally connected to other elements of the Church's
institutional and sacramental life. Claims of a "return to orthodoxy"
notwithstanding,[48] young adult Catholics, in particular, have loose connections with institutional Catholicism. For many — in a revealing
symbolic shift in identity construction — the appellation "Christian"
has come to qualify or supplant "Catholic" as a first-term indicator of
their religious identity.[49] Although most American Catholics have no
intention of leaving the Church, the numbers who see it as important
in their lives have gradually declined, as have overall levels of religious
practice.[50] Those actually involved in parish life outside of parochial
school connections and Sunday liturgies also remain relatively small.[51]
In our study of young adults, only 17 percent had been active in any
group or committee in their parish or in another Catholic group in the
last six months; nearly 25 percent were not registered in any parish.[52]
In addition, few individuals had overlapping memberships in Catholic
organizations that would work to reinforce Catholic identity. Little wonder that post-Vatican II Catholics rank the "spirit of community among
Catholics" lower than other religious groups.[53] Other venues of social
connectedness among Catholics have also diminished. Catholic enroll-
ment in Catholic educational institutions at all levels has declined,[54] as
has the number of Catholic professional organizations and apostolic
associations. The number of Catholics embracing religious life (a distinct
but preeminent expression of Catholic communalism) has also shrunk
significantly.

The destabilization of Catholic family life — following broader cultural patterns of marriage and divorce — is also relevant to Catholicism's
weakening social ecology. Outside of its celibate ranks, Catholicism has
traditionally been based on the two-parent, heterosexual, nuclear family. As more Catholics are raised in single-parent, blended, or otherwise

nontraditional families, exposure to formalized Catholic social patterns will likely decline. In addition, nearly half of all non-Latino Catholic marriages are now to non-Catholics.[55] This trend, along with increasing numbers of "irregular" Catholic marriages (Catholics to Catholics outside the Church)[56] and divorce rates paralleling national trends, will have serious long-term implications for Catholic solidarity and identity.

Catholic social and institutional ties have also been weakened by broader mobility dynamics, by the demise of dense neighborhood networks among Catholics,[57] and by the presence of more differentiated age cohorts within the Church — a reality that makes religious socialization more challenging. The erosion of Catholicism's social basis is also related to ethnic dynamics.

Ethnicity once created a complex social ecology that reinforced Catholic identity. That impact, especially among Euro-American Catholics, has been greatly diminished today.

I take it as self-evident that in the case of Latinos and Asian "new immigrant" Catholics, a relatively tight bond exists between ethnic and religious identity. New immigrants see their religion as a primary means of preserving their cultural heritage and particularity.[58] Among Euro-American Catholics, however, it is far less clear that ethnicity now operates as anything more than a residual carrier of Catholic identity.

The social networks of most Euro-American Catholics today are multiple and hardly confined to the ethnic group. Regional variations notwithstanding, ethnic societies and associations have declined. The so-called "new ethnic consciousness" that arose in reaction to the Civil Rights Movement was short-lived and essentially over as a self-conscious movement by the late 1980s. Most of the Euro-American ethnic-based forms of folk theology, piety, and devotionalism have disappeared, or continue to decline. In addition, studies such as Davidson's (1997) show that generational or cohort effect is a stronger predictor of Catholic belief and practice than race or ethnicity. Another dynamic also erodes the oneness of ethnicity and religion.

The postmodern milieu is a "multicultural" one. Multiculturalism can mean the promotion of ethnic pride and group identity, the highlighting of cultural boundaries and differentiation or, in more exaggerated forms, ethnic separatism.

Paradoxically, however, multiculturalism can also signal a "post-ethnic" sensibility. Cultural fluidity today means that cultural identities (like religious ones) are increasingly adopted, exchanged, and shed. Individuals can lay claim to multiple identities with varying degrees of commitment to each depending on the psychic economy of the individual relative to evolving circumstances. As Mayer and his co-authors note in their studies of Jewish identity, in such an environment it is difficult to speak of anyone's identity as a permanent fixture of the self.[59] For growing numbers of Americans, individual identity is a function of cultural *preference* rather than race or ethnicity per se; post-ethnic young adults eschew identifying exclusively with any group or race. They refuse to claim a single cultural or racial identity. The rising numbers of mixed-race marriages, along with the generational decline of native languages are but two of the more obvious causes and consequences of these trends.[60] Another is an alteration in the interplay of religion and ethnicity, especially the role of the latter in reinforcing the former.

A final factor to which I want to draw brief attention as an illustration of the individualist impulse among American Catholics is an emerging evangelical temper. David J. O' Brien pointed to this trend over a decade ago and linked it to the "realities of voluntarism" influencing American Catholics.[61] William Portier has recently written a lengthy and subtle exploration of the topic.[62] The aspect of evangelicalism with which I am concerned here is not its emphasis on personal conversion, subjective emotionalism, public witness, belief in biblical literacy, or its potential for sectarianism; it is evangelicalism's accentuation of the primacy of the *individual's* relationship to the divine.

Like O'Brien, Portier roots the emergence of Catholic evangelicalism in the cultural embrace of American religious voluntarism following the demise of the Catholic ethnic subculture. Portier emphasizes that until early in the second half of the twentieth century, an extensive immigrant subculture buffered American Catholics from the full effects of religious voluntarism. Predictably, the dissolution of that subculture has led to the emergence of more evangelical forms of Catholicism — especially in the context of American pluralism and as the social, demographic, and behavioral differences between Catholics and other Americans have evaporated. Vatican II accelerated these trends. However, the dissolution of the subculture and not the Council per se is the more significant factor. Portier contends — and I concur — that *the* pressing issue today is how to be Catholic under the full weight of America's voluntaristic and pluralistic milieu minus this subculture.[63]

The concern I want to voice here is that this "evangelical impulse" harbors an anti-institutional bias. As Portier puts it, while Catholic evangelicalism may promise a religious revival, "the evangelical Catholic future simultaneously threatens church unity with consumerist individualism."[64] As Miller illustrated in his study of the new paradigm churches, the issue for many individuals today is not denominational affiliation; it is, "Is Christ living in you?"[65] Given Catholicism's current institutional weakness, the decline of its ethnic sources, and the tenuous connection of many of the young to it, "Jesus" or a "personal relationship with the Lord" holds the allure of becoming more popular than the Church and, following broader cultural patterns, *de facto* replacing it — for at least some American Catholics.[66]

Conclusion

To be Catholic is to be part of a community. In Vincent Miller's adept phrase, it is a "work of community over time."[67] Catholicism is not an individual appropriation driven by self-interest, or a purely private one — even where, in a deep existential sense, Catholic identity (like all authentic religious identity) requires personal self-appropriation. To be Catholic is to be communal, institution- and tradition-centered. It is to be a *communio*, to be one in Christ and united in the bonds of human love and community. It is to be social.

Over the last half century, individualism has become a more conspicuous feature of Catholic religious self-understanding. Catholicism's institutional identity has become weaker, more diffused, and less salient to American Catholics. Many live today as self-defined Catholics without depending on the Church for normative authority to do so. They practice more of a consumer Catholicism than an institutionally validated one. Furthermore, many Catholics, especially post-Vatican II ones, have had fewer experiences of Catholicism, not only as a coherent symbol and linguistic system, but also as a vibrant *social reality* of groups, organizations, and associations.

Like Bellah and others, my comments about American individualism have emphasized its corrosive impact on community. Individualism among American Catholics, however, is not an entirely negative development.[68] I take the influence as positive when it is associated with personal maturity, with a sense of "ownership" and critical appropriation of the faith, and where it illustrates a laity rightfully acting as producers as well as consumers of the tradition. However lay agency is related to the cultural currents of American individualism, it is also theologically legitimated in the Vatican II emphasis on the dignity of the human person, respect for the primacy of informed conscience, the compatibility of faith and reason, the necessity of an enculturated Catholic identity, and the emphasis on a living faith relevant to a particular social and historical context.[69] Lay agency is also integral to the "universal call to holiness" (*Lumen gentium*, Dogmatic Constitution on the Church, #39) and to the recognition that there are diversely legitimate ways of being Catholic.

My concern here, however, is with the weakening of Catholic social structures and community ties — beyond the demise of the ethnic subculture with which this loss is usually linked. Fewer Catholics experience social solidarity with other Catholics in ways that would reinforce a strong Catholic identity. Fewer experience the tradition as a *social* reality. Catholic identity is not consistently reinforced by ritualized solidarity. While there are exceptionally good parishes, participation rates in many parish programs are low. Many Catholics do not invest significant amounts of time and energy in parish life. Their spirituality is parish-formed or parish-bound in only limited ways. These developments — compounded by the influence of religious individualism, privatization, and cultural commodification — represent a serious fracture of Catholicism's social ecology, a "hollowing out" of the experience of Catholicism *qua* community.[70] They pose obvious challenges to the maintenance of a "Catholic ethic," a "Catholic imagination," and to Catholicism's possibilities as a vital tradition capable of engaging and transforming the culture. Minus the experience of Catholicism as a vibrant social reality (symbolically understood in the imagery of the "Body of Christ"), young Catholics are less likely to be successfully socialized into the tradition, less likely to find it compelling, less likely to have a bounded sense of identity, less likely to develop a Catholic vocabulary to interpret their experiences, and less likely to find the tradition's plausibility structures credible.

I assert that "Handing on the Faith" today is not a purely cognitive task. It is not solely the passing on of a formulaic "content." Nor is it a nostalgic exercise for a lost world, or a matter of configuring the tradition so that it might appeal as another "life-style enclave."

The task is a profoundly sociological one. It means addressing the atrophy of communal participation and the need for a socially embedded Catholicism. It includes the creative (re)construction and intensification of Catholicism as a *communal* reality of habit, prayer, reflection, dialogue, and debate. It necessitates the (re)creation of more cohesive social bonds, shared memories, mutual responsibilities, permanent relationships, and other experiences of connectedness. The problem today is not only that younger Catholics have not had passed on to them a good synthesis of the old and new Catholicism so that they might do a discerning engagement of the culture. It is that they (and many older Catholics as well) see less connection between "faith" and church or community. Too often their experience of Catholicism as a social reality that actualizes an ecclesial reality intrinsic to their identity as Catholics remains impoverished.

Young people must have opportunities for involvement in the structures of the Church, and for the creation of their own structures for sharing their gifts and talents. They must be *socially* anchored (ministries, associations, societies, prayer, and formation groups) as Catholics. Minus such experience, it is not clear how their commitment will be maintained in other than anemic ways. Nor is it clear how effectively Catholic spirituality and Church teachings rooted in a social vision and sensibility — the common good, the importance of solidarity, international relations, and social responsibility — can be sustained.

Parish life, small faith communities, and the liturgy are obviously means for meeting the need for greater Catholic communal solidarity. In the wake of the postconciliar dissipation of other Catholic social structures the liturgy, in particular, has increasingly carried the burden of meeting this need. This is a necessary and legitimate function of the liturgy. It is not, however, its sole function and will be inadequate minus other supporting experiences of church and community building.

"Handing on the Faith" in a culture of individualism, choice, and an unfettered market economy is a daunting task. To be successful, it must be attended by a "handing on (of) the community."

Chapter 3

Culture's Catechumens and the Church's Task

Paul J. Griffiths

Prolegomena

How MAY the Catholic faith be handed on in the early years of the third millennium in the USA? That is the general topic of this volume. It is a large and troubling question, for the church is, now as always, only a generation away from the extinction guaranteed by failure to pass on the faith with which she has been entrusted; and now, as always, there seems to the pessimistically and apocalyptically inclined (like me) little evidence that the church has the resources or the will to manage this difficult task. We have God's promise, however, of the continued guidance and blessing of the Holy Spirit, which is good, for we're going to need it.

Thought about handing on the faith requires thought about the cultural context within which this occurs. If it seems that the ambient culture is benevolent and hospitable, then it's likely that a correlationist model, according to which the church should discern what is good in the culture and cut its catechesis and proclamation according to that cloth, will seem attractive. This is not a view of the current relations between church and culture I hold. Quite the contrary: so far as I can tell, the ambient public culture of the United States is profoundly pagan in the sense that it has been formed either in ignorance of or in opposition to the self-revelation of the God of Abraham. Furthermore, the political order in America is now, largely because of the pagan nature of its ambient culture, increasingly difficult to distinguish from a tyranny, by which I mean a political order whose public law in significant measure directly and explicitly contravenes the natural law and whose foreign policy has unjustly bathed all Americans in innocent blood. The public culture of the United States is, therefore, inhospitable to both the practice and the transmission of the Catholic faith. If this is right (and of course it's disputable, although not, I think, reasonably so), the primary question is not how to correlate, harmonize, and accommodate but how to resist.

My task is to address context, and this I'll do by making some comments upon the cultural catechesis undergone in America by the members of what's come to be called "Generation Y" (roughly, those born between 1978 and 1991) — Catholic and otherwise. This generation includes most of today's high-school and college students and a few of its graduate students, professionals-in-training, and young adults already embarked upon working for a living. Relatively few of its members are yet married or deeply enmeshed in child-bearing and raising; almost none yet occupy positions of leadership in church or world; none, until the events of the last few years, has lived through a war or a serious economic depression — though many are nonetheless poor, and the poor among them are disproportionately represented by those now in military service; many are recent immigrants or the children of such; few of them can recall the presidency of Ronald Reagan, and some can't recall Bill Clinton; and most of them learn more happily and easily from visual and aural artifacts than from written ones. The events of September 11, 2001, will, for most of them, be the first event of major international significance to have made a lasting impression.

My expertise on the formation of this generation is limited: I've undertaken no quantitative studies and have no training in sociology, economics, or cultural theory. What I know or am willing to speculate about the matter is drawn from recent experience (2000–2005) teaching this generation at a large multiethnic and multireligious state university in the American Midwest, and from the fact that my own children belong to this generation (I have a daughter born in 1983, a recent graduate from a state university on the West Coast and now in service in the Peace Corps in West Africa; and a son born in 1986, now an undergraduate at a Catholic university in Chicago).

The Catechumenate of Culture

Culture educates desire. Desire without culture's pedagogy is intense but inchoate, unformed, without goal or purpose: the newborn sucks as the nipple touches its lips; it startles, rigid and staring, if support is removed from its body and it feels itself suspended over the void; its eyes move to the light, irresistibly drawn. But without culture's pedagogy that's about as far as it goes. Everything else is taught and learned: the gurgle and the scream become words; the boundary between the body and the world gradually becomes sharp and clear; the moving shapes — like trees walking — resolve themselves slowly into the mother, the father, the siblings, the friends. A world is learned as the house of language is entered and its taxonomies (this is a dog, that is a sunset, here you fall to your knees, there you curse, this is disgusting, that is beautiful) spin the child's cognitive and affective web with threads so strong that they seem given rather than made, natural rather than a matter of technique and artifice. Culture thus brings, experientially, the very order of things into being and shapes the individual's desires to harmonize with that order. This is how it must be: it is the inevitability of the order of knowing here below.

Culture's catechumens submit willingly, eagerly, inevitably to this pedagogy. There is nothing else they — we — can do. Without such submission, such urgent embrace of language as culture's principal gift, we remain not only mute and inglorious but also not fully human. The extent to which we are human is the extent to which our desires — for thought, for making, for sex, for love, for beauty, for reputation, for pleasure, for God — have been educated and, thereby, formed. And, the precise shape of my particular humanity (and yours), what makes it possible for someone to treat me as this particular person and not some other, is given by the idiosyncratic burden of my catechized desires and the history by which they have assumed their specific gravity. I, for example, desire books, pictures, poetry, wines from southern Italy (that rough savor), women, well-turned English sentences, Handel's keyboard music at the hands of Keith Jarrett, Arvo Pärt's ecstatic musical minimalism, the Agnus Dei chanted slowly as prelude to the gift of flesh and blood, the cleansing rush of the words of absolution in the confessional, the litany of the saints, the rapid equatorial sunset, and above all else God, the *summa essentia* (*una quaedam summa res,*[1] says Augustine, carefully) whose gift made me and whose lineaments I now see enigmatically, *per speculum,* but will soon see, I hope, with all possible clarity. This particular burden of desire has extended catechesis as its necessary condition. The same is true for the desires of us all.

But the catechumenate of culture is, since the fall, not benign. Prospero's gift of language to Caliban brought with it the capacity and the desire to curse; learning the arts of making with tools brings with it always an increase in the capacity to kill and, therefore, in the number of those killed by violence — since Abel, the earth has soaked up so much innocent blood that no step can now be taken without the foot's impress causing the blood to bubble redly from the soil; the *libido dominandi,* the chief mark of culture's deforming pedagogy, is everywhere, intertwined with the fleshly concupiscence of sensual desire wrongly educated and the ocular concupiscence of intellectual desire disordered.[2] We live now as people outside Eden have always lived, which is as eager catechumens of a culture that trains us carefully, with exquisite refinement and precision, to kill, to rape, to torture, to dominate, to control — and, above all, to obscure from ourselves that this is what we are doing. There has been, since the cherubim's flaming sword barred the way back into the garden, no golden age when this was not so, no time of simplicity and peace to which we should look back with nostalgia and longing. It's a characteristic error of conservatives (ecclesiastical and political) to think that there was — that the story we should tell is one of declension. The equal and opposite error of liberals is to think that the right story is one of progress, ever upward from the night of savagery into the day of democracy's civil society. In fact, culture's catechumenate has always been largely malign; the task of diagnosis is not to show how much better or worse things are now than once they were, but instead carefully to attend to the particulars of contemporary malignities. That always gives us quite enough to do.

The church is also a culture and so has its own pedagogy of desire. This pedagogy begins with death: the drowning of the old Adam and the old Eve in the baptismal bath, the renunciation of the blandishments of the world, the flesh, and the Devil (which is shorthand for pagan culture's pedagogy in all its complexity), the overwriting of all natural identities — gender, ethnicity, nationality, and so forth — by Christ's script, the script of the cross.[3] These old identities remain, of course, as a palimpsest; but for the Christian they are no longer determinative or exhaustive: they have been overwritten. We are Christians first and everything else (American, male, female, old, young, gay, straight) a very long way second. What we were remains only as ornament upon Christ's body. Grace perfects nature without destroying it, certainly. But

the perfection granted is sufficiently scarifying that the nature perfected
is to the nature fallen as the praise-shout of the angelic choir is to the
beehive's drone.

All this means that the church is not only a culture with its own
pedagogy, but also and necessarily a counterculture with a counter-
pedagogy. What the church under the Holy Spirit's guidance teaches
its catechumens to desire assumes that the weight and pattern of their
already-formed desires needs to be transfigured, at least, and often simply
killed. The city of God has always its other, the human city; and the loves
that inform the first are scarcely recognizable to those weighted with the
loves characteristic of the second. And so the church must always strive
to keep the catechumenate of culture closely in view. This is not because
the church seeks to accommodate itself to that world; it is because the
church seeks to transfigure it by drawing it into itself, baptizing what is
good and consigning to the fire what is not. This is the proper meaning
of inculturation. It cannot, however, be done without close attention to
the particulars of the pedagogy of the pagan culture (it is always more
or less pagan) in which the church finds herself. If the church's catechists
do not know these particulars they fumble in the dark: what has already
been written needs to be known if it is effectively to be overwritten,
and this is not as easy as it seems because culture's catechesis is, now as
always, in flux, changing rapidly, difficult to pin down and understand.

Aural Buzz and Visual Flood:
The Sensory Ambience of Contemporary Culture

Generation Y lives and moves and has its being in an artificial sensorium
of vast, stimulating power. Silence is rare: public space is almost always
saturated with background music; moments without conversation, one's
own or someone else's, have become ever rarer since the deep penetration
of the cell phone into public life (most of Generation Y does not recall
a world without this device); and when neither background music nor
conversation are easily available, the personal music of the Discman or
the iPod will at once be resorted to. Silence is not sought and not much
liked when found.

An illustration: If I arrive for class five minutes early, those already in
the room will be doing one or several of the following: sleeping; reading

in preparation for my class or some other; listening to music via earphones; talking on a cell phone; or chatting to someone sitting nearby. If reading is being done, it's almost always together with the cell phone or the music. Sleeping, in fact, is the only one among the activities I've mentioned that usually excludes the others — though I have seen instances of students apparently asleep with music still playing through their earphones. Often, then, the room will appear to contain a collection of largely isolated individuals, each being intensely and idiosyncratically stimulated through the ears, and each combining this with at least one other task.

Visual stimuli of a man-made and deliberately stimulating sort are almost as omnipresent. Most come through a screen: every dorm has large-screen TV lounges as important elements of its public space; every dorm room has multiple screens — often two computers and at least one TV for a small room shared between two people. A typical dorm room of perhaps 150 square feet will often include, during evening social hours: half-a-dozen people; a movie playing on a DVD player; two or three cell phone conversations; music being downloaded and played, moderately loudly, through a computer hooked to a high-speed web connection, together with visual display on the computer's screen; and, of course, several different face-to-face conversations.

Some of the circles of Dante's Hell would be preferable. But many members of Generation Y swim in this visual and aural environment like fish in a warm, salt sea. For the most part they have done so since childhood.

There are many things that could be and have been said about this aural buzz and visual flood. Often, the tone of such sayings is one of lament, like Plato's about the invention of writing. I've no intention of adding to those laments, and I note these facts about the Generation Y sensorium not to criticize them but only to register them, together with their likely causal connection to an indubitable set of facts about how Generation Y learns and studies, for these facts are, or should be, of great interest to the church's catechists and liturgists.

Generation Y's members, as this sketch of their environment suggests, are not creatures of the written word. They are, instead, creatures of the image and the sound, and of visceral response to both. Few of them have the ability or the desire to read or listen with attention to subtlety and nuance; fewer still have the patience for lengthy, complex argument.

Faced with prose from Aristotle, Augustine, Aquinas, Henry James, Don DeLillo, or even Dave Eggers, they will pass their eyes over the sentences and will for the most part construe them accurately; but they will have little idea of the shape of a lengthy passage's argument as a whole, and will as often as not be unable to say, having read, what the author has argued. Text-fragments (sentences, paragraphs) dance before them as discrete entities. Weaving them together into a whole, keeping one fragment in mind as key to the meaning of another many pages later — these are not skills widely possessed by the generation, nor actively sought and valued by its members. I often teach, for example, Augustine's *Confessions* (mostly in Henry Chadwick's translation). At least three-quarters of an average class finds it impossible without very extensive guidance to read a book of the *Confessions* and offer a written summary of its content. This is not because they can't read the sentences; it's because they can't keep the beginning in mind long enough to see its relevance to the end, and because they find Augustine's rhetoric a dazzling bafflement.

By contrast, image and sound are familiar and loved. Response to them appears effortless, and does not generate resistance and tension. This is in part because image and sound are consumed recreationally, while the written word is not. Probably less than 10 percent of Generation Y reads for pleasure — and I mean reads anything at all. This is certainly true of my students. But more than 90 percent (probably almost all) consume images and music recreationally, and have done so since early childhood.[4]

These claims are not a lament. I mean them only descriptively. The church, certainly, has (or should have) no particular stake in encouraging literacy: the vast majority of Catholics have always been illiterate, and this is not a problem. It may even make the practice of Christianity easier. But the facts mentioned in the two preceding paragraphs (if they are facts) do raise some questions for the church's catechetical practice.

The first such question has to do with comprehension of and response to the spoken (rather than the written) word. In this, I believe, the church does have an important stake. Proclamation requires that the Gospel's word be spoken and understood; the liturgy makes proclamation of the scriptural word of quite central import. But I do not think that most of Generation Y's desires, formed as they have been by a culture in which the paradigm for oral communication is the fifteen-word sentence (active voice, indicative mood, no sub-clauses), give them the capacity to understand St. Paul or St. John read from the ambo. The words flow over and around them as ambient vibration. (It must also be said that the way in which Scripture is read aloud in most Catholic churches does not help: we read as though we have no expectation that what we read will or should be comprehended; we certainly provide little or no silence in which we might think about it.) I have no immediate recommendation to make about this, other than to note that the ability to comprehend complex prose by ear is articulated in complex ways with the capacity to recall what one has heard. And this capacity has received almost no training by the culture's pedagogy, and is effectively not practiced by the church—not many in Generation Y can easily and without book recite the Gloria, the Credo, the Sanctus, and the Agnus Dei (and I don't mean in Latin). Our churchly catechesis has lost sight of the importance of memory, and this is both mistaken and quite unnecessary. As we make the transition from a culture in which book-literacy is valued and aspired to, to a culture in which it is not, we need badly to recover the techniques developed for other times and places in which such literacy was largely absent; and so far as I can tell, we are not doing so.

The second related question has to do with the increasing (as it appears to me) removal of visual pedagogy from our churches. If Generation Y is not a generation of the word but of the image and the (musical) sound, then this would seem a strong reason to increase—to maximize, even—the presence of icons in our churches. I use the term "icon" in a relaxed sense to include statues, stained glass, frescoes, paintings, and so on: the more of this the better, so far as Generation Y is concerned. And yet, American church buildings designed and constructed since 1970 have moved in the opposite direction, stripping away visual stimuli and visual complexity. This makes little sense. The pre-verbal child in church is instructed in complex ways by abstractedly gazing at stained-glass images of the saints, plaster statues of the Virgin, bloody images of Christ on the cross, and so on. So would be the members of Generation Y, but too often we deny them the chance.

Pagan Pedagogy of Identity: The Brand[5]

A company called QuotableMugs markets an expensive ($10.95–$12.95) line of coffee mugs branded with inspirational slogans. One of these is: "Life isn't about finding yourself. It's about creating your-self." The distinction between invention and discovery has of course a long and interesting intellectual history. This slogan, although not subtle, appears to affirm the significance of that history and of the dif-ference between invention and discovery by promoting the former over the latter. But the very same company also markets a mug that reads "be who you are," which promotes discovery over invention. The purposes of QuotableMugs, it seems fair to assume, are entirely commercial: what they think will sell is what they make and market. Intellectual consistency is not the point. But these two mugs, and the company that makes them, may nonetheless serve as emblematic of some important facts about the pagan catechesis of identity: that this catechesis is fun-damentally and essentially interested in identity; that it wants to mark that identity by branding; and that it is equally at home with tropes of discovery and tropes of invention in undertaking the branding process. This has deep effects, I think, upon Generation Y's sense of itself.

The fundamental desire of the members of that generation is to be thoroughly branded.[6] It is to this end that almost all the energies of cul-ture's catechesis are bent, and to this end that the burden of educated desire tends. The brand is the mark of identity: cattle have it burned into their hides; consumer goods are branded to make it possible for buyers to remember and identify with them; and the brand is an essential ele-ment of corporate culture by which corporations identify themselves to the public and maintain and manipulate their public profile. The brand, then, is both a public fact and a communal fact: it marks those branded as human beings of a certain sort, but also, and at the same time, as members of a community of those of like sort. There is a Christian ver-sion of the brand, of course: in baptism we are marked as Christ's own forever and thereby incorporated into the community of those also so marked. It is likely (as is usual) that corporate and commercial under-standings of the brand are debased derivatives of this Christian usage (and the Christian usage is in turn an appropriation and remaking of the Jewish brand of circumcision).

The members of Generation Y have been taught by entertainers, advertisers, and educators (the difference between the latter two is increasingly hard to discern as commercial culture makes inroads into our public schools) that branding itself is important, indeed that it is the only thing of real importance, and that all their desires should be bent toward it because from it all else flows. But, as QuotableMugs has already shown us, the tropes and images used to send this message are various and not entirely coherent. I'll try to disentangle them.

The first set of tropes embroiders upon the ideas of making and cultivation. This is the point of the first of my QuotableMugs slogans. Grade-school teachers often tell their charges that they can be anything they want to be, that they are limited only by their imaginations. The United States Army tells its potential recruits the same thing. The claim is of course outrageously false, though no doubt well-enough intentioned: the truth is that each of us is finite, limited, damaged, and constrained by very many factors, and this means exactly that we cannot be anything we wish to be. It is a mark of adult and reasonable humanity to acknowledge this, and it is a catechetical malformation of our young people to tell them otherwise. Nonetheless, this is what they are repeatedly told, and they have, to a considerable extent, internalized it. The message is that what they've been given (their ethnicity, their social class, their sex, their physical appearance, their tastes) can be remade. Where you end need not be where you began: plasticity has no limits, and the given can always be resisted or jettisoned by energetic cultivation of something different.[7]

The remakings can be mild. Perhaps you're a Vespa-riding vegetarian Goth with multiple body-piercings: you can jettison that and become without too much trouble a White-Sox-loving beerswiller who drives a pickup truck (the piercings will heal gradually). Or, perhaps you're a straight oenophile with Republican leanings: it's not too hard to become a gay vodka-drinker who votes for Ralph Nader. Or, perhaps you're a Polish Catholic with a taste for kielbasa: a few short steps, a little study, the cultivation of some new religious and culinary tastes and voilà, you're a Conservative kosher-keeping Jew whose only connection to things Polish is excoriation of that ethnic group's traditional anti-Semitism (this remaking may involve cutting your family ties, but that too is always possible). Or, perhaps you're an academically underachieving bodybuilder with a record of making bad movies: as we've seen, you can remake yourself into the governor of the wealthiest state in the union. But the remakings can also be drastic, involving surgery, transplants, drugs, and genetic manipulation. Perhaps you're a woman: you can become a man. Perhaps you're five feet three and two hundred pounds: liposuction and shin implants can do wonders. Perhaps you have small breasts or a small

penis: either can be made larger. Perhaps you're no longer interested in
sex: drugs can change that. Perhaps, until now, your children have been
ugly or stupid or crippled; manipulation of the genome may soon be able
to give you only Harvard-bound world-class athletes.[8] And so on.

Holding up the shining image of becoming anything you want to be
educates desire to seek to transform the given by the cultivation of taste.
Such an education creates a burden that weighs heavily upon the members of Generation Y. I mean the burden of an excess of possibility, too
many glittering images of what one might become. Am I to be a gay
Latina or must I remain a straight Hispanic? Do I need surgery to transform my body? True, I'm now an Asian biker chick, but I could be a
Jigger (full explanation of these interesting niche-identities would divert
us too far from the matter at hand). Should I try on the rôle of an aspir-
ing banker (poring over the *Financial Times* as I drink my latte), or is
the retro campus Maoist (clutching the Chairman's little red book) more
my style? Our culture's script provides so many rôles, so many kinds of
possible identity. They multiply as fast as cold remedies, cereal varieties,
and weight-loss products on the supermarket shelves, and each is given
its means of public visibility, representation, and support: its 'zines, its
sartorial style, its food, its chat rooms, its logo-bearing credit card, and
its argot by which its afficionados recognize one another as Freemasons
used to know one another by the secret handshake. All this, to Generation Y, is both dazzling and oppressive: so many possibilities and so
many difficulties in deciding which to embrace. As I freeze before the
excess of possibility represented by the supermarket's cereal shelves —
so many of them freeze before the excess of possibility represented by
market-driven human plasticity.

But the pedagogy of the brand is not exhausted by considering tropes
of making and plastic possibility. These are intertwined with another set
of tropes of a broadly essentialist sort. These tropes have to do with discovery, with finding the glassy, jewel-like essence that defines your true
identity. This explains the second of my QuotableMugs slogans. Practitioners of this second way of talking share with those who prefer the first
way (they are, naturally, usually the same people) an interest in providing those whose desires they're educating a means of resisting the given.
But now such resistance is grounded not upon an appeal to imagination
and the plasticity of body, mind, and soul; it is grounded instead upon
an appeal to a genuine identity that makes the one who has it essentially

different from what she seems to be. The effort of resisting the given is now grounded upon the discovery of the true self. So, for example, I hear students say, "I was fourteen when I realized I was gay," or, "I knew that I was an artist when I first picked up a pencil." Another form of this rhetoric, much more common at the level of the educational establishment, is talk of discovering oneself as African-American or Latino. This talk assumes (and communicates) that there really are ethnic, racial, and gender identities of this sort, and that they can be discovered rather than made. It's interesting to note that transformations as radical as any envisaged by the advocates of imagination can be grounded upon this essentialist rhetoric. It's become a commonplace of the sex-change memoir that the woman-who-was-once-a-man knew from a very early age that her masculinity was not who she really was, and that such a realization was why she altered her body.

The same trope is equally common in matters of sexual preference and practice: people will say that they discover their gayness or straightness, as if it were a property indistinguishable from their height or their eye-color (both, of course, now changeable, at least in theory).

The pedagogy of the brand is, then, rhetorically quite complicated and almost certainly incoherent. Who propounds this rhetoric? Who forms desire in this way? The answer is, of course, almost everyone: Generation Y talks to itself in these terms because it has learned them so well, which means that the peer group reinforces the pedagogy of desire already received. There is constant reinforcement from mass-media entertainment (television, Internet, movies), as there also is from the educational industry and the forces of the market. I can't explore all these pedagogical forces here, but I will say a few words about the latter two.

The educational industry begins the pedagogy of the brand at very young ages. Even before students can read, they are encouraged to look at pictures that reflect their sex and ethnicity, to identify with the people so represented, and to draw sustenance from that identification. A little later, a similar tack will be taken with representation of families: the child will be encouraged to perceive and identify with representations of his or her own family structure (one-parent, two-parent, same-sex, opposite-sex). And then there is the offering by the schools of festivals and feasts in celebration of particular ethnicities, particular gender-identities, particular sexual tastes and practices, and so on. By the time students arrive

at higher education (those who make it that far) they find a proliferation of new (meaning post-1980, for the most part) programs of study
that also offer a pedagogy of the brand: Catholic Studies, Jewish Studies,
Native American Studies, African-American Studies, Latino and Latin-
American Studies, Women's and Gender Studies, and so on. None of
these programs closes its courses to those not of the relevant persuasion;
but all tend to speak more to those who are or plan to be of that persuasion than to those who aren't and have no interest in being. Some
proselytize overtly and strenuously. (I underscore that Catholic Studies belongs in this list, a matter to which I'll return.) Such brand-specific
programs contribute to the pervasive sense that the brand is indeed what
counts, even though this is never the professed purpose of such programs.
And such an impression is only reinforced by the necessity that all secular universities (and to an increasing extent religiously affiliated ones as
well) find themselves under pressure to provide extracurricular nurture
and support to students who've already branded themselves. Thus we
find such things as offices for gay, lesbian, and transgendered students;
university contribution to the pastoral presence of particular religious
denominations; and the formation of ethnic- or nation-specific student
associations usually also with active university support.

Much more important in branding than the pedagogy of the educational establishment, however, is the pedagogy of the market. Capitalism — the market economy — has moved on from its early phase, which
was constituted by the discovery of mass production, the concentration
of population in cities, and the fostering of mass markets for standard-
ized products (the Model T is the paradigm of this phase). It has become,
now, what's often called "late capitalism," and in that form the increasing segmentation of markets is essential to the stimulus of desire.[9] Success
in marketing means the creation, *de novo,* of a new niche, to which all
the markers of identity can be sold. This is the very hallmark of late
capitalism, and so all the considerable forces of the advertising industry
are brought to bear upon the nurturing of the kinds of identities mentioned above. The nurture in question involves, of course, the feeding
with product of those captured by the catechesis of the brand. The pedagogy of the market is powerful because it is omnipresent: the vocabulary
and patterns of thought that it provides are dominant for Generation Y.
Desire runs in these channels, strong and deep.

The apparent contradiction between the two QuotableMugs slogans with which I began this section is resolved by the deeper grammar of market segmentation and the identity-construction that goes with it. The trope of discovery and the trope of invention are both devices in the service of branding. Generation Y's members, then, are encouraged to know who they are, and they will indiscriminately use both tropes. What they are doing is responding to a bastardized, late-capitalist deformation of the Apollonian injunction. To know oneself according to this pagan model is to brand oneself: to mark oneself as a particular kind of human being (the brand as trademark), and also as a creature of a particular community (the brand as mark of ownership).

The Omnipresence of the Lockean Church

So far, then, we have Generation Y floating in an aural and visual flood, catechized by the late-capitalist market into seeking and finding its identities in increasingly segmented communities of taste whose existence is justified by tropes of quasi-genetic identity. Such communities are Lockean churches. John Locke, in the 1685 *Letter Concerning Toleration*, defined a church as "a voluntary society of men, joining themselves together of their own accord in order to the public worshipping of God, in such a manner as they judge acceptable to him, and effectual to the saving of their souls."[10] This is a community of taste and choice, constructed by a particular catechesis of desire. It is in all important structural respects like the community of those who mourn the passing of Phish (a latter-day Grateful Dead), those who read *qvMagazine* (a 'zine for gay Latinos), or those who like to go to monster-truck demolition derbies. The world of late capitalism has made all communities seem to those who inhabit them to be of this sort. The use of tropes of discovery to explain and justify membership in these communities ("I read *qvMagazine* because I really am a gay Latino") is, now, only a device to cement habits of consumption.

If this diagnosis is right, it follows at once that Generation Y Catholics will understand their Catholicism in this way. They have been catechized by their culture to understand all identities in this way, and there is no reason to think that Catholic identity will be exempt. The proliferation of cultural studies programs at universities, mentioned above, fits perfectly into this profile: Catholic Studies is there in just the same way and for just the same reasons that (e.g.) African-American Studies or Asian-American Studies is there — which is to say as the intellectual arm of a Lockean church.

But what does it mean to understand the Catholic Church as a Lockean church, and why is this a problem (if it is) for the Catholic Church's handing on of its tradition? The central point, I think, is that inhabitants of Lockean churches will typically understand their community and their membership in it by subsuming the order of being into the order of knowing. They will be aware, inchoately, that they have come to be Catholic (or gay or straight or Republican) by means of a catechesis of desire; they will be aware, too, that this could have been otherwise — that if local variables had been different their desires would have been formed differently and the Lockean churches in which they would then have found themselves would be different from the ones in which they now find themselves. These are claims in the order of knowing: they say something about how habit and identity are formed, including the habits of assent required by membership in any Lockean church. But they are not yet claims in the order of being: those are claims about what a particular Lockean church actually is. For late-capitalist Lockeans, however, claims in the order of being are not separate from those in the order of knowing. If membership in a community requires a catechesis of desire; if, too, that catechesis is contingent (it could have been otherwise) and not coerced, then it follows at once that the community in question just is a community of taste, preference, and predilection. It makes no sense from a late-capitalist-Lockean perspective to identify a community so joined as a community of truth, to say of it that it in fact is the community that preserves and transmits more fully than any other the truth about human beings and the world in which we live.

And because the cultural catechesis undergone by Generation Y does not permit such claims — makes them seem irretrievably and puzzlingly odd — the members of that generation will inevitably (for the most part) not understand their Catholicism in terms of them. They will find it difficult to understand that anyone can seriously make such claims, for they will construe all claims about a community's nature — about what it is — by reference to the paradigm I've already discussed. An example: I often teach selections from Aquinas's questions on virtue in the *Summa*. Some students will make a serious attempt to understand what he's arguing, and some will succeed. But almost always, and often with the force of a puzzled epiphany, there will be a moment in class when some (usually a brighter) student will raise her hand and say (something like): "But doesn't that mean he thinks that everyone should think like he does about these virtues?" Well, yes, it does: he thinks it's the truth. But to most members of Generation Y that is an extraordinarily odd thing to think. For them, the community of Aristotelian-Thomist virtue theorists (they wouldn't put it like that, of course) is one that might reasonably have its slogan-branded sweatshirts, and its own credit cards whose every transaction yields a small donation to Peter's Pence (they'd have an image of the Dumb Ox and the slogan *virtus animam facit optimam* in the top-right-hand corner). But they can't think of it as one that it makes sense to say teaches the truth, *simpliciter*. This reaction is neither coherent nor (usually) thought through: it is just what someone formed by the catechesis of a late-capitalist culture is almost inevitably going to say and think. The grammar of the culture does not permit the Catholic Church's view of itself the dignity of being a well-formed utterance. Teaching that view is therefore difficult, and provides what I take to be the deepest level of challenge for the church's transmission of itself in the U.S.A. in the first centuries of the third millennium.

But I should end on a hopeful note: *Oculus non vidit, nec aurus audivit, nec in cor hominis ascendit, quae praeparavit Deus his, qui diligunt illum.*[11]

Part Two

THE CONTENT OF
THE FAITH HANDED ON

Chapter 4

On Taking the Creed Seriously

Luke Timothy Johnson

S PEAKING OF THE "content of faith" demands a willingness to tread carefully between two extremes represented by each of the terms in the phrase and by different parties within the Christian family. One extreme emphasizes content as though it were objective fact. The other extreme stresses faith as though it were subjective feeling. Putting the terms in the same phrase creates a space for thinking.

We would all agree, I think, that "faith" in its fullest sense is indeed subjective in the sense that it is a personal witness. Faith in full is the response of humans to the living God involving belief, trust, obedience, and loyalty, a response that remains always flexible and creative even as the one to whom it responds is living and active in the world. In this sense, "handing on the faith" is not like transmitting an ideology or philosophy, a matter of ideas clearly communicated and precisely preserved. Rather, "handing on the faith" means the transformation of life from one generation to the next, the mysterious leaping of a divine spark from person to person through the agency of the divine person who is the fire. It is in this sense that we can speak of the true history of Christianity being the lives of the saints, for if faith is not a faithful life then it is nothing.

But we would also all agree, I think (at least within this room), that faith as response is a response to something or someone real. Christian faith is *not* subjective in the sense that it is simply an interesting opinion, or that it is a projection of individual desire. Quite the opposite. Faith claims that it responds to what is most real about the world, and claims furthermore that what is most real about the world is not the result of human calculation but is the gift of divine revelation. If faith is certainly subjective in the sense that it is personal and perspectival and cannot persuade on the basis of universally agreed-upon evidence, it is also certainly intersubjective in the sense that it is public and makes genuine truth claims about reality — even though such claims cannot be supported by universally agreed-upon evidence. Christian faith is public both in the sense that it is exoteric rather than esoteric — it speaks of the world as everyone sees it if not as everyone experiences or understands it — and in the sense that it is the profession of a people, a people, moreover with a past and future as well as a present. It is in this sense that we can properly speak of "the faith" and "the content of faith," as a way of designating the public and consistent claims about the world made by Christians in the past and in the present.[1]

Our language must be sensitive both to the public profession by which Christians stake a claim to the truth about the world, and the personal commitment through which such claims are shown to be plausible or not on the basis of the sort of life they engender. If we fail to respect the public profession, then we sink into utter solipsism and sentiment. But if we fail to honor the personal commitment, then we sink even lower into a form of ideology.

The Creed as Articulation of Faith

I have recently proposed that Christians recover a sense of their public profession as well as their personal commitment through the frequent recital, close study, and theological reflection on the Nicene-Constantinopolitan Creed, which is, together with the Apostles' Creed, the most familiar, accessible, and adequate articulation of classic Christian faith.[2] I have suggested that the creed performs several identity-formative functions with admirable directness and brevity. It narrates the Christian myth, interprets the Scripture, constructs a coherent understanding of the world, guides Christian practices, and, because of its placement in the Mass between the Liturgy of the Word and the Liturgy of the Meal, prepares a faithful people for worship.

The creed is particularly pertinent as an instrument of Christian self-definition in the present cultural context, and also particularly provocative. For some contemporary Catholics persuaded that everything undefined is also unsafe, the classic creed falls far short of adequacy. It is far too parsimonious in its profession. The creed elaborates no theory of sin or atonement, provides no definition of Eucharist or priesthood, and is absolutely silent on ecclesiastical authority. For those who identify Christian with Catholic, and Catholic faith with an itch for ever-more expansive definition, the creed appears as too dangerously reticent and ecumenical a profession.

On the other side — and it is a far larger side — many Christians have deep anti-creedal sentiments. Some from within free-church traditions despise creeds as the instruments of theological tyranny imposed by ancient ecclesiastical authority. They claim the authority of Scripture alone. Others have erected the acute individualism and consumerism of contemporary American culture into a new Gnosticism that neglects and sometimes scorns classic expressions of Christian faith. They consider spirituality more important than religion.[3]

Both Catholicism and mainline Protestantism in America have suffered the erosion of clear boundaries between the saints and the world. On every side we see the struggle between those who seek to eliminate such boundaries altogether, and those who seek to make such boundaries into barriers. The extreme positions are both abetted by an inadequate grasp of the essentials of faith as found in the creed. Those who have no sense of what is truly essential cannot be flexible at any point; they need to define everything as essential precisely because they can't tell the essential from central from the peripheral. And on the other side, the willingness to scuttle even the heart of the Christian confession clearly reveals the unwillingness to acknowledge some truths as nonnegotiable.[4]

In a crisis of Christian self-definition, the creed has the advantage of defining without confining, of challenging the world while at the same time challenging those who recite it. In an obvious way, the recitation of the creed challenges the ethos of the world. In my book, I speak of those who say the creed at Mass every Sunday: "In a world that celebrates individuality, they are actually doing something together. In an age that avoids commitment, they pledge themselves to a set of convictions and thereby to each other. In a culture that rewards novelty and creativity, they use words written by others long ago. In a society where accepted wisdom changes by the minute, they claim that some truths are so critical that they must be repeated over and over again. In a throwaway, consumerist world, they accept, preserve, and continue tradition. Reciting the creed at worship is thus a counter-cultural act."[5]

At the same time, the creed also challenges those who speak its words. Cognitive psychology has again taught us what we were first taught by ancient moral philosophers (including Paul) and should never have forgotten, namely, that humans act upon their genuine and deep beliefs concerning the world and their place in it. The creed constructs a vision of the world as created and saved by God, guides the reading of the Scriptures that reveal such a vision, and provides the basis for practices consistent with that vision. The challenge the creed presents is whether those who speak its words truly believe what they say and truly act in accordance with its profession.[6]

I do not mean to suggest that the creed is significant only because of its efficacy as an instrument of coherent ecclesiology. Just the opposite: I suggest that the creed deserves attention and study because it can shape Christian communities in accordance with the truth of revelation. It is not simply that the creed functions to shape identity. Any statement of convictions can do that. It is that the creed shapes Christian identity according to the truth of God's self-revelation. The implication of the rejection or distortion of faith's content according to the creed is not only the rejection or distortion of the entire Christian tradition, but as well the rejection or distortion of the creed's claim to speak truly about the human experience of God in the world.

The Case of Christology

The creed reminds us, moreover, that the convictions that make up "the content of faith" are more than a set of discrete opinions concerning reality. They are, rather, deeply interconnected aspects of the same story, which I have called "the Christian myth." It is not possible to reduce or reject one part of the story without a commensurate effect on every other part of the story. The denial or distortion of one truth leads to the denial and distortion of the entire set of truths, or the truth of the entire story.

Nothing so clearly shows such interconnectedness than the understanding of Jesus, or Christology. And nothing so dramatically reveals the crisis within Christianity concerning the "content of the faith" than the way in which the truth of the Gospel concerning Jesus the Lord has been challenged and eroded over a period of centuries, not through direct attack by Christianity's cultured despisers, but through a steady process of revision by theologians who seem either unaware of or not to care about the consequences of their capitulation to the premises of Christianity's cultured despisers.

I am speaking of the variety of "Christologies from below" that have, in different ways, sought to capture a more accessible and attractive Jesus for contemporary Christians, through the use of historical methods, while failing to recognize that a "Jesus within the bounds of Reason" may be accessible and attractive, but is much less than the Jesus proclaimed from the beginning as the good news by which humans are saved. The most benign form is taken by liberation theology, which seeks to base a message of social betterment on a "historical Jesus."[7] The most malign form is undoubtedly found among the liberal Christians who are represented by Bishop Spong,[8] and the essayists anthologized several decades ago in *The Myth of God Incarnate*.[9] Among such authors, the Enlightenment critique of classic Christian belief is the unquestioned starting point for the dismantling of the Christian faith in the name of modernity or relevance.

Between these extremes are the various versions of "the historical Jesus" that have been on offer since the time of Reimarus and D. F. Strauss,[10] down to (on the left) Funk, Crossan, and Borg — the three most famous members of the Jesus Seminar[11] — and (on the right) N. T. Wright — the most famous champion of the evangelicals.[12] The diversity of images of Jesus generated by what is supposedly an "objective scientific" method is, to be sure, one of the standard observations concerning these efforts, revealing them to be, on the whole, much more an exercise in apocryphal imagination than in sober historiography. Stated motivations, to be sure, range widely. Funk and Crossan are clear in their hostility toward traditional Christianity — from the start a distortion of the "real Jesus" — and their desire to dislodge the creedal Christ in favor of their "historical" reconstruction, with the express intention of reshaping a "Jesus for the New Millennium."[13] Borg and Wright appear far more pious, regarding their respective reconstructions of Jesus (based entirely on the Gospel of Luke) thoroughly compatible with traditional belief.[14]

Whatever form taken, four aspects of such "Christologies from below" are noteworthy, no, astonishing. The first is the thoroughly uncritical acceptance of "critical history" as an adequate epistemological framework for interpreting the mystery by which millions of Christians through the ages have interpreted their lives. The second is the assumption that "bracketing" the resurrection perspective of the Gospels in order to present Jesus "as he really was" or "bracketing" the theology of the incarnation for the sake of "real history" is any more intellectually honest than "bracketing" the fact that a woman is my mother in order to present her more historically. The third is that so many ordinary Christians, certainly including many Catholics, regard such Christologies from below as entirely positive, precisely because they render Jesus "more like me," and have real difficulty in understanding why someone should object to such theologies and histories. The fourth is that, despite the creedal confession concerning Jesus being under such constant attack over a period of some three hundred years (now the longest-lasting christological controversy in the church's history) and creating such confusion among lay and ordained Christians alike, there has been little or no concerted effort to identify what is erroneous or destructive in such efforts, little or no concerted effort to identify the truth of the Gospels for the present generation. I will say a word about each of these *thaumata* before moving forward.

1. The uncritical acceptance of critical history as an adequate way of thinking about Jesus and as an adequate framework for reading the Gospels reveals the remarkable compression of acceptable modes of knowing after the Enlightenment. After Bacon, only the potentially verifiable can seriously claim to truth about the world.[15] For the present, natural science trumps all; for the past, historiography alone counts. Everything else is opinion, legend, myth, error. I call this compression remarkable not only because of the narrowness of its focus but because of the range of its success. How can ontology so completely have disappeared? For that matter, how could mathematical and musical and aesthetic and moral ways of knowing be regarded as irrelevant to grown-up life? But the results are all around us. Lay readers and scholars alike seem to think that "historical" equals "real." Among the historical Jesus books, only John Meier's first volume takes up the epistemological problem with this equation, and in his actual questing, not even he entirely avoids the slippage between the terms.[16] Similarly, despite all the ways in which the phenomenology of religion and philosophy has tried to rehabilitate the term *myth* for language that expresses what surpasses the empirical,[17] common usage (again both lay and scholarly) tends to reduce the meaning of myth to "non-historical" and therefore "non-real."

2. The "bracketing" of the resurrection and incarnation in order to "recover" a historical Jesus is more problematic than it first appears. What appears as a simple methodological decision quickly becomes a substantive exclusion or denial. When D. F. Strauss declared already in 1835 that historical method could not deal with the supernatural — since history deals only with human events in time and space — he was absolutely correct.[18] History's scan captures only what is at least potentially verifiable. Therefore nothing "supernatural" in the Gospels can be handled historically, including Jesus' miraculous birth, exorcisms, healings, transfiguration, and resurrection. But the fact that history cannot deal with miracles slips easily into the denial that miracles occur or can occur — especially when history has been elevated into the only legitimate way of knowing. This is, to be sure, the simplest sort of fallacy, namely, equating reality with our capacity to know it. But that does not keep it from being widespread. Such "bracketing" of the divine in Jesus — for that is what it is — is problematic in two further ways.

One further problem is its historiographical naïveté. Everything we know about Jesus (apart from those few outsider sources that confirm the basic facts about his life and death) comes from those who believe in him as the resurrected and exalted Lord, not merely the one who came back to life but who became "life-giving spirit" (1 Cor 15:45). Not only the shape but also the very selection of Jesus' words and deeds derive from that conviction. Even if we could scrape away all redaction and get back to bedrock, we should still be within the framework of tradition. We have nothing that comes directly from Jesus. Everything comes from those who heard and saw him, and whose view of what they heard and saw was fundamentally altered by the reality of his continuing presence in their midst.[19]

Questers for the historical Jesus show themselves most historically naïve in their willful "bracketing" of all evidence about Jesus in our earliest Christian sources, not only the letters of Paul but also such early compositions as 1 Peter and Hebrews: all of them attest to the importance of the humanity of Jesus, but all of them speak even more powerfully of the reality of Jesus' exaltation to the presence and power of God.

The other problem with such bracketing is in fact the most severe. If Jesus is the incarnate word of God, then his story is, from beginning to end, mythic, for no other language can contain the activity of God within the frame of human existence. The language of myth is, to be sure, connected to a historical figure. But to claim to render Jesus "historically" by eliminating the language that seeks to convey his divinity is an exercise not in historical fastidiousness, but a form of theological denial. Similarly, if Jesus is the raised and exalted Lord who not only lives but continues to be life-giving spirit even now, then his share in God's life is what is most true about him. "Bracketing" the truth that Jesus now sits at the right hand of the Father as Lord and will come to judge the living and the dead is to "bracket" the existential and ontological truth about Jesus. It is because historical critics operate with such a methodological bracketing that they consistently miss the literary richness and religious profundity of the Gospel stories, and appear, in the end, to be verifying what does not matter while leaving everything that does matter unexamined, and worse, unengaged.

3. Astonishing also is that Christology from below has been so universally applauded by ordinary Christians. Most Christians are little disturbed by the various and sometimes contradictory versions of "historical" Jesus on offer at Barnes & Noble, and consider anything "historical" an improvement on "doctrine." Indeed, as the success of books by Elaine Pagels[20] and Dan Brown[21] make obvious, virtually any account of Christian origins is to be preferred to that handed on by the Christian tradition. How do we account for this remarkable phenomenon? The causes are undoubtedly multiple, but they must include the failure of preaching and teaching within the church to powerfully communicate the true significance of the resurrection life and the transformation of human identity by Christ, the corresponding success of scholars to position themselves as mediators of truth more trustworthy and uncorrupted than priests or ministers, and, finally, the breakdown of a creedal consciousness among most Christians, who no longer have a sense of the connectedness of the truths of faith, or their inner logic, so that a purely human Jesus "just like us" seems to them like an unexpected addition rather than a fatal subtraction.

4. That this long-standing christological tendency has generated so little official response from the church is also astonishing.[22] The failure adequately to address the erosion of the heart of the Gospel stands in stark contrast to the church's willingness to engage issues of morality great and small, especially those having to do with sexuality. Bishops can gather to issue statements on war, on the economy, and on sexual

scandal. But the collapse of classical Christology seems scarcely to be noticed, least of all by the many ministers who week by week continue to erode the integrity of the good news by preaching as though the resurrection were an event of the past concerning Jesus that is celebrated each year at Easter rather than the most pressing and present circumstance of all human existence — and the premise of all preaching.[23] That ecclesial groups in America are gathering in solemn assembly to debate the homosexual body but would find ludicrous the proposal that they gather to debate the resurrection body says all that needs to be said about the state of creedal faith today.

Corollaries of Christological Collapse

We might add as a fifth astonishing thing that the corollaries of such christological collapse do not seem to concern anyone overmuch either, even though they represent a thorough revision of traditional (creedal) faith. Recitation and study of the creed might at the least alert Christians to the fact that they continue to affirm as truths things that cannot be true if what they now think about Jesus is true.

If the resurrection is denied or reduced to a form of resuscitation, then humanity has not entered (through Jesus) into a share in God's life, humanity has not been gifted with the transforming power of the Holy Spirit, and Jesus cannot come again as the judge of the living and the dead. Jesus remains simply a dead Jewish teacher of the past. Everything else is fantasy, everything Christians do "in the name of Jesus," including worship. It is literally nonsensical to pray to God "through Jesus Christ our Lord," if Jesus is not "Lord." And to the precise degree that Jesus does not have a present in the presence of God, believers have no future in the presence of God. Thus, "looking forward to the resurrection of the dead and the life of the world to come," as the creed concludes, is at best a form of poetry, and at worst a sad example of self-deception.

Likewise, if Jesus is not the divine Word of God made flesh, if God does not, in Jesus, enter fully into human existence, then the claim that "Jesus reveals the human face of God" is again true only in the way that it is true of any human being. And if God has not entered into human existence, then neither has God shared fully in human suffering and death, nor has God transfigured human suffering and death. Nothing fundamental has changed in the human condition.

Without incarnation and resurrection, contemporary Christians are in effect the heirs of the radical Arians of the fourth century, and, whether knowingly or not, Unitarian rather than Trinitarian. Jesus has not revealed God but only a way of being human. The spirit of Jesus is not the one that leads us into God's own life but is at most a form of enthusiasm.

Without incarnation and resurrection, with a purely "historical" Jesus as the basis of Christian commitment — who knows why? — the understanding of sin and salvation necessarily adjust as well, as we have seen them adjust. Sin is no longer a matter of the rebellion of the human will against God but a matter of unjust social systems harming people. Salvation is, correspondingly, not the transformation of human existence, a process of sanctification leading in the end to a share in God's glory, but a process of political change, seeking just social structures in place of alienating ones.[24]

If the shape of human hope is confined to the rearrangement of human institutions, it is small wonder, in turn, if Christianity appears to some observers as a fairly incoherent club for moral betterment, and to still others — among them many calling themselves Christian — as a moral force that could be more effective if it stripped away the last inhibiting vestiges of myth. We have arrived back in the land of Bishop Spong and Robert Funk. Jesus liberated from the tentacles of the creed leads to a Christianity liberated from any coherence and from any reason to continue in its present (diminished) form.

The Corollaries of Taking the Creed Seriously

One consequence of reading the creed and studying the creed is the discovery of how little contemporary Christians actually understand what the creed says and, once they understand it, how little they actually believe in what it says. Taking the creed seriously would, I think, first create a crisis in a Christian consciousness that has steadily been eroded under the influence of modernity. Being forced to engage the gap between what Christians have always professed and contemporary Christians actually think should generate a healthy cognitive dissonance. The scandal of Christian faith will prove to be a scandal first of all to Christians. The cognitive dissonance cannot be resolved in a positive fashion, moreover, unless those who have induced the crisis through taking the creed

seriously also have the ability to lead others to a more robust appreciation of classic Christian confession, and the way of life that follows from
that confession.

It is here, I think, that the real challenge is posed to those of us who
are participating in this conference on "handing on the faith." If we want
to be prophets, teachers, pastors, within a church that takes the creed
seriously, if we want to be theologians within such a church, then much
will be demanded of us, both personally and intellectually.

Personally, we must find some way of witnessing to the faith that
combines deep piety, social passion, and intellectual openness. Deep and
authentic piety is necessary, because words about the transformation of
life that are not backed by a life in the process of being transformed are
empty. An active and committed passion for social justice is required,
because the logic of the creed demands practices that are at least as
radical as those bruited by liberals. Intellectual openness is mandatory,
because adherence to tradition by those who are not even aware of
modernity's charm as well as challenge is otherwise mere stubbornness.

When orthodoxy is represented only by the humorless and the bland,
by those patently interested in power and privilege, by those who show
no real engagement with thought and little real engagement with the
lives of the suffering, then orthodoxy is naturally (and perhaps justly)
regarded as the protected turf of the safe and comfortable. It is therefore,
I think, an essential dimension of the contemporary witness to orthodox
faith that it combines largeness of vision, sharpness of mind, and a joyous
embrace of legitimate diversity. Above all, theologians must reveal in
their lives as well as their words that the power of the resurrection is
present and the miracle of transforming grace is real. Otherwise, the
content of faith articulated by the creed will indeed appear removed
from life, and an imposition from the fossilized past on the problematic
present.

Beyond the demands of such personal witness, theologians seeking
to cultivate a creedal Christianity face severe intellectual challenges. If
the creed is to be intelligible and credible (and attractive) to contemporary believers, far more than a historical explanation of its terms will be
required. A historical explanation of why Nicene theologians considered
it necessary to assert belief in "one" God, or affirm that God is creator
"of heaven and earth, of all things visible and invisible" does not, by
itself, make those words either true or pertinent today. In fact, the basic

intellectual challenge facing teachers in the church today is recovering a sense of critical thought that is not constrained by the epistemological contraction of the Enlightenment, and this means refusing to accept that history is always and everywhere the censor of acceptable discourse about God and the world.

Three aspects of this epistemological challenge are fairly obvious. First, theologians must once more embrace, eagerly, gladly, and without apology, the language of myth as appropriate for the story of salvation rather than that of history. This is clearly a delicate and difficult step, for we must also declare that the story of which we speak has historical dimensions, and the study of history is pertinent to the responsible reading of Scripture. History as such is not rejected as a way of knowing. But history cannot adequately contain the truth of which faith speaks. When Paul declares that "God was in Christ reconciling the world to Himself" (2 Cor 5:19), not a single word in that sentence is even potentially verifiable as historical. Yet it speaks the truth about Jesus more profoundly than any historical statement could. When history is the only means of knowing, the truth of faith is necessarily reduced. Resurrection must be reduced to resuscitation, for only resuscitation fits within the framework of empirically verifiable fact, whereas exaltation to the right hand of God does not. But if Jesus' resurrection is merely a resuscitation, it is not good news, it is not a new creation.

Second, theologians need to recover ontology. In fact, it may be possible to speak of myth as a form of narrative ontology. The story told by the creed is not that of merely human events in time and space, but the story of God's entry into human existence and God's transformation of human existence. If all our language can address is the factual and the empirical, then we cannot speak the content of the faith. Without being able to speak of being and of existence, we cannot speak of the reality of which the creed speaks. It is certainly the case that philosophical language entered the creed as a way of responding to the philosophical idiom introduced by Arius. But it is not true to say that philosophical language (either that of the Arians or the Nicene theologians) was alien to the language of the New Testament. The story told by the New Testament is not that of historical fact alone but of divine presence and activity through Jesus. The language of myth ("God was in Christ reconciling the world to Himself") is itself ontologically dense, and requires for its explication a language capable of dealing with more than the empirical.

Once more, the contemporary discussion of the resurrection reveals the consequences of a loss of philosophical sensibility. Those who can speak only in a historical idiom are helpless in the face of the New Testament's assertions. Typically, they end up either eliminating the somatic dimension of the resurrection, reducing it to a vague "spiritual" survival (through teaching, memory, imitation), some sort of psychological adjustment occurring in the minds of Jesus' followers, or, in the attempt to assert its "realness," reduce it precisely to its somatic dimension, ending up with a resuscitation of Jesus' empirical body. But resuscitation only defers rather than overcomes mortality. Yet Paul speaks of the resurrection as a mystery in which "this perishable body must put on imperishability, and this mortal body must put on immortality" (1 Cor 15:53).

Similarly, Paul speaks of the resurrection in terms of a *soma pneumatikon* (1 Cor 15:44). But if we have no phenomenology of the body, and no phenomenology of spirit, how can we possibly address Paul's language? If, in order to fit within the framework of modernity, we think of the body in terms of physical extension and think of spirit in terms of the mind in the machine (or, today, in terms of brain chemistry), we cannot begin to engage Paul's statements. Only if we have some way of thinking about spirit as a capacity to transcend individual somatic boundaries and enter into the bodies of others can we begin to approach the mystery of which Paul speaks.[25] If we insist that revelation must fit within the bounds of reason, as reason is defined by modernity, then we cannot but reduce revelation.

Third, theologians must be willing to read Scripture in ways other than historically. I spoke earlier in this paper of the creed as a guide to the reading of Scripture, and if the creed itself is to become intelligible and credible to Christians, then theologians must again learn to read as the Nicene theologians read.[26] Even at its very best, the historical approach to the Bible is necessarily reductive, simply in order to be properly historical. The historical approach necessarily reads the writings of the Old and New Testaments as human writings that stay in the past. The historian can perhaps declare on the reliability of the compositions with reference to events of the past that are in principle verifiable, although even this occasion is rarer than we might wish. But the historian as historian is simply not in the position to declare on the truthfulness of the compositions when they speak of the identity and character of Jesus, or of his resurrection and exaltation to the right hand of the Father, or of his future coming as judge, or of the manner of life that is "worthy of God." Indeed, methodological consistency demands of the historian the bracketing or screening of such language: that may be what Paul said and thought, but as to its truth, as a historian, I cannot judge.

What happens when the historical approach to Scripture is considered to be the only legitimate approach? Inevitably, the conversation between Scripture and theology is adversely affected. At best, biblical scholars have little to offer theologians and pastors, since their approach works only to describe what the compositions might have meant in the past and not what truth they may have for the present. At worst, theology is made captive to the historical approach to Scripture, because of the exclusive claims to competency asserted by scholars who are historians but not theologians, and thereby theologians either accept the reductionistic (historical) version of the resurrection, for example, as what Scripture actually teaches, or accept one of several versions of a "theology of the New Testament" that is itself simply another version of reduction through history.

Learning to read Scripture not simply as a record of the past, but as compositions that speak prophecy to the present — speak the truth about the presence and power of God at work to transform the world in the communities reading these texts — will not be easy. It will demand of us the humility to learn from readers of the past. It will require of us the learning of skills and of sensibilities that are not professionally rewarded. It will require of us the willingness to exegete the complexities of contemporary human experience as well as the complexities of ancient language. It will ask of us that we become theologians rather than historians.

Taking the creed seriously will not, I think, make things easier. In many ways, it will make things more difficult. But it may also make things in the church more truthful. And it may be a way in which we can once more put together a commitment to orthodox doctrine and a generous humanity, a love for the content of the church's faith as well as a passionate witness to the life that faith enables.

Chapter 5

The Metaphysics of Co-Inherence

A Meditation on the Essence
of the Christian Message

ROBERT BARRON

ROUND THE YEAR 750, scribes, artists, and illustrators of the monastery of Iona, situated on an island just off the western coast of Scotland, produced a book of the Gospels. We know that, for a time, it rested at the shrine of St. Brigit in Kildare, where a visitor referred to it as "the High Relic of the Western World." A twelfth-century pilgrim to Ireland gave us a vivid description of its pages: "If you take the trouble to look very closely...you will notice such intricacies, so delicate, so subtle...so involved and bound together...that you will not hesitate to declare that all those things must have been the work not of men but of angels."[1] This remarkable sacred object is now known, from the last place that it rested, as the Book of Kells.

One of the most famous of its pages is the "Chi-Rho" page, the opening of the Gospel of Matthew. Sinuous lines cross one another, twisting, turning, overlapping, intertwining, forming tightly woven patterns. Often within an already densely textured design, a smaller and even more intricate pattern can be picked out. Animals abound (including two mice who tug at a consecrated host!), and they find their place alongside of human figures, who in turn are implicated in the structure of the letters. The playful, colorful, and interlacing style of the Book of Kells has been called typically Irish, and this may be so, but at a much more basic level it is Catholic and Christian.

Charles Williams, who was, along with J. R. R. Tolkien and C. S. Lewis, a member of the Oxford writers' group the Inklings, claimed that the master idea of Christianity is co-inherence, by which he meant the implication of the being of one in the being of the other, the intertwining and interlacing of reality. He saw it in the *circumincessio* of the Trinitarian persons, in the coming-together of divinity and humanity in Jesus, in the dynamics of Christ's atoning death, and in the corporate life of the Church, the way the members of the body of Christ bear each other's burdens.[2] Like the lines and patterns of the Book of Kells, reality, seen through Christian eyes, has a stubbornly co-inherent structure.

That co-inherence is metaphysically basic is the content of our catechesis and teaching; it is one way of stating the core belief that we Catholic Christians want to communicate to the next generations. I stand with Hans Urs von Balthasar in claiming that the most effective starting-point for our teaching and proclamation is the beauty of our message, a beauty very much like that of the Book of Kells: engrossing, fascinating, intricate, and deeply involving. When Charles Ryder, the narrator of Evelyn Waugh's great Catholic novel *Brideshead Revisited,* comes to Brideshead for the first time, he is overwhelmed and attracted by the mansion's beauty. It is only in time, as he interacts with the various people that inhabit the home that he comes to appreciate that living there carries with it an intellectual and moral demand. Brideshead — how like Paul's Christ who is head of his bride the church — is symbolic of the mystical body of Jesus. Waugh seems to be teaching us that the optimal way to lure the nonbeliever into the communion of the church is through the attractive quality of Christianity's beauty, trusting that, once captured by beauty, he will be led to truth and goodness as well.[3] Thus, in the course of this presentation, I will attempt to show the compelling doctrine of co-inherence as it is displayed paradigmatically in the Incarnation of the Lord and then to demonstrate the implications of this teaching for Christian metaphysics, epistemology, and ethics.

The Distinction and the Connection

G. K. Chesterton said that even those who reject the doctrine of the Incarnation are different for having heard it.[4] The claim that God became one of us changes the imagination, compelling a reassessment of both God and the world. This odd assertion is made, implicitly or explicitly, on practically every page of the New Testament. When, in Mark's Gospel, Jesus says to the paralytic, "my son, your sins are forgiven," the onlookers respond, "but only God can forgive sins," thereby, despite themselves, stating the evangelical faith. In Luke's Gospel, Jesus says, "unless you love me more than your mother and father, indeed your very life, you cannot be my followers," implying that he is the Good that must be loved above even the highest created goods. In Matthew's Gospel, Jesus asserts, "heaven and earth shall pass away, but my words shall never pass away" — a claim which can consistently and sanely be made if and only if the speaker is himself the eternal Word. And that, of course, is precisely what the prologue to the Gospel of John explicitly affirms: "in the beginning was the Word and the Word was with God and the Word was God...and the Word became flesh and dwelt among us" (see Jn 1:1–14). John's magnificent confession is echoed in the hymn that has found its way into Paul's Letter to the Colossians: "in him [Christ] all things hold together; all were created for him and in him all things are maintained in being" (see Col 1:15–20). As this unprecedented and intellectually provocative assertion made its way across the centuries, it proved both illuminating and deeply disconcerting, as is evident from the boisterous debate that it inspired among Christians. How, many wondered, is God capable of such an act of condescension?

The classic doctrinal statement of the Church's faith in the Incarnation is the formula hammered out at the Council of Chalcedon in 451. Battling both Monophysitism and Nestorianism, the council fathers maintained that in Jesus two natures — human and divine — are grounded and instantiated in the person of the Logos, effecting thereby a hypostatic union of divinity and humanity. Though the natures are realized in the one person, they come together without "mixing, mingling, or confusion," that is to say, without losing their ontological integrity and distinctiveness.

According to the logic of Chalcedon, it is decidedly not the case that God turns into a creature, ceasing to be God and transforming himself into a created nature; and it is assuredly not the case that a human being stops being human and turns into the Creator. Rather, divinity and humanity come together in the most intimate kind of union, yet non-competitively. But such non-competitiveness is possible only in the measure that God is not, himself, a creaturely or finite nature.[5] Due to their metaphysical structure, finite things, despite the numerous ways in which they can find communion with one another, remain, at the most fundamental level, mutually exclusive, so that one can "become" another only through ontological surrender or aggression. Thus, a wildebeest becomes a lion only by being devoured; a building turns into rubble and ash only by being destroyed; and you "become" me only through some act of enormous psychological manipulation.

Since, in the Incarnation, God becomes a creature without ceasing to be God or compromising the integrity of the creature that he becomes, God must be other than a creaturely nature. But the divine otherness is not simply the kind of otherness that obtains between two creatures, a standard over-and-againstness. Rather, God must be "otherly other," to borrow Kathryn Tanner's phrase.[6] God is not one being among many, caught in the nexus of contingent relations, but rather, as David Burrell has argued, that which is responsible for the whole of finite reality, the one who, as Herbert McCabe has said, sustains the world the way a singer sustains a song. We are skating on the edge of a paradox, for it is this very transcendence to the world that allows God to effect an incomparable closeness to worldly things. Nicholas of Cusa expressed this by saying that God, even as he remains utterly other, is the *non-aliud,* and Augustine gestured toward the same metaphysical tension when he observed that God is, simultaneously, *intimior intimo meo et superior summo meo.* No theologian has more beautifully evoked the non-competitive transcendence of God than Irenaeus, who said: *gloria Dei homo vivens,* the glory of God is a human being fully alive, implying that God's majesty is entirely compatible with creaturely flourishing.

The closeness of God to the world is also a function of God's radical self-sufficiency. The otherly other Creator, who continually gives rise to all of finite reality, could not, even in principle, stand in a relationship of neediness vis-à-vis what he makes in its entirety. As Whitehead quite rightly saw, a process view of God is incompatible with a theology of creation. When Anselm described God as "that than which no greater can be thought," he signaled a break with the classical understanding of the divine, for the gods of ancient mythology and philosophy are superior beings to be sure, but they remain in the world alongside of other things. Therefore, they could not be characterized as "that than which no greater can be thought," since they plus the world would be greater than they alone. Anselm's peculiar description reflects precisely the non-contrastive and non-competitive transcendence that we have been describing, for it implies that God plus the world is not greater than God alone. The true God could not possibly need the world since nothing in creation could ever add to God's perfection.

Implications for Metaphysics

This unique understanding of God, rooted in the paradox of the Incarnation, shapes the way Christians view the whole of existence. Precisely because God stands in no need of the world, all that exists apart from God is an expression and embodiment of sheerest love. Thomas Aquinas defines love as the willing of the good of the other as other. Since creatures are finite and imperfect, they remain, in regard to one another, to a certain degree in a relationship of need, and hence their capacity to will the good of the other will always be partially mitigated or compromised. But this cannot be true of the self-sufficient Creator. Therefore the very being of the universe is testament to the purest possible act of willing the good of the other as other. The First Vatican Council (1869–70), in its polemics against forms of Hegelianism that were creeping into Catholic thought in the nineteenth century, asserted that God did not make the world out of need but simply to manifest his glory.[7] Whatever has come to be, therefore, has been loved into being. Love is not an accidental relationship that a creature may or may not enter into with God; instead, love — being from and for the other — is the relationship which constitutes any and all things from the beginning.

The ontological irreducibility of relationship appears as well when we look more closely at the doctrine of *creatio ex nihilo*. As Robert Louis Wilken has indicated, one of the major points of demarcation between the metaphysical account of the earliest Christians and that of the pagan philosophers was the teaching regarding the origins of the world.[8] In most forms of classical philosophy, order comes into the universe through a divine shaping influence on some preexisting element. Thus, Aristotle's first mover draws prime matter into shape through its irresistible attractiveness, and Plato's demiourgos manipulates the primal chaos after consulting the patterns of the forms. But the Christians proposed something new — a doctrine of creation from nothing, according to which God brings the whole of finitude in all of its dimensions and aspects into being, without reference to a preexisting substrate. This implies in turn that there is nothing substantial and external with which God enters into relationship, but rather that all that is not God is, essentially, a relationship to God.

In his densely textured analysis of creation, Thomas Aquinas is compelled to twist and break the language of Aristotle in order to articulate this radical teaching. In response to the question whether creation is something in the creature or perhaps between the creature and God, Thomas makes the Zen-like remark that that which receives the act of creation is itself a creature.[9] Operating beyond the categories of substance and accident, Aquinas says that creation is *quaedam relatio ad creatorem cum novitate essendi* (a kind of relation to the Creator with freshness of being).[10] The creature does not have a relationship with God; instead, it is a relationship with God. This novelty and distinctiveness was well expressed in the poem *God's Grandeur* by Gerard Manley Hopkins when he spoke of God as "the dearest freshness deep down things."

John Milbank and his radical orthodoxy colleagues have helped us to see that this teaching implies, furthermore, the primordiality of nonviolence. If creation is truly *ex nihilo,* then there is nothing about it that is invasive, interruptive, or interfering, for there is no antagonistic other upon which God works. Order does not occur through any type of intrusion or conquest; instead, God brings the world to be through an entirely gratuitous and nonviolent act of love.[11] James Alison has suggested that the metaphysical doctrine of creation from nothing flows from the surprise of the Paschal Mystery, more precisely from the moment when the risen Jesus restores order to the frightened community of his disciples who had betrayed and abandoned him, not through answering violence, but through forgiveness.[12] All of this shows that the world to the very roots of its being exists in God by means of a relationship, and that God can reach most intimately into things, as Aquinas puts it, "by essence, presence, and power." The intertwining, the co-inherence, of God and the universe is a principal metaphysical consequence of the non-contrastive transcendence of God.

And from the co-inherence of God and creation follows the co-inherence of created things with one another. Because all finite reality — from archangels to quarks — comes forth here and now from the same divine generosity, the ontological ground of any one thing is identical to the ontological ground of any other. Like islands in an archipelago, we are all, despite our surface differences, connected at the depths. All creatures are ontological siblings. When he stood at the corner of Fourth and Walnut Streets in downtown Louisville in 1958, Thomas Merton realized this truth and in his *Conjectures of a Guilty Bystander* gave famous expression to the realization. Seeing all of the ordinary people bustling past him, it suddenly dawned on him that he loved them all, not in a sentimental or emotional sense, but mystically, even metaphysically. Waking from what he called "a dream of separateness," he knew that they all belonged to God and hence to each other, connected through a *point vierge,* a virginal point where each was being created by God.[13] Understanding this co-inherence for the first time, Merton exclaimed: "there is no way of telling people that they are all walking around shining like the sun."[14]

It is precisely this connectedness of all creatures to one another through God which Thomas Aquinas articulates in his doctrine of analogy. Because all created beings participate in God who is *ipsum esse subsistens,* they are unavoidably related to one another by means of that shared participation. It has been central to the intellectual projects of Louis Dupré, Hans Urs von Balthasar, Alisdair MacIntyre, and many others to show how this metaphysical vision fell apart through the introduction of a univocal conception of being, which effectively placed God and creatures side by side under the general heading of existence and thereby separated them from one another. In a word, the univocal understanding of the concept of existence blinded us to the centrality and primordiality of co-inherence.

Implications for Epistemology

The non-competitive coming together of divinity and humanity in Jesus also has implications for the way we know. If, as the prologue to the Gospel of John insists, Jesus Christ is the visible icon of the Logos through which God has made all things, and if, as the Letter to the Colossians makes clear, Jesus is the one in whom and for whom all things exist and through whom they are maintained, then Jesus is the interpretive lens through which reality is properly read. Jesus Christ is, for Christians, epistemically basic, which is to say, that he functions as an epistemic trump: any account of reality which runs essentially counter to what is disclosed in the narratives about Jesus must be false. Lest this sound like sectarianism, we must bear in mind that both Augustine and Aquinas maintain that even "natural reason" is subject to Christ in the measure that the first principles and operations of the mind are nothing but a participation in the reasonability of the divine Logos, which became incarnate in Jesus. We Christians claim to know in a distinctive way, but this does not exclude us from the general human conversation, quite the contrary. It allows us to enter it more honestly, effectively, and creatively.

So what does it mean more precisely to have the mind of Christ? First it means to hold to the radical intelligibility of being. If God has made all creation through the Logos, then all existence must be stamped with form, the mark of a knower. As many have pointed out, it is by no means accidental that the hard physical sciences emerged and came to flourish in a Christian culture, for only those who have a mystical confidence that being is intelligible will endeavor to know the world through observation, experimentation, and the forming of hypotheses. A universe without rational structure could never be the correlate to a scientific spirit.[15] But that upon which all scientific activity rests cannot itself be the subject of scientific investigation; it must rather be the fruit of an intuition which can only be called religious in its depth, range, and breadth. Christians name it exactly as the faithful grasp of the doctrine of creation through the Word. This is the ground for the confident human- ism that has characterized Christianity at its best over the centuries. We who hold precisely on theological grounds to the intelligibility of being have nothing to fear from the honest and careful practice of any and all intellectual disciplines, just the contrary. When Aquinas was challenged by certain of his contemporaries who were concerned that his use of Aris- totle amounted to the diluting of the wine of revelation with the water of pagan science, Thomas responded, "No, it is rather the changing of water into wine."

But Christians know, in light of Christ, how to specify more exactly the structure and content of the world's intelligibility. Because all things are made through the Logos, which is itself nothing but a subsistent relation to the Father, co-inherence, and not substance or individual- ity, must be the basic truth of things. The wager of the Christian faith is that any philosopher, scientist, social theorist, or psychologist look- ing, within the confines of his own discipline, at the structure of reality will find something like being-for-and-with-the-other. Connection rather than separation, relationship rather than substance, will be disclosed as the most fundamental constitutive features of reality. In his writings on religion and science, physicist-priest John Polkinghorne has dem- onstrated that recent investigations of quantum physicists and chaos theorists reveal just this co-inherent quality at the most elemental level of matter, a finding, he suggests, that should not surprise Christians.[16]

A further epistemological implication of the non-competitiveness of the natures in Christ is that the act of knowing is not so much individualist but inter-subjective. Over and against Descartes's insistence that proper philosophy commences with the private ruminations of the isolated thinker, cut off from received tradition, sense experience, and assumption, Bernard Lonergan implied that it is not so much the *cogito* that matters as the *cogitamus*. Lonergan knew that Descartes's program of radical doubt was a fantasy, a hopelessly unrealistic and self-defeating exercise, since the act of doubt itself is made possible only through a rich complex of language, supposition, and shared conviction. More to it, no philosopher or scientist would ever get her project off the ground had she not accepted a whole congeries of findings, data, principles, and assumptions that she herself had not verified directly.[17] In a word, every responsible intellectual project involves, willy-nilly, a community of knowers seeking the truth together: the *cogitamus* rather than the *cogito*.

One of Lonergan's intellectual heroes was John Henry Newman. In his *Essay on the Development of Doctrine*, Newman maintains that ideas exist, not on the printed page, but in the play of lively minds. The human intellect does not take in notions dumbly or passively, as though it were a *tabula rasa*; instead, it analyzes, judges, compares, assesses, and questions them. More to it, by a sort of inner compulsion, it seeks to deepen and intensify this process through the establishment of a conversation with other minds.[18] In the playful, game-like exchange of insight, information, questions, and answers — beautifully exemplified in the dialogues of Plato and the treatises of Aquinas — ideas develop and human beings come to deeper understanding. This inter-subjective, communitarian manner of knowing is congruent with the metaphysics of co-inherence that we have been outlining. We know the complex truth of things precisely by wrapping our minds, Book of Kells-like, around one another.

A final epistemological consequence of an Incarnational sensibility is a thoroughly participative view of knowing. As we have seen, the intelligibility of being is a sign that all finite reality has been thought into existence, produced through the Logos of God. But this means that at the most fundamental level, there is a correspondence between knower and known, God's knowledge, as it were, informing and actualizing what it knows. Karl Rahner reiterates this idea when he says, in *Hearers of the Word,* that the meaning of existence is knowing and being known in an original unity.[19] Now this primordial co-inherence of divine knower and creaturely intelligibility obtains analogically in all human acts of intellection. For Thomas Aquinas, the human subject comes to know precisely when his mind is illumined and stirred to act by an objective form, and that form is realized, illumined, stirred to act precisely in the act of being known.[20] Knowing happens, in short, through a sort of mutual participation of knower and known, each one calling out to and perfecting the other. This mutuality is caught in the marvelous medieval dictum *intellectus in actu est intelligibile in actu,* the intellect in act *is* the actualization of the intelligible. It was this participative and mystical epistemology that was set aside in the modern period when the distantiation of subject from object, necessary for analysis, was emphasized. Descartes's concern with mastering nature through the mind is utterly alien to, say, Thomas Aquinas's desire to contemplate nature through intellectual participation. The former is made possible by a breakdown in the co-inherent Christian worldview that thoroughly informed the latter.

Implications for Ethics

When the young Gregory Thaumaturgos came to Origen to seek instruction in Christian doctrine, the great teacher told him that first he must share the life of the Christians and become their friend. Only in that way would he begin to understand what Christians teach.[21] Origen shared the assumption of most sages in the ancient world that philosophy is not an academic discipline but a form of life, a *bios*. A disciple at Plato's academy was not so much a student of Platonic theory as a practitioner of a way of life centered on the pursuit of truth.[22] This tight connection between knowledge and ethical practice was maintained by Christian thinkers throughout the patristic period and into the high Middle Ages. Augustine, Bernard, Anselm, Bonaventure, and Aquinas took for granted that real advancement in knowledge of Christian mysteries is a function of an accompanying advancement in the practice of the Christian virtues. If one were to pose to any of those figures the characteristically modern question about relating theology to ethics or spirituality, I trust he would not understand the question.

Nowhere is this connection between knowledge and practice clearer than in the *Summa Theologiae* of Aquinas. The great second part of the work, centered on the journey back to God, is predicated at every point upon the theological moves made in the first section, and the third part, dealing with Christ and the sacraments as the definitive way to God, is but a further specification and concretization of the second part. To speak, therefore, of Aquinas's "ethics" in abstraction from his doctrine of God or his Christology would be anomalous.[23] All of this is an elaborate way of saying that, for the classical Christian tradition, the doctrine of the Incarnation and its accompanying metaphysics of co-inherence have clear implications in regard to ethics and that correct moral behavior itself conduces toward a deeper appreciation of a distinctively Christian ontology.

In order to appreciate the moral and behavioral consequences of a Christian worldview, I would like to look first at what followed ethically from a breakdown in that unified *Weltanschauung*. As I have already noted, in the late Middle Ages, figures such as Duns Scotus and William of Ockham put forward a univocal conception of being, replacing the analogical understanding found in Aquinas. The most telling ontological implication of this epistemological shift was the placing of God and the world under the same metaphysical umbrella, turning God thereby into a supreme being among beings. No longer the deepest ground of whatever exists, God necessarily appeared as a rival to the world which he confronted. When this supreme existent was viewed in relation to human beings, he was construed as a threat to freedom. One rubric under which modernity can be viewed is that of the struggle — sometimes explicit, more often implicit — to defend human liberty against the invasive authority of God.[24] Thus the materialist Thomas Hobbes asserted that proper political order flows, not from a sense of the transcendent good, but rather from individual rights grounded in desire and fear. Though he softened this view to a degree, John Locke remained in a fundamentally Hobbesian framework, arguing that legitimate government exists to defend rights, defined as those things that one cannot help but desire. A consequence of this approach, perfectly in line with the nominalist assumptions that undergird it, is that citizens are seen as individuals jealously guarding their prerogatives over and against others who threaten them.

This strain of modernity came to even more radical expression in the nineteenth and twentieth centuries. For Feuerbach, Marx, and especially

Nietzsche, human flourishing is made possible only through the elimination of the competitive God. Feuerbach's formula is "the no to God
is the yes to man"; Marx's dictum is that religion must be sloughed off
like a snake's skin before human beings can aspire to maturity and political liberation; and Nietzsche bluntly declares that God is dead, because
the *Ubermensch* in the sheerest exercise of his power has killed him.
Jean-Paul Sartre elegantly states this conviction in terms of a compelling
syllogism: "if God exists, I cannot be free; but I am free; therefore God
does not exist."[25]

Lest we think that these claims remain on the level of academic
abstraction, consider the decision of the United States Supreme Court
in the 1992 matter of *Casey v. Planned Parenthood of Pennsylvania*. In
a breathtaking defense of human freedom over and against any power
that might condition or direct it, the justices wrote: "at the heart of liberty is the right to define one's own concept of existence, of meaning, of
the universe, of the mystery of human life."[26] According to this formula,
the true and the good are projections of human subjectivity, constructs
of an arbitrary autonomy. What we see in all of this is the playing out
of the shift to a univocal conception of being and a rivalrous view of
the God-world relationship. The "no" to God is the "yes" to man only
in the measure that God's existence stands over and against the world,
impinging upon it intrusively and invasively.

However, when God is perceived, not as a competitive supreme being,
but as the subsistent act of existence itself, then authentic human flourishing is appreciated as tantamount to a surrender to God and God's
purposes. When God is correctly understood along Chalcedonian lines,
then the co-inherence of humanity and divinity, of subjective freedom
and objective truth, becomes evident. Over and against what they perceived to be the heteronomy inherent in the classical tradition, the
Enlightenment philosophers advocated a bracing autonomy. Paul Tillich,
reflecting the Augustinian-Christian spirit, characterized that dichotomy
as simplistic and called instead for theonomy, the realization that one's
deepest sense of freedom is coincident with an embrace of the God who
is the ground of one's being. He knew, along with the great tradition,
that the true God is not a threat to freedom, but the condition for the
possibility of freedom properly exercised.

In the seventh century, the monothelite controversy raged within the
Christian church. This was a dispute over the nature of will in Jesus

Christ. Theologians of a more monophysite bent maintained that there was but one divine will in Jesus, but others held that a key implication of the two-natures doctrine of Chalcedon is that there must be two wills, divine and human, in the Lord. After much wrangling, the fathers of the Third Council of Constantinople in 681 determined that Christ possesses two wills and two natural operations, not opposed to one another, but cooperating in such a way that his human freedom finds itself precisely in surrender to his divine freedom. It might seem odd to rehearse the details of this ancient theological battle, but I believe that it sheds considerable light on the problematic that we have been exploring. In some ways, the monothelites — those who held to the unicity of will in Jesus — anticipated the philosophers of modernity, since they seemed to hold that divine authority and real human freedom are incompatible. In resolving the dispute as they did, the fathers of third Constantinople antecedently answered Hobbes, Feuerbach, Marx, Nietzsche, and Sartre: humanity is enhanced rather than diminished when placed in tight co-inherent relationship with the non-competitive God. Divine freedom and human freedom can interlace and overlap as thoroughly as any of the designs in the Book of Kells.

Again, the proper relationship between God and human freedom is on clear display in the second part of Aquinas's *Summa Theologiae*. Most of the moral philosophies and theologies of the late medieval and modern periods commence with a consideration of obligation. They are preoc-cupied with the limits set to freedom by the commands of God. What lies behind such a starting-point is the assumption that God and human beings are alien to one another and that divine and human freedoms are mutually antagonistic. But the moral section of the *Summa* does not commence with obligation, duty, or law, but rather with happiness.[27] Thomas wonders what makes human beings joyful and determines that neither power, nor riches, nor reputation, nor glory, nor any finite good could ever do so. It is, he concludes, only the infinite, inexhaustible good of God that could possibly satisfy the infinite longing of the human heart. Thus, like Augustine, he shows that there is a correspondence between human desire and divine desire, between human nature and divine nature. His moral theology is predicated, not on the struggle between an autonomous finite freedom and an arbitrary infinite free-dom, but rather on the co-inherence between a human soul that finds its beatitude in God alone and the God who delights in sharing his being with creation.

We must draw one further ethical implication from the non-competitiveness of God and the world. When asked why God creates, Thomas responds typically with the formula of the pseudo-Dionysius: *bonum diffusivum sui*. The good God creates because it is his nature to give. And when asked why God became incarnate in Jesus Christ, Aquinas turns to the same formula. Because it is the nature of the good to give of itself and because God is the supreme good, it is only fitting that God should give himself utterly, superabundantly, and this explains the fittingness of the Incarnation. The being of God, in a word, is a being that gives. But this means that when a human being clings to God as her ultimate good, thereby finding happiness, she is conforming herself to this divine generosity. This is why, in a wide variety of his ethical writings, Karol Wojtyla, John Paul II, speaks of the centrality of the law of the gift in the Christian tradition: one's being increases and is enhanced in the measure that one gives it away. To achieve the ultimate end of the moral life is not to attain a prize that gratifies the ego; rather, it is to enter into the gracious way of being characteristic of God. One of the tragedies of our time, in my judgment, is that our presentation of the moral life remains conditioned by the assumptions and language of modernity — obligation, law, autonomy/heteronomy, divine demand — rather than by the much more traditional language of grace, co-inherence, and joy.

Conclusion

In our understanding of God, the universe, the act of knowing, and human ethical behavior, we Catholics are unique. Though we can discern family resemblances in the other great religions and even in the best features of the secular culture, the Catholic vision of things is distinctive. It is born of what Chesterton called the "jest" of the Incarnation, the utterly incongruous and unexpected juxtaposition of divinity and humanity. In this great co-inherence of Creator and creature, we spy the Pattern, the basic structure of reality; we touch and see, to borrow the language of St. John, what was from the beginning, the Word of life. Our task, as I see it, is the work taken up by every Christian generation: to narrate the story with joy and panache, to tell again and again the joke which is delightfully on us.

Chapter 6

The Church's Way of Speaking

Robert Louis Wilken

"Thy words were found, and I ate them, and thy words became to me a joy and the delight of my heart." (Jer 15:16)

WHEN ST. AUGUSTINE abandoned the teaching of rhetoric in Milan to enroll for Baptism he asked Ambrose, the Bishop of Milan, what he would recommend to read in the Scriptures "to make me readier and fitter to receive so great a grace." Ambrose told him to read the prophet Isaiah. Augustine took his advice, but as soon as he took the book in hand he was perplexed by what he read. "I did not understand the first passage of the book," he writes, and "thought the whole would be equally obscure." So Augustine laid it aside, as he explains, "to be resumed when I had more practice in the Lord's style of language."[1] *In dominico eloquio!* An arresting and beguiling phrase!

For the Christian reader Isaiah is a demanding and difficult book once one strays beyond the familiar passages cited in the New Testament or read in Christian worship, Isaiah 9 at Christmas, Isaiah 53 during Holy Week. To the uninitiated the first chapter is particularly daunting with its arcane oracles against Judah and Jerusalem: "Ah, sinful nation, a people laden with iniquity, offspring of evildoers, sons who deal corruptly. They have forsaken the Lord, they have despised the Holy One of Israel" (Is 1:4–5). For someone like Augustine, formed by the poetry of Virgil and the philosophy of Plotinus, the opening verses must have seemed embarrassingly parochial, taken up as they are with the fortunes of the ancient Israelites centuries earlier. Words such as "sinful nation," "holy one of Israel," "daughter of Zion," "new moon and sabbath" would have sounded alien to his ears, and anthropomorphisms like "I will vent my wrath on my enemies," or "turn my hand against you" would have offended his cultivated spiritual sensibility.

Yet Augustine called Isaiah's language the Lord's way of speaking and recognized that if he were to enter the Church he would have to learn this new tongue, hear it spoken, grow accustomed to its sounds, read the books that use it, learn its idioms, and finally speak it himself. He had to embark on a journey to acquaint himself with the mores of a new country. Becoming a Christian meant entering a strange and often alien world.

The title of this conference is "Handing on the Faith," and in the early Church the occasion for the handing on of the faith was the Rite of Baptism at the great vigil of Easter beginning on Saturday evening. There the creed was "handed over" to the catechumens. Ambrose realized there was more to becoming a Christian than putting the creed to memory and being instructed in the "mysteries." It also meant learning the distinctively Christian language whose lexicon was the Bible. And among the books of the Scripture, Isaiah was preeminent. Jerome said Isaiah was an evangelist as well as a prophet.

Ambrose recognized that "the faith" is not simply a set of doctrinal propositions, creedal statements, and moral codes; it is a world of discourse that comes to us in language of a very particular sort. And language, as we all discover studying a foreign tongue, is not simply a vehicle, an instrument for ideas, beliefs, and sentiments. Language defines who we are. How a people think, how they see the world, how they respond to persons and events, even how they feel are all molded by language. Thinking and understanding, like memory, are not solitary acts — they are mated to the language we share with others. If we forget how to speak our language we lose something of ourselves. As the Polish poet Czeslaw Milosz once wrote: "What is pronounced strengthens itself. What is not pronounced tends to non-existence."

Language, however, is not only the language of a people or a country. There are languages within languages. Just as there is a language proper to science or to medicine, so there is a language proper to Christianity. Our beliefs, our moral convictions, our attitudes are carried and transmitted by very specific words and images. Words, not ideas, bring into focus with compactness and intensity what is honored and cherished. They are the necessary carriers in which the Church's faith is handed on from generation to generation.

Think, for example, how many terms Christians use in a distinctive way: Father, Son, Spirit, faith, hope, love, grace, sin, mercy, forgiveness, image of God, flesh, kingdom, lamb of God, righteousness, repent, see (as in blessed are the pure in heart for they shall see God), know (as in know the truth), believe, truth (as in I am the truth), creation, "male and female he made them," passion (as in the passion of Christ), face of God, kyrie eleison, and so on. And that is not to mention the many proper nouns, Jerusalem, Mt. Zion, Egypt, Galilee, Sinai, Carmel, Damascus, Mt. of Olives, Bethlehem, Nazareth, and the names of persons, Abraham, Isaac, Jacob, Sarah and Rebecca, Moses, Samuel, David, Solomon, Isaiah, Paul, James, Mary, Mary Magdalene, Peter.

All of these words come from the Scriptures, and one might say that the lexicon of Christian speech is the Bible.[2] Indeed with some few exceptions, the Greek term *homoousios* (one in being with the Father) in the Nicene Creed, for example, the distinctively Christian vocabulary is almost wholly drawn from the Bible. Though Christians may speak English or Spanish or Arabic or Russian, they nevertheless use another language, a language within their native language, that is uniquely and recognizably Christian.

Consider the difference between the phrase "Happy Easter" and "He is Risen. He is risen indeed. Alleluia." The one is the language of our society, the other the Church's speech. Or take the words "nature" and "creation." The one is the conventional term in our society to refer to the world of plants and animals and mountains and oceans, what we call the natural world, the other the term used by the Bible and Christians to point to a creator and the world as ordered and purposeful. Instead of revered ancestors Christians speak of saints, instead of the birth of Christ we speak of the Incarnation. Even some of our prosaic terms are unique: instead of president we say pope; instead of governor, bishop; instead of convention, council or synod. Christians even have a unique term to refer to the community to which they belong: church.

Augustine said there was a *consuetudo loquendi ecclesiastica*, the church's customary way of speaking.[3] As an example he gives the word "martyr"; the term used by Christians for what the Romans call *vir*, or hero. Recall the opening words of the *Aeneid: Arma virumque cano*, of the making of war and of a hero I sing. Though the term *vir* had a venerable history in Latin, and from one perspective it seemed fitting for the martyrs, Augustine thought Christians should avoid it and use a distinctively Christian word for their valor. "Martyr" bore overtones that were absent from "hero," and "hero" carried connotations offensive to "martyr."

"Martyr" is of course a biblical term meaning witness, and it is used with a very specific sense in the book of Acts. Again and again the disciples are called "witnesses of the Resurrection" (Acts 2:32), that is, someone who knew Christ during his earthly sojourn and to whom the risen Christ appeared. Accordingly a martyr is one who knows Christ and bears witness in death to the living Lord. By comparison the term *vir* or hero seemed colorless and anemic when applied to the martyrs.

In a sermon Augustine highlighted another feature of Christian language for the martyrs. The Church used the term *natalis*, birth date, to refer to the day of martyrdom:

> Today we celebrate the birthday of the most glorious martyr, Cyprian. This expression, *natales* (birthdays), is regularly employed by the Church in this way, so that it calls the precious deaths of the martyrs their birthdays. This expression, I repeat, is regularly employed by the Church, to the extent that even those who don't belong to her join her in using it. Is there anyone to be found, I ask you, and I don't mean just in this city of ours, but throughout the whole of Africa and the regions overseas, and not only any Christian, but any pagan or Jew, or even heretic, who doesn't call today the birthday of the martyr Cyprian?
>
> Why is this, brothers and sisters? What date he was born on, we don't know; and because he suffered today, it's today that we celebrate his birthday. We wouldn't celebrate that other day, even if we knew when it was. On that day he contracted original sin, while on this day he overcame all sin. On that day he came forth from the wearisome confines of his mother's womb into this light, which is so alluring to our eyes of flesh; but on this day he went away from the deep darkness of nature's womb to that light, which sheds such blessing and good fortunes upon the mind.[4]

Another suggestive example is the Latin word *passio,* passion. It occurs in a verse from 1 Thessalonians, "that each one of you know how to take a wife for himself in holiness and honor, not in the passion of lust like heathens who do not know God..." (1 Thes 4:5).

Augustine thought this translation unacceptable to Christians because "passion" was the word used for Christ's suffering and death. "In the church's customary way of speaking," he said the term "passion is not used in a pejorative sense" (as it is here, the "passion of lust"). It should be reserved for the suffering of Christ and of the martyrs.

Augustine even thought that Christians should avoid the Roman custom of referring to the days of the week, for example, Monday, the moon's day, or Wednesday, the day of Mercury (as in the French *mercredi*). "We do not like this practice," says Augustine, "and we wish Christians would amend their custom and not employ the pagan name." And then he adds: "They have a language of their own that they can use."[5] Augustine preferred the simple numeration of the first, second, third day of the week, a practice that is kept to this day in the Latin breviary, *feria prima, feria secunda, feria tertia*.

The faith, then, is handed on embedded in language. It is not a set of abstract beliefs or ideas, but a world of shared associations and allusions with its own beauty and sonority, inner cohesion and logic, emotional and rhetorical power. The Church's way of speaking is a map of the experience of those who have known God, and the beliefs it hands on cannot be abstracted from the words, nor the words uprooted from the persons that used them. Christian thinking is inescapably historical.

Christian speech is not primarily the technical vocabulary of Christian doctrine — words such as substance, essence, one person and two natures, prevenient grace, atonement, transubstantiation, and so forth. It is the language of the psalms, the stories of the patriarchs, the parables of the Gospels, the moral vocabulary of Paul's Epistles. Though Christians became very comfortable with the Greek vocabulary of the cardinal virtues — prudence, justice, fortitude, and temperance — their native language for the virtuous life comes from St. Paul who spoke of "fruits of the Spirit," "love, joy, peace, patience, kindness, goodness, faithfulness, gentleness, self-control" (Gal 5:22–23). We, in using the Church's language to live together as a community, to breathe together if you will, to think the Church's thoughts, share its loves and live by its precepts.

One of the most beautiful words in the Christian lexicon is "hyssop," in "purge me with hyssop and I shall be clean" (Ps 51:7). In Christian speech it has overtones of repentance and forgiveness, and calls to mind the beautiful line of the psalm, "a humble and contrite heart God will not despise" (Ps 51:17). Nothing is more characteristic of Christian life than repentance.

Another is the term "patience" in its Old English rendering in the King James translation, "longsuffering" or "slow to anger," as in the verse: "The Lord is slow to anger, and abounding in steadfast love, forgiving iniquity and transgression" (Num 14:18). Peter says that "God's patience [that is, long suffering] waited in the day of Noah" and out of mercy God refrained from punishing those who had done wrong (1 Pet 3:20). The ancient Greeks and Romans had no word for this virtue; they spoke not of patience, but of endurance, meaning perseverance in adversity.

About the year A.D. 200 Tertullian, the first Christian to write in Latin, wrote a little treatise with the title *de patientia* (On Patience), and Cyprian and Augustine also wrote works with that title. In his little book Tertullian keenly observed that patience was not only a divine but a human virtue. The supreme example of patience was Christ's Passion, an observation later echoed by Augustine: "The passion of our Lord is a lesson in patience." For Christians the mark of patience is not endurance, sticking it out, but hope grounded in the Resurrection and directed toward an end. For Tertullian (himself an impatient man) it is the premier Christian virtue because it signifies a life oriented toward a future that is God's doing. Its distinctive feature is longing, not so much to be released from the ills of the present, but yearning for the good to come. Even love, said Tertullian, cannot be practiced, he says, "without the exercise of patience."

"Mercy" is another beloved Christian word taken from the Bible. St. Caesarius of Arles called it a *dulce nomen*, a sweet word.[6] I recall some years ago sitting in the cathedral of Christ Church at the University of Oxford during morning prayer. I noticed on the stone floor several medallions with the terms *justitia, prudentia, fortitudo* and realized the medallions represented the four cardinal virtues. But then I noticed that there was a fifth. When the service was over and I could make my way to the front, sure enough I found *temperantia* but the fifth was *misericordia*, mercy, a biblical word. Clearly the designers of the church thought that the cardinal virtues (a heritage from the Greeks) were not complete without the addition of a distinctively Christian term, mercy. As early as the third century the Christian writer Lactantius, recognizing the indispensability of *misericordia* for thinking about the Christian life, chided the Stoics because they had no place in their moral universe for the affections.

Without the distinctive Christian language there can be no handing on of the faith. For that reason the words that embody what we believe and practice, words handed on to us by those in whom Christ was present, cannot be frivolously tampered with, translated into another idiom, or discarded. Language is a defining mark of the Christian polis. As Augustine reminded us centuries ago, the appropriate metaphor for the Church is a city. Like a city the Church draws its citizens into a shared public life, marked by its central cultic activity, the Eucharist, and by other rituals such as the imposition of ashes on Ash Wednesday, and processions on Palm Sunday or Corpus Christi. The Christian polis has its own calendar that sets the rhythms of the community's life, its own polity, the office of bishop, institutions like monasticism, its own law, architecture, art, music, its own customs and mores, history and memory. Christ entered history as a community and over the course of history this community has created a distinctive social and cultural space.

One of the most significant features of the transformation of the Roman world in the fourth and fifth centuries was that Christianity occupied and then re-oriented public space. The classical city with its agora and temples and theaters gave way to a new city plan with the church located at the center. With the Christianization of space came the sacralization of time as the church's calendar marked the days for celebration and fasting and resting. In the early Middle Ages when kings and their people embraced Christianity, conversion was more than adherence to a new set of beliefs, it brought about a change in public practice.

Over the last hundred years, however, the Church has gradually given up this public face, relinquishing the public square to other rituals, to other calendars, to other buildings, and to other languages. There has been an alarming decline in communal rituals and practice. The Church's way of life is being chewed up and spit out by the omnivorous society that surrounds us. A good example of the attenuation of Christian life is the use of the term "culture." We tend to use the term "culture" not of the Church, but of the society in which we live. But the Church has its own cultural identity and forms an alternate society. Like the society in which it lives it constitutes a complex social world of practices and institutions with its own symbols, inherited sentiments, beliefs, and behavior. The task of handing on the faith is not primarily a question of how "Christ" relates to "culture" but how the Christian culture is to be sustained and deepened in the face of another culture that is increasingly alien and hostile.

Implicitly the Christ and culture paradigm assumes that the secular culture is the arbiter of meaning. Consequently a high premium is placed on "translation." By translation I do not mean from Greek or Latin into English or Spanish, but translation from one idiom to another within the same language. Translation of course is inevitable in any religious transaction, whether it be telling a story from the Bible to a youngster, explaining the sacraments to a recent convert, or preaching the gospel to a people who know nothing of Christianity. If, however, Christianity is a culture in its own right, translation can never be a one-way street. The Church must insist on its way of speaking and there must be translation *into* the Lord's style of language, i.e., adopting and learning to use the Church's language. More frequently, however, the task of handing on the faith is understood to mean rendering Christian language into the patois of modernity — even in liturgy, the one area where one would expect to preserve the uniqueness and idiosyncrasy of the Church's way of speaking.

The point can be illustrated by considering the way some prayers in the liturgy were rewritten after Vatican II. Here, for example, is the prayer for Pentecost XI prior to the reforms of Vatican II: "Look mercifully upon our service, O Lord, I beseech you, that what we offer may be a gift acceptable to you and a support to our frailty" (*nostrae fragilitatis subsidium*). In the new version, for Sunday XI in ordinary time it reads: "Look mercifully upon our service, O Lord, we beseech you, that what we offer may be a gift acceptable to you and an increase of our charity" (*nostrae caritatis augmentum*).[7]

On first reading the alteration seems innocuous, and the reason given by the compilers reasonable: they wished to render the petition positive rather than negative, thereby, it was assumed, making the prayer more dynamic. (What is at issue here is not translation from Latin to English, but the new Latin version.) But the result was the elimination of a vivid word found in early liturgical texts and used for centuries. In its place one gets "love," obviously a good Christian word, but one that focuses the prayer on the goal while ignoring what stands in the way of attaining the goal, our "frailty." The prayer as it stands borders on the trite (one should love others), making the language of the liturgy indistinguishable from countless other contemporary sentiments and suffocating genuine religious feeling. Frailty, however, a word one is likely to hear only in the liturgy (except perhaps in speaking of the frailty of age), is sacrificed to a banal platitude.

Another example is the collect (a good Christian word that has been jettisoned) for the Sunday of the Pasch: "O God, who unlocked for us the gate of eternity through your only begotten Son who conquered death, grant, we beseech you, that we who celebrate the solemnity of his resurrection may through renewal of the Holy Spirit, rise from the *death of the soul* (*a morte animae*)." The revised version reads: " . . . through renewal of the Holy Spirit, rise *in the light of life* (*in lumine vitae*)."

The new version is not only vacuous, it borders on incoherence. What does it mean to "rise in the light of life"? Here the faithful are deprived of two precious Christian words, soul and death, both biblical, each having connotations that are central to Christian faith. And most important the new version ignores a fundamental truth about Easter — it is not only a celebration of Christ's Resurrection, but a time of interior renewal for the Christian, a truth that is expressed metaphorically in the phrase "rise from the death of the soul." I don't see that the phrase "death of the soul" is any less intelligible to people living in our age than in previous ages. The original plunges the faithful into the deeper caverns of the spiritual life where we struggle against the forces that hold us in bondage. The revision offends Christian sensibility by injecting the fatuous language of new age religion into the Church's worship.

The changes, mind you, are deliberate, an attempt to accommodate the words of the liturgy to "the modern mentality," in the words of one of the revisers. The translators display an embarrassing lack of confidence in what Christians believe and practice. Some texts were judged "shocking for the man of today" and "difficult to understand" and for that reason were "frankly corrected."[8] What we have here is a kind of "inculturation" in Western modernity. Though the term "inculturation" is used more often in relation to adapting the gospel to the genius of a native people, it fits just as well for the kind of adaptation that marks this kind of liturgical revisionism. Anscar Chapungco, one of the leading exponents of inculturation, put it this way: "Liturgy must not impose on culture a meaning or bearing that is intrinsically alien to its nature."[9] What this represents, to use John Milbank's phrase, is a kind of "policing of the sublime."

The unique gift of liturgy, wrote Roman Guardini in his *The Spirit of the Liturgy*, is to "create a universe brimming with fruitful spiritual life." Liturgy does not "exist for the sake of humanity, but for the sake of God."[10] If the Bible is the lexicon of Christian speech, the liturgy is its grammar, a place to learn to know and love the idiom of Christian speech and to be formed by it. For Augustine the reciting of the psalms was a way of making the words of the psalmist his words, and he talked about what the words of the psalms "had done to me."[11]

Obviously there is always a place for translation, even in the liturgy, but in our present situation the Church has a much greater responsibility to preserve and practice its own way of speaking, to tend to the architecture of the Church's interior life. Its goal should be to draw people into an alternate way of life, to teach the beauty, truth, and, one might add, usefulness of the biblical and Christian language.

Let me give one example: the phrase "image of God." Of course it comes from the creation narrative in the book of Genesis. After the creation of the heavens, the sun and moon, the birds and fish, the creeping things and beasts of the earth, God said: "Let us make man in our image, after our likeness. . . . So God created man in his own image, in the image of God he created him" (Gen 1:26–27). There is no biblical expression more central to Christian faith than this. That human beings are made in the image of God is the foundation for the whole drama of salvation: made in the image of God, the image defaced and tarnished, Christ restoring the image in those who live in fellowship with him. It is also the pillar on which rests the Christian understanding of the human person. "Image of God" brings into focus what is unique about human beings. Without the phrase "image of God" Christian witness to the truth about man is hamstrung and crippled.

But does it have a place in our public discourse? Most certainly! Christians must insist on the phrase, for several reasons. First, it is biblical and it occurs in one of the most familiar passages of the Bible. The Bible still has emotional as well as intellectual power. Second, image implies that there is something other than the image, the thing which the image reflects. It points beyond itself to a reality that is more perfect, more true, more beautiful. The image depends on the original, but it can never be the same as the original. Yet without the original there can be no image. Third, it names that reality as God. The term "image of God" helps keep our speech mindful of the transcendent and opens space for deeper reflection on the nature of the human person.

Paul Griffiths has recently shown that one does not have to believe what Christians believe to make use of Christian language and ideas. Within the last few decades four European philosophers, all atheists, have written major works that draw on Christian thinkers: Terry Eagleton on Thomas Aquinas, Jean-François Lyotard on Augustine's *Confessions,* Alain Badiou on St. Paul, and Slavoj Žižek on Christ's willing acceptance of suffering and death. None of these writers embraces the theological views of Thomas or Augustine or Paul, but they employ their language, their ideas, their stories for their own ends. These writers exhibit a "yearning" for something more than what modernity has to offer and the only place, finally, to turn is to Christianity, its language, its mode of thinking, its texts. "This should not surprise Christians," writes Griffiths. "Our intellectual tradition is long-lived, rich, and subtle, and any attempt by European thinkers to do without it is not likely to last."[12]

Griffiths's observations lay to rest the canard that the Church must abandon its unique language to enter the public square. It is the plenitude, depth, and durability of the Christian language that make it attractive to outsiders. Even when they do not believe the things Christians believe, it offers resources and support for their own work.

Like language, Christian ritual has always fascinated outsiders. I was reminded recently when I heard a thrilling performance of Rimsky-Korsakov's *Great Russian Easter* by the National Symphony Orchestra in Washington. Rimsky-Korsakov was not a believer — he was probably a pantheist — but the *Great Russian Easter,* one of his most popular and stirring compositions, draws deeply on the Orthodox Liturgy and the Scriptures. The subtitle of the piece is "Overture on Liturgical Themes" and it is based on the Obikhod, a collection of Russian Orthodox canticles, biblical texts such as "let God arise, let his enemies be scattered" from Psalm 68, and hymns. The piece is ablaze with colors and lights as well as brooding darkness, at once awesome, majestic, austere, and carnival-like effects that would not be possible without the Orthodox Liturgy.

For too long Christianity has relinquished its role as teacher to society. At the beginning of the twenty-first century the time has come for the Church to rediscover herself, to savor her speech, delight in telling her stories, and confidently pass on what she knows. Only then can she draw people away from the coarse and superficial culture surrounding us into the abundance of life in Christ.

This is not a new strategy but one that has marked Christian thinking from the beginning. Origen of Alexandria was one of the most brilliant Christian apologist of the first three centuries of the Church's history. His most famous work is a debate with Celsus, a Greek philosopher who had lived seventy years earlier. In his book *Against Celsus,* Origen gives his opponent a full and fair hearing, citing him extensively and verbatim. At the very beginning he quotes Celsus who said: "Greeks are better able to judge the value of what the barbarians [i.e. the Christians] have discovered.... " Celsus believed that the truth of Christianity should be measured "by the criterion of a Greek proof."

Origen too had been trained in the Greek intellectual tradition, and he knew a thing or two about argument. But he rejects out of hand Celsus's assumption that the Church's faith should be measured by an alien standard. The truth of the gospel, Origen insists, is to be judged by a "proof that is peculiar to itself, and this is more divine than Greek argument." This, says Origen, is what St. Paul was referring to in 1 Corinthians when he spoke about a "demonstration of the Spirit and of power" (1 Cor 2:4).[13] Here is a strategy to be commended at the beginning of the twenty-first century — let the Church appeal to what is peculiar to herself, not to presumed notions about what is meaningful or intelligible or relevant to the society. A robust Christian witness can only be forged by drawing on the fullness of Christ as known in the Church.

At this time in the Church's history in the United States, it is less important to communicate the gospel to American culture than to rebuild the Church's distinctive culture, to relearn "the Church's way of speaking." There is no dearth of "communication," whether it be the homilies of the clergy, the catechesis of the young or the formation of catechumens through RCIA, the one-to-one conversations of friends and neighbors, the public statements of bishops, or encyclicals of the Holy Father. But while these many and diverse activities go on, there is another urgent task — to restore thickness and density to Catholic life.

I end with two examples of the "Church's way of speaking," one from the arts and the other from liturgical language.

The Church of St. Patrick is the oldest church in the District of Columbia, located in the center of the city in what is now a vital neighborhood of apartments, shops, restaurants, theaters, and clubs. St. Patrick's is a handsome American Victorian Gothic-style building with fine and intricate stained-glass windows including a sequence on the life of St. Patrick in the chancel, a Pieta, several statues of St. Patrick, St. Anthony of Padua, St. Thomas More, and others. When one enters the church, however, it is not the windows that draw one's attention, but a series of large paintings in the chancel that occupy sixteen tall narrow niches. Painted by the artist Tatiana McKinney in 1996 they depict the saints and blesseds of the Americas: St. Elizabeth Ann Seton, St. John Neuman, St. Frances Xavier Cabrini, St. Rose of Lima, St. Rose Philippine Duchesne, St. Isaac Jogues, St. Martin Porres, Bl. Kateri Tekakwitha, Bl. Juan Diego, Bl. Andre Bessette, and others. On a long shelf at the rear of the church the pictures of the saints are reproduced with a brief account of the life of each holy person.

Two things strike the viewer at once. These saints represent Christian holiness of the most varied sort — a religious woman, a bishop, a Native American, a missionary, for example — and they all come from the New World. They present models of the Christian life for the faithful to admire and emulate, but they also help forge a Christian identity that is distinct from the national cultures. By combining saints from North and South America, Canada, the United States, Peru, and other countries, one is reminded that as Christians we are part of another city.

Finally I return to where I began — with language. One Pentecost I was in South Bend, Indiana, and attended a solemn and festive Liturgy in Sacred Heart Church on the campus of the University of Notre Dame. Though the university was out of session and it was the weekend of Memorial Day, there was a full choir. Much to my delight they sang in its entirety the sequence appointed for Pentecost, *Veni, Sancte Spiritus.* This sequence was written almost a thousand years ago, yet its language was as fresh as if it were composed this spring. It is an example of the *ecclesiastica loquendi consuetudo,* the Church's way of speaking, the kind of language that burns the soul with the searing flame of the Spirit. Here are some of the strophes followed by a free translation:

> *Veni, Sancte Spiritus*
> *et emitte caelitus*
> *lucis tuae radium*

Come, Holy Spirit
send out from heaven
the beams of your light

Veni, pater pauperum
Veni, dator munerum
Veni, lumen cordium
Come, father of the poor
come, giver of gifts
come, the light that enlightens our hearts.

Consolator optime
dulcis hospes animae
dulce refrigerium
Dearest and best comforter
the soul's delightful guest
sweet refreshment

In labore requies
in aestu temperies
in fletu solatium
In labor rest
in noonday heat a cooling place
in grief solace

Lava quod est sordidum
riga quod est aridum
sana quod est saucium
Wash what is filthy
with rain refresh what is dry
heal what is wounded

Flecte quod est rigidum
fove quod est frigidum
rege quod est devium
Bend what is stiff
warm what is cold
redirect what has strayed

Da virtutis meritum,
da salutis exitum,
da perenne gaudium.
Amen, Alleluia.
Give the reward of virtue,
Give a blessed end,
Give eternal joy.
Amen. Alleluia.

Part Three

COMMUNICATING
THE FAITH

Chapter 7

Communicating the Faith

Conversations and Observations

Michael J. Himes

O<small>N SEVERAL OCCASIONS</small> I have been asked to speak to graduate students in theology about teaching techniques. I have invariably excused myself from doing so, for I am embarrassed to admit that, after thirty-three years of preaching and twenty-seven of teaching theology, I have no theory about how to do what I do. I fear that all I have to say to fledgling teachers is a variant of the advice given to beginning actors: speak clearly and don't trip over the furniture. So, to reflect on how to communicate the faith, I must turn to those whose wisdom about leading others into the tradition I have found most helpful over these years of preaching and teaching. What follows is in two parts: the first being a series of brief "conversations" with four great communicators of the faith from whom I have learned, and the second being a few observations on the task of communicating the faith to young adults, the college-age men and women whom I teach. I hope, even if I have no right to expect, that these observations may have relevance to others as well.

Conversations

Thomas Aquinas

Saint Thomas offers perhaps the most important observation for consideration in thinking about how to communicate the faith: teaching is necessary but insufficient. In addressing the question of the cause of faith, Thomas observes that there are two requisite elements for faith.[1] The first is that what is to be believed must be proposed to human beings.

This is necessary if faith is to be explicit. Faith is not simply a subjective disposition, a kind of universal credulity ready to accept anything.
Faith has content, and since faith refers to the things of God, its content
must be revealed by God. To some God reveals the truths of revelation directly, e.g., the apostles and prophets; to others these truths are
communicated by the preachers and teachers whom God sends to them.
So teaching is necessary for faith. But, Thomas reminds us, there is a
second requisite: the person taught must assent to what is taught. He
mentions two causes that can bring about the assent of the believer to
what is taught. The first, external cause could be an external inducement to belief, such as a miracle. But, Thomas notes, this cannot be the
primary cause of the believer's assent because not everyone who sees a
miracle is moved to faith. There must be an internal inducement. Some,
e.g., the Pelagians, have mistakenly thought that this internal inducement is an act of the believer himself; a free choice on the part of the
one to whom the truths of God's revelation are taught. This cannot be
because the truths are supernatural and, in assenting to them, the hearer
is raised above the limits of human nature. So the internal cause of faith
must be a supernatural principle accorded to the believer; in short, it is
an act of God. Thus, the primary cause of the assent of faith is the grace
of God.[2]

What does a teacher of the faith teach? At the outset of the *Summa
Theologiae,* Thomas indicates that what God reveals is Godself, and the
way God reveals Godself is complex. In the very first question of the
Summa Thomas announces that his subject is *sacra doctrina,* which he
distinguishes from *theologia,* which, in one sense of the term, may be
included in *sacra doctrina.*[3] "Sacred doctrine" is a very inclusive term in
Thomas. It is preeminently Scripture, the record of God's self-revelation
to the apostles and prophets, but Scripture was not simply an inspired
book or a collection of texts. For Thomas, as for virtually all medieval
Christian teachers, Scripture was embedded in and foundational to a
tradition of thought and practice, of prayer and action. Sacred doctrine
includes for Thomas not only the Bible but also those interpretations of
the scriptural texts that had accrued over the centuries in the Fathers
of the church and the tradition of preaching and the liturgical contexts
in which texts were read.[4] Teaching sacred doctrine meant presenting
the hearer with the full richness of the church's prayer, preaching, and

practice. Thomas recognized, of course, that not every believer could be taught the full richness of sacred doctrine. As he wrote:

> The truth necessary for salvation is summed up in a few brief articles of faith. To characterize the word that we proclaim, Saint Paul cited Isaiah: "A short word shall the Lord make upon the earth" [Rom 9:28, quoting Is 28:22]. Human ends are clarified in a brief prayer in which our Lord instructs us how to pray and teaches us what we ought to desire and hope for. Human justice, which consists in obeying the law, he completes with one commandment of charity: 'Love is the fulfillment of the law' [Rom 13:10].[5]

The teacher of the faith is primarily a teacher of Scripture, but Scripture as interpreted in the *glossa ordinaria,* the standard commentary of patristic exegesis, as well as the liturgical uses to which biblical texts had long been put and their authoritative ecclesial interpretation (usually drawn from conciliar and canonical sources). The essence of this scriptural teaching is encapsulated in the articles of faith, the official creedal statements of the church, the Lord's Prayer, and the commandments, preeminently the commandment of love. It is not hard to see already developed here what became the typical homiletic cycle of topics by the close of the Middle Ages and so widely used in post-Tridentine Catholic preaching and catechesis — indeed, which still provides the outline for the new *Catechism:* the creed, the Lord's Prayer, and the commandments. The all-important qualification, however, is that the teacher of the faith, let him or her be ever so qualified and skilled, will not lead the hearer to believe unless the hearer is moved by God to assent to what is taught, i.e., unless the grace of faith is infused. We shall return to this central condition for the communication of the faith. For the moment we will concentrate on the work of the communicator.

Augustine

Augustine was a rhetorician, a professional communicator, by education and profession until his conversion and short-lived retirement. Only a few years after his baptism, he was chosen as a priest of the church in Hippo Rhegium, and three years later became its bishop. Thus he once again found himself in the role of teacher but no longer of rhetoric, now a communicator of faith. Because of his fame as a teacher and preacher, he was consulted on several occasions by people seeking advice on how

to teach the faith truly and effectively. One of those persons was Deogratias, a deacon of the church in Carthage, who around the year 400
requested Augustine's counsel on how to instruct people with little or no
background in Christianity and apparently equally little general education. The busy bishop responded by writing *De catechizandis rudibus,*
his treatise on the religious instruction of the unlearned.

Augustine offers advice both on what should be taught and how to
teach it. On the subject matter, he is in agreement with virtually all the
Fathers of the church, so many of whom were bishops and charged with
the ministry of preaching: the source and subject of all Christian teaching
is Scripture. Augustine insists that this means that the Christian teacher is
first of all to teach a narrative because the Bible is primarily the account
of a story beginning with the origin of all things in God and ending in
the vision and promise of the union of creatures with God. But when
speaking to the kind of audience that Deogratias envisions, the *rudes* or
unsophisticated, the teacher ought not to try to give a detailed account of
all of salvation history. He should rather give a summary of major events
and turning-points in the narrative, selecting these key moments with an
eye to being able to connect with them the central issues in the Christian
faith which arise from the biblical history.[6] Augustine does not envision
a catechism structured according to the articles of the creed. Instead,
he presumes that the creed is structured according to the narrative of
salvation history. He would be in full agreement with Nicholas Lash
who, observing that "the Creed is not a list of theses, a catalogue of
chapter headings for a textbook of theology," has written, "What the
Scriptures say at length, the Creed says briefly."[7] One might think of
books 11 through 22 of Augustine's own *De civitate Dei,* that vast,
discursive compendium of Christian teaching, which, while dealing with
central doctrines and not a few theological disputes, is basically a history
of salvation from creation to the eschaton. *De civitate Dei* is, of course,
an instance of what Augustine calls a "longer" or "fuller" narrative,
not the summary presentation that is appropriate to the unsophisticated
beginners that he and Deogratias so often taught. In either case, however,
the organizing principle of the presentation is that of Scripture, namely,
the narrative of salvation history out of which doctrines have developed
and through which they can be made intelligible to those being instructed
in the faith.

How can one summarize salvation history into a shorter narrative and be certain that one is not omitting something essential? Augustine offers a simple hermeneutic for reading and so for teaching the narrative: the centrality of Christ. All the events prior to the Incarnation are recorded in Scripture in order to point us toward the coming of Christ, and everything that has happened since is the fruit of that coming. The key to understanding the Scriptures, and therefore the standard by which the wise teacher determines what to include in his summary narrative, is Christ.[8] But what precisely does this Christocentrism of Augustine's teaching mean? Why Christ? What do we learn from Christ? Augustine's (entirely typical) answer is that Christ came both to teach and to demonstrate that God loves us so that we might be moved to love God.

> If, therefore, the principal reason for Christ's coming is this: that human beings might learn how much God loves them, and that they might learn this so that they would be drawn to love him by whom they were loved first and might also love their neighbor according to the commandment and example of him who became our neighbor because he loved them when they dwelt far from him, and if all the divine scriptures written in earlier times were written to signify the Lord's coming, and if everything written subsequently and established by divine authority is a testimony to Christ and teaches us to love, then it is clear that on the two commandments to love God and to love our neighbor depend not only the whole law and the prophets, which were the only sacred scriptures at the time when the Lord taught, but also all those books about divine matters written later for our well-being and cherished in our memory.[9]

So this is how Augustine understands Jesus' words that the two great commandments are the key to all the Scriptures. If this is true of the Hebrew Scriptures, he reasons, it is also true of the Christian Scriptures. Indeed, I think that, in the context of his treatise to Deogratias, we are correct in understanding Augustine as claiming that any Christian writing, i.e., the whole of patristic literature, is of permanent value to the extent that it is rooted in the two great commandments. And so this is the Christian teacher's guide for the summary presentation of salvation history: the whole of the narrative leads up to and foreshadows Christ and flows from him and points to him, and Christ is the demonstration of how God loves us and how we are to love one another. According to Augustine, this is the sum and substance of the teaching of the faith.

If this is what must be taught, how does one communicate it effectively? Augustine turned to his rhetorical training to answer that question. Around 396, a few years before his treatise written for Deogratias, he wrote the first, second, and most of the third book of *De doctrina christiana,* which in the Middle Ages became one of the most widely read of his works and has had a deep effect on preaching and catechesis in Western Christianity. Thirty years later, in reviewing his work, he decided that it was incomplete and added what are now the end of book three and the whole of book four. "The first three books help in understanding scripture," he wrote; "the fourth shows how one who has understood it should express himself."[10] The first three books are, indeed, the clearest statement of his hermeneutics for scriptural exegesis; the final book is the advice of a rhetorical master on how to communicate with an audience. Paraphrasing Cicero, Augustine tells us that effective communication involves teaching, delighting, and persuading.[11] One might think that in presenting hearers with what is true expressed clearly and accurately, one has done enough as a teacher. But for the communication of faith more is needed. Pastoral zeal cannot allow the teacher of faith simply to announce the truth, for he or she wants to move the audience to love. That is, as we have seen, the whole point of the Gospel — to kindle in one's hearers love for God and neighbor by presenting the story of God's love for us. So the teacher of faith wants to hold the hearer's attention, wants to delight the hearer. It is not enough to say the truth; one must lead one's hearer to want to listen to the truth. But even that is not enough.

> For if the things that are being taught are of the kind which it is sufficient to believe or know, consenting to them simply means admitting that they are true. When, however, something is being taught that has to be done, and is precisely being taught so that it may be done, in vain does the way and style in which it is said give pleasure, if it is not put across in such a way that action follows. It is the duty of the eloquent churchman, when he is trying to persuade the people about something that has to be done, not only to teach, in order to instruct them; not only to delight, in order to hold them; but also to sway, in order to conquer and win them.[12]

Faith is an assent that leads to action, namely, the action of loving God and neighbor. One might say that the assent of faith leads the hearer to love what ought to be loved, for in the first book of *De doctrina christiana* Augustine had drawn his distinction between use and enjoyment, *uti* and *frui,* the key to clarifying our loves. Throughout his writing, however else he changed his mind on issues, he remained convinced that the central reality and driving force of the human person is love. The great question is not whether we love, but what we love. So, delighting the hearer, bringing him to love what he ought to love, is an essential part of the communication of faith. Since love is the impetus to action, persuading the hearer is also essential.

So, the teacher of faith must know the truth that he seeks to communicate, present it in a way that will attract and hold the hearer's interest, and energize and inspire the hearer to act on what he has heard. In short, the teacher must be knowledgeable, interesting, and energizing. As any teacher knows, this is easier said than done. Augustine, however, has an even more interesting requirement for teachers of the faith and a remarkable suggestion about how to achieve it. It is interesting that, in the formal treatise on instructing people in Christianity, *De doctrina christiana,* Augustine omits a subject that had occupied a large part of his attention in *De catechizandis rudibus.* In seeking his advice on teaching the faith, Deogratias had written that he often found himself disappointed in his own performance and discouraged by his hearers' lack of response. This is surely a familiar experience to every teacher of any subject, and Augustine regarded it as sufficiently important to devote a large part (sections 14 to 22) of his response to it. A disheartened teacher lacks what Augustine considered an all-important quality, *hilaritas.*

Hilaritas, as Augustine used it, is a difficult word to translate. He takes it from the Latin translation of 2 Corinthians 9:7, which he quotes twice in his reply to Deogratias: *hilarem datorem diligit Deus,* and which we are accustomed to translate into English as "God loves a cheerful giver." "Cheerfulness" does not quite get at what Augustine means, however. A better translation might be "enthusiasm" or "enjoyment." The teacher of faith must be enthusiastic, must enjoy what he or she is doing. Without this quality, it is highly unlikely that faith will be communicated to one's hearers, whether they are worshipers listening to a sermon or students in a classroom.

At some length, Augustine discusses six factors that can sap enthusiasm and hinder the teacher's enjoyment and offers ways to counter them. First, the teacher may find it burdensome to adapt his or her presentation to the hearers' level. This is especially the case when one is instructing *rudes,* the unsophisticated in the subject presented. Second, one can be dissatisfied with one's own performance as a teacher, feeling that one has not been able to do justice to what needs to be taught. Third, introductory presentations for newcomers to a subject are necessarily repetitive, which may well weary the teacher. Fourth, hearers may not be responsive for one reason or another, which cannot fail to disappoint the presenter. Fifth, the instructor may well have other responsibilities that require time and attention. And finally, teachers are human beings who may well be preoccupied with problems that others have caused them or that they have caused themselves and that have nothing to do directly with teaching at all. While Augustine has interesting things to say about each of these hindrances to enjoyment of teaching, one theme appears in each of his responses: teaching must always be about the hearers, not the speaker. If the teacher is bored by accommodating his or her presentation to the level of the students, he or she should remember that teaching is for the good of the students, not the teacher. If one is unhappy with how one is teaching, one should recall that the students are the ultimate judges of one's performance, not oneself. If teaching fundamentals becomes boring, the teacher should recall that though he or she may have taught the lesson for the umpteenth time, it is the first time that the students have heard it. Teachers should not assume that the way they would respond to something is the way their hearers will respond. The work of communicating to people who do not react in the way we would is precisely the great challenge of teaching. Everyone has a multitude of obligations, but if one is a teacher (and preeminently a teacher of faith), then nothing is a more pressing responsibility than the instruction of one's students. And if one finds oneself distracted by worries and problems, the teacher must re-center himself or herself on the students. The key issue is that teaching is a service, an act of love, and so long as the lover is focused on the beloved and not on himself or herself, the lover cannot fail to be enthusiastic.

Being knowledgeable, interesting, and energizing are not enough in teaching the faith; one must be enthusiastic or, to put it another way, one must enjoy what one is doing. This enjoyment comes naturally from centering attention on those taught, not the one teaching. The teacher cannot help but be enthusiastic about teaching if the students and their needs remain the focus of his or her attention. I do not think it is doing an injustice to Augustine to hear in his advice to Deogratias an echo of Marshall McLuhan's dictum that the medium is the message. One cannot teach the Gospel, which is first and foremost the story of God's love for creatures to which we should respond by loving God and our neighbor, unless one clearly and obviously loves one's students.

John Henry Newman

On more than one occasion in his long life, John Henry Newman cautioned his contemporaries in an age entranced by the doctrine of Progress that education is not religion. In his caustic series of essays, "The Tamworth Reading Room," in which he dismantled the claim that education in the sciences and literary culture would necessarily lead to moral improvement,[13] as well as at length in Part 1 of *The Idea of a University*, he reminded his readers again and again that liberal education has its own ends and purposes that may and should prove of use to religious faith but are distinct from it. This caution must be kept in mind if we are to draw any suggestions about communicating the faith from Newman's observations on education. Nevertheless, Newman is so astute an educator that I think it both appropriate and important to draw from him, especially on two points.

Throughout the nine "discourses" collectively entitled "University Teaching," which make up the first part of *The Idea of a University*, Newman describes the goal of liberal education in several ways, culminating in the eighth discourse, "Knowledge Viewed in Relation to Religious Duty," with his often-quoted picture of a "gentleman." The opposite of a gentleman in Newman's sense of the term is what he earlier in the fourth discourse, "Bearing of Other Knowledge on Theology," calls "a man of one idea."[14] The "man of one idea" is the person who absolutizes one way of knowing or one field of knowledge and so devalues or distorts all other ways of knowing.

> Hence it is that we have the principles of utility, of combination, of progress, of philanthropy, or, in material sciences, comparative anatomy, phrenology, electricity, exalted into leading ideas, and keys, if not of all knowledge, at least of many things more than

belong to them, — principles, all of them true to a certain point, yet all degenerating into error and quackery, because they are carried to excess, viz., at the point where they require interpretation and restraint from other quarters, and because they are employed to do what is simply too much for them, inasmuch as a little science is not deep philosophy.[15]

In this fourth discourse, Newman is at pains to demonstrate that an education which ignores theology will inevitably lead to some one or more other fields encroaching on properly theological issues and concerns and so pretending to knowledge that they cannot rightly claim. This overextension of fields of knowledge is what produces people of one view.

The goal of university education, according to Newman, is the attainment of a philosophical cast of mind. He describes this as the "only . . . true enlargement of the mind," by which he means "the power of viewing many things at once as one whole, of referring them severally to their true place in the universal system, of understanding their respective values, and determining their mutual dependence."[16] The "man of one idea" is an instance of what the lack of philosophy in this sense produces. Because he has no overview, no architectonic principle by which his knowledge and experience can be ordered, a person allows a particular viewpoint, a field in which he is especially knowledgeable or adept, a perspective that he finds particularly comfortable or genial, to become the organizing principle of his life. At worst, he becomes a fanatic; at the least harmful, he will be a crank. The lack of what Newman calls "philosophy" can produce another extreme: the person who believes himself to be "tolerant" because everything is equally valuable — or valueless — to him. Newman gives a striking image:

Perhaps [such people] have been much in foreign countries, and they receive in a passive, otiose, unfruitful way, the various facts which are forced upon them there. Seafaring men, for example, range from one end of the earth to the other; but the multiplicity of external objects, which they have encountered, forms no symmetrical and consistent picture upon their imagination; they see the tapestry of human life, as it were on the wrong side, and it tells no story. They sleep, and they rise up, and they find themselves, now in Europe, now in Asia; they see visions of great cities and wild regions; they are in the marts of commerce, or amid the islands of the South; they gaze on Pompey's Pillar, or on the Andes; and nothing which meets them carries them forward or backward, to any idea beyond itself. Nothing has a drift or relation; nothing has a history or a promise. Every thing stands by itself, and comes and goes in its turn, like the shifting scenes of a show, which leave the spectator where he was. Perhaps you are near such a man on a particular occasion, and expect him to be shocked or perplexed at something which occurs; but one thing is much the same to him as another, or, if he is perplexed, it is as not knowing what to say, whether it is right to admire, or to ridicule, or to disapprove, while conscious that some expression of opinion is expected from him; for in fact he has no standard of judgment at all, and no landmarks to guide him to a conclusion. Such is mere acquisition, and, I repeat, no one would dream of calling it philosophy.[17]

The absence of philosophy, then, makes one either a fanatical "man of one idea" or leaves one adrift in a life that is experienced merely as one thing after another. In the former case, all things are related to one another by subordinating everything to one way of thinking, one vision, one perspective; in the latter, nothing is connected to anything else at all. This is reminiscent of Paul Tillich's description of the idolater and the atheist. Tillich famously described "faith" as "the state of being ultimately concerned."[18] An "ultimate concern" makes ultimate demands upon us and promises ultimate fulfillment to us. It is possible — indeed, Tillich thinks, all too possible — to assign ultimacy to something that is, in fact, not worthy of ultimate loyalty and that cannot offer ultimate fulfillment. Such false objects of ultimate concern are idols, false gods that shatter at moments of testing. Virtually everyone has some form of faith in Tillich's definition of faith, although most often faith turns out to be idolatrous. There seems, however, to be the limit case of atheism. The atheist is the denier of any ultimacy. Nothing is of ultimate concern; everything is equally important — or unimportant. Newman's "man of one idea" is an idolater; his person who passes through life like a tourist is an atheist.

The teacher of faith obviously does not want his or her hearers to be atheists, but neither should they become people of one idea. Worshiping false gods is not necessarily preferable to refusing to worship anything. Thus to communicate the faith to others, the teacher of faith must encourage in his or her hearers the development of what Newman meant by philosophy. This may appear to be an extraordinary demand to make of the teacher of faith since Newman thought such a philosophical cast of mind to be the product, not often achieved, of university education. Indeed, to insist that believers be people of such a philosophical mind-set may well seem elitist. I certainly do not intend to suggest that every preacher and religion teacher must provide his or her hearers with the kind of liberal education that Newman so wonderfully describes in *The Idea of a University.* But it is incumbent upon the teacher of faith to show how the Gospel connects with all the dimensions of the hearers' lives. As Newman envisioned "philosophy" as an understanding of the interconnections of fields of knowledge so that no one of them trespassed into the proper domain of any other, so the believer must be helped to see how religious faith and its doctrines and practices relate to all the areas of his or her life. Unless the believer has some sense of how Christianity affects and is affected by science and the arts, politics and economics, history and psychology, the believer may well either mistakenly identify religion with one of those fields or subordinate religion to them or assume that religion replaces them. The faith is catholic not only in that it is to embrace the whole world but also in that it embraces the whole human person and the whole of his or her experience. This may be a difficult task, but if it is not addressed, the results of its absence become ever more destructive.

Not every teacher will be able to make explicit the connections between Christian faith and all these dimensions of human experience, of course, and not every student will be able to hear the lesson if the teacher could do so. Few people, however, have been so acutely aware of the many ways in which human beings come to knowledge and to faith as Newman, and he certainly recognized that not all of them were clear and explicit. Indeed, sometimes for some persons the most fruitful ways of knowing and believing are not at all clear and explicit ones. In a remarkable passage from a sermon preached at Oxford in 1840, a passage presaging in an extraordinary way some of the central elements in both *An Essay on the Development of Christian Doctrine* and *An Essay in Aid of a Grammar of Assent,* Newman wrote that reason, defined as "the faculty of gaining knowledge without direct perception, or of ascertaining one thing by means of another,"[19] is "a living spontaneous energy within us, not an art."[20] I do not think that violence is done to Newman's point if we read his description of the implicit working of reason as in large part a description of the mental working of human beings more generally, including the ways in which one may be brought to faith.

> In this way [reason] is able, from small beginnings, to create to itself a world of ideas, which do or do not correspond to the things themselves for which they stand, or are true or not, according as it is exercised soundly or otherwise. One fact may suffice for a whole theory; one principle may create and sustain a system; one minute token is a clue to a large discovery. The mind ranges to and fro, and spreads out, and advances forward with a quickness which has become a proverb, and a subtlety and versatility which baffle investigation. It passes on from point to point, gaining one by some indication; another on a probability; then availing itself of an association; then falling back on some received law; next seizing on testimony; then committing itself to some popular impression, or some inward instinct, or some obscure memory; and thus it makes progress not unlike a clamberer on a steep cliff, who, by quick eye, prompt hand, and firm foot, ascends how he knows not himself, by personal endowments and by practice, rather than by rule, leaving no track behind him, and unable to teach another. It is not too much to say that the stepping by which great geniuses scale the mountains of truth is as unsafe and precarious to men in general, as the ascent of a skillful mountaineer up a literal crag. It is a way which they alone can take; and its justification lies in their success. And such mainly is the way in which all men, gifted or not gifted, commonly reason — not by rule, but by an inward faculty.[21]

In *An Essay in Aid of a Grammar of Assent,* Newman described "notional assent" as the acceptance of the truth of an inference and "real assent" as the acceptance of the truth of an experience.[22] Communicating faith is not primarily a matter of supplying propositions and information (although that is part of faith) but rather evoking and naming experiences. The teacher of faith should help his hearers examine their experience and offer categories to them for understanding that experience. Teaching faith is, in a sense, offering people a hermeneutic for interpreting what they experience within and around themselves so

that disparate parts of their experience begin to connect and emerge as a
meaningful whole. In terms of the passage from the *University Sermons,*
the teacher of faith evokes and helps interpret the indications, prob-
abilities, associations, received laws, testimonies, impressions, inward
instincts, memories — in short, the living experience — of his or her
hearers.

Karl Rahner

Karl Rahner's rich reflection on the salvific agency of the word is part
of his theology of symbol, one of the central links in Rahner's systematic theology. Entering that reflection is much too vast a project for my
purposes. There is one strand of Rahner's thought about the word that
will be helpful for my purposes: his discussion of the relationship of the
internally and externally spoken word of God, "the essential connex-
ion between the inner word of grace and the external, historical, social
('ecclesiastical') word of revelation."[23] The external word of revelation
is the account of salvation history, the proclamation of the apostles, the
doctrinal teaching of the church, and the worship of the community;
it is the instruction in faith that parents give their children, the homily
the pastor preaches, the lesson taught by the catechist, and the lecture
delivered by the theologian. The external word is, in short, the concrete
expression of God's self-communication that comes to us in countless
shapes in our time and place.

> The external, historical word expounds the inner one, brings it to
> the light of consciousness in the categories of human understand-
> ing, compels man definitely to take a decision with regard to the
> inner word, transposes the inner grace of man into the dimension
> of the community and renders it present there, makes possible the
> insertion of grace into the external, historical field of human life.[24]

The internal word of God is the grace by which the hearer of the
external word is enabled to assent to it as the self-communication of
God. It is the internal inducement to faith that Thomas Aquinas wrote
of as the primary cause of faith. As Rahner wrote, "It is only the inner
grace, as light of faith and inward connaturality with God, that makes it
possible for man to hear the external, historical word of God strictly *as*
the word of God, without subjecting it to the *a priori* of his own human
spirit and thereby debasing it."[25]

Fruitful faith, faith that brings forth righteousness that is formed by love and issues in works of love, is the result of the coming together of the internal and external words. The external word gives shape and direction to the inner longing of the human person for life and purpose and hope and forgiveness, i.e., for God. To use Saint Thomas's term, it is what makes faith "explicit."[26] But the external word without the internal word is a lifeless letter without the Spirit. The inner action of God giving Godself to the human person is the power that enables us to receive the externally proclaimed word with the profound "yes" of acceptance and obedience and joy. Without the external word, the internal word remains implicit; it is (to borrow a famous image from Rahner) "anonymous"; it is unnamed. Without the internal word, the preaching and teaching of the faith remains, at most, the imparting of more or less interesting information. "In a word, for the full normal accomplishment of the personal self-disclosure of God to the personally self-actualized man, the inner word of grace and the external historical word come together, as the mutually complementary moments of the one word of God to man."[27]

The teacher can never know when the internally spoken word of God is, as it were, aligned with the externally spoken word. There is no way to be certain that the moment is right for the external word to give shape and explicit form to the impetus to assent within the hearer. Therefore the communicator of faith must speak the word "in season and out of season" because he or she can never be sure when the season is. More often than not the teacher or preacher will find that the word of faith that he or she offers is out of season. Augustine warned Deogratias that lack of receptivity in his hearers would be a discouragement. One does not usually associate *hilaritas* with Rahner, but I suspect that he would have thoroughly understood and agreed with its necessity for the external teaching of the word.

At the risk of disjointedness, I will add one further observation drawn from Rahner that may seem unconnected to his reflections on the internal and external words of God. Although his "fundamental course" in Christian faith may seem to presume a more sophisticated audience than most preachers and teachers of faith face, Rahner maintained that "in today's situation all of us with all of our theological study are and remain unavoidably *rudes* in a certain sense, and that we ought to admit that to ourselves and also to the world frankly and courageously."[28] The complexity of the world in which we live has rendered the *rudes* in the classical sense of the term virtually extinct. *Rudes,* as Augustine used the term, were not people who were unintelligent or even uneducated; rather, they were persons of very limited experience, people who had not traveled and who were unaware of other contexts and customs than those they had lived in all their lives. Mass communication and easy transportation have almost eliminated such *rudes* from our society. No one who has access to a television or who has a radio in his or her car or who reads a newspaper or who has ever glanced at the cover of *Time* or *Newsweek* is a *rudis* in this classical meaning of the word. Rahner suggests, however, that there is a modern *rudis* and that the description fits almost all of us. Because of the explosion of knowledge and information and the complexity of the world in which we live, all of us are people of more or less narrow experience. Even the most knowledgeable person in one field is at a loss in other fields. In this sense, any one seeking to communicate the faith today still faces the task of Deogratias fifteen centuries ago in Carthage, that of catechizing the *rudes.* Rahner's suggestion about how to do so is interestingly very close to Augustine's.

Noting that a reader of a book described as "foundations" of faith and claiming to offer "an introduction to the idea of Christianity" might be surprised not to find it a work of fundamental theology, Rahner explains that, however useful the classical arguments for the credibility of Christian faith may have been at one time and may still be in certain circumstances and purposes, no one has ever claimed that such arguments are necessary for faith or even likely to be conducive to it for most people. For today's *rudes,* i.e., virtually everyone, a different course is required.

> By its very nature the foundational course must necessarily be a quite specific *unity of fundamental theology and dogmatic theology.* ... [The] particular characteristic of the traditional fundamental theology from the nineteenth century until our own day consists in this, that the facticity of divine revelation is to be reflected upon in a purely formal way, as it were, and, in a certain sense at least, is to be proven.... The point of our foundational course in theology is precisely this, to give people confidence from the very *content* of Christian dogma itself that they can believe with intellectual honesty. In practice it is the case that a fundamental theology of the

traditional kind, despite its formal clarity, precision, and cogency, very often remains unfruitful for the life of faith because the concrete person, and with a certain theoretical justification, has the impression that the formal event of revelation is not really all that absolutely clear and certain.[29]

In other words, the best apologetics is a good dogmatics. The most persuasive communication of the faith is an account of what Christians believe that shows how the various articles of faith hold together and the ways they shape and interact with the many dimensions of human life. This is not far from Augustine's insistence that the narrative of salvation is the content of the teaching of the faith. This is who we are, this is how we got here, this is what we have experienced, and this is where we are going; however different their language and thought forms, Augustine and Rahner would both recognize this as the content of the teaching of the faith.

Observations

George Bernard Shaw famously claimed, "He who can, does. He who cannot, teaches," and my corollary is that he who cannot teach, teaches others to teach. With that salutary caution in mind, I make bold to offer some reflections on communicating the faith based on these brief conversations with Thomas, Augustine, Newman, and Rahner.

1. No teacher of the faith should have too exalted a view of his or her usefulness. Faith is not something that one can give to another unless one happens to be God. Faith is a theological virtue, i.e., it is a habit infused by God into the heart and mind of the believer. First, foremost, and always, the teacher must remember that faith is a grace, an act of God's self-giving. The teacher can exemplify this grace. He or she may sacramentalize it. He or she may inspire the hearer to desire it. What he or she cannot do is give it to the hearer. Grace is given by God alone because grace is the self-communication of God to creatures.

The teacher cannot be the cause of faith, but he or she may be the occasion of faith. The grace of faith leading to the assent of belief remains formless, implicit, and incapable of communal expression and proclamation without the word of God taught to us by others. The word of faith taught by parents, friends, catechists, pastors, and theologians makes explicit the impetus toward belief that the Spirit of God enkindles in the heart and mind. The historical, public forms of faith — doctrines, liturgy, forms of prayer, devotional practices — concretize the unspeakable groanings of the Spirit.

Since the teacher cannot cause faith in the hearers apart from the grace of faith given by God, the teacher's first work for his or her hearers must be to ask that this grace be given them. The first duty of a communicator of faith to his or her hearers is to pray for them. It is also the one work at which a teacher is always successful.

2. The teacher of faith is a storyteller. The faith that is taught is a narrative. Even in its most abbreviated form — "Christ has died, Christ is risen, Christ will come again" — the proclamation of faith is a story. Before he or she is an instructor in doctrines or moral precepts, the teacher of faith tells a story. The best advice about how to tell the Christian story is that of the King of Hearts in *Alice in Wonderland*: "Begin at the beginning and go on till you come to the end: then stop." I am convinced that the way to introduce people into the faith is to show them how they fit into a story that, quite literally, begins "in the beginning" and continues without end. I know no greater service that a teacher can do for students (certainly contemporary American students) than to help them discover that history is their biography, that their life-stories began long before their lives, that they are part of a universal narrative.

Obviously this Christian narrative is, in large part, Scripture. But it is a serious mistake to tell this story in such a way that, after reaching its central moment in the life, death, and destiny of Jesus Christ, we jump to the eschaton. The narrative is the story not only of patriarchs and prophets and apostles but also of martyrs and church fathers and monks and reformers, of saints and scholars and builders of communities and servants of the poor. The history of the church is as much a part of the story of God's self-communication to creation as the history of Israel. To try to teach the faith without teaching the story of the Christian community may not be quite performing *Hamlet* without the prince, but it is at least comparable to performing *Romeo and Juliet* without Juliet.

3. For many centuries, Christian preachers and teachers made the narrative of salvation the story of their hearers by employing an allegorical exegesis of salvation history in which types and antitypes answered to one another across centuries. That may not be especially persuasive

to hearers today, but the goal of those teachers from Origen to Dante to Erasmus (not a bad lineage, that) remains important: to show how the past of the story of salvation is still present. I suggest that today this should be done by introducing students into conversation with their predecessors in the story.

The communion of saints is a powerful image in our tradition, and one that has multiple meanings (as do all really powerful images). One of those meanings that may be useful to recover is communion as communication or conversation. I have just suggested that to introduce people into the faith is to introduce them into a community that has a history. To be truly a participant in a historical community is to enter into conversation with persons who do not happen to be living at the same time as we are. Many of the most important, interesting, and insightful conversation partners happen to be dead at the moment. Being dead in no way diminishes their value as members of the tradition. In one of my favorite passages from Chesterton, he writes:

> Tradition may be defined as an extension of the franchise. Tradition means giving votes to the most obscure of all classes, our ancestors. It is the democracy of the dead. Tradition refuses to submit to the small and arrogant oligarchy of those who merely happen to be walking about. All democrats object to men being disqualified by the accident of birth; tradition objects to their being disqualified by the accident of death. Democracy tells us not to neglect a good man's opinion, even if he is our groom; tradition asks us not to neglect a good man's opinion, even if he is our father.[30]

Believers have a right to enter into the ongoing conversation within the tradition that we sometimes call the commun[icat]ion of saints. It is my firm conviction that in communicating faith, i.e., introducing others into the narrative of salvation, we must do so by bringing them into conversation with other believers who are not present to them at this time and place. I do not mean simply that they should be told about them — what they did and thought and said — but rather that they ask them questions and open themselves to be questioned by them, that they fight with them and agree with them on some things and disagree with them on others, in short, that they do all the things people do when they talk with one another. (It will not have escaped the reader, I hope, that the first part of this paper is a series of four brief conversations with people who do not happen to be breathing at the moment.)

4. All successful communication is conversation. I fear that this may be thought a trendy statement of contemporary adult educational theory. Far be it from me to suggest that communicating the faith is an extended question-and-answer session, still less a matter of breaking into discussion groups. What I am suggesting is at least as old as Plato. I do not think that it is merely a matter of literary form and flair that Plato wrote dialogues. I suspect that it is rooted in something he had learned from Socrates, namely, all real learning takes place in conversation. A homily or a lecture should be as much a conversation as a small group session. The speaker is in conversation with the text and, equally importantly, with his hearers who should be talking back, albeit within themselves: "What does he mean? Do I agree? If not, why? How does this cohere with what I have experienced or heard in the past? What ought I to do if this is the case?" The communicator of faith must be in conversation with predecessors within the tradition and able to introduce others into that conversation.

5. The absolutely necessary requirement for all successful preaching and teaching is joy. Augustine is quite correct: the communicator of faith must be characterized by *hilaritas,* must be enthusiastic, must enjoy what he or she is doing. As he knew, however, there are many things that sap enthusiasm. Weariness, discouragement, the nagging fear of pointlessness, all can poison one's joy. And again Augustine is quite correct about the (in my experience) one and only way to hold on to one's enthusiasm for teaching or preaching: center on one's hearers. Communicating faith is not about the speaker; it is about the hearers. Preachers or teachers who are passionately devoted to the people in front of them will not necessarily be eloquent or knowledgeable, but they will be convinced of the importance of what they are doing and excited about doing it because those for whom they do it matter so much. At the beginning of this paper, I mentioned that I have little to say when asked to advise graduate students about teaching. For many years the one counsel I have given them is that they must love what they teach and whom they teach.

6. Finally, preachers and teachers of faith should never forget that the primary resource for their teaching lies not in them but in their hearers. The restless heart that Augustine recognized as the longing for God in each and every human being drives us all, some faster, some slower,

some by a more direct, some by a more circuitous path, toward God. Preachers and teachers simply give names to the inner experience of their hearers, what Rahner described as the fruitful meeting of the internally and externally spoken words of God. That deep and abiding hunger, that restlessness of the heart, that ache for God is the preacher's and teacher's greatest ally and primary resource. My favorite statement both of the privilege of communicating faith and of the ground of confidence for doing so is taken from Wordsworth:

> what we have loved,
> Others will love, and we will teach them how.[31]

Chapter 8

Handing on the Faith
to the "New Athenians"
in the American Catholic Church

CHRISTOPHER AND DEBORAH RUDDY

"Athenians, I see how extremely religious you are in every way."
(Acts 17:22)

I

ON JUNE 18, 2004, near the end of a weeklong special assembly in Colorado, the United States Conference of Catholic Bishops (USCCB) released "Catholics in Political Life."[1] This 970-word statement, prompted by the controversy over the reception of the Eucharist by Catholic politicians who publicly support abortion legislation, received significant media attention for its position, based upon canon law and pastoral discernment, that each diocesan bishop retained the right to deny or to offer the Eucharist to such politicians.

The statement's terseness — even blandness — was complemented by the release, on June 23, of the more expansive interim reports of the USCCB's Task Force on Catholic Bishops and Catholic Politicians. These three reports, presented to the bishops on June 15 as guides for their discussion, addressed the theological and pastoral concerns underlying the public controversy.[2] Archbishop William Levada of San Francisco, in his theological reflection, noted that, despite more than three decades of consistent Catholic teaching on abortion in the aftermath of *Roe v. Wade,* the dialogue between the Catholic bishops and both Catholic politicians and American culture at large still seemed not to have been "effectively engaged." Ignorance abounds, particularly among Catholic

130

politicians on the relationship of their faith and their public service. The archbishop thus encouraged the bishops to recognize that, as "naïve" as it might seem, the dialogue is still at a " 'beginning' stage." He added, in a subsequent interview, that "we bishops have a lot to learn about the practicalities and the steps involved in political judgments, including political platforms and party relationships. We have to envision a dialogue that is not just one way."[3]

Cardinal Theodore McCarrick of Washington, D.C., speaking on behalf of the Task Force, noted that the committee had its origins in the bishops' "common frustration and deep disappointment" at Catholic political leaders whose voting "ignore[s] or contradict[s]" church teaching. The bishops could not shirk their responsibilities as teachers, pastors, and leaders. As teachers, they faced the challenge of a comprehensive "evangelization and catechesis" on human life and dignity, ranging from schools and parishes to adult faith-formation and RCIA programs. The cardinal also spelled out the shape of persuasion more explicitly than did the USCCB's statement: "Relationships matter. We cannot communicate and persuade simply through newspaper columns or issuing statements. We need to dedicate ourselves to dialogue with those in public life, especially those who do not follow the Church's teaching." For these reasons and others, the Task Force did not generally recommend the denial of communion to Catholic politicians or Catholic voters whose stands on life issues contradicted the church's. Such measures are permitted, said McCarrick, but they "should be applied [only] when efforts at dialogue, persuasion, and conversion have been fully exhausted."

Unmentioned by both the brief "Catholics in Political Life" and the lengthier interim reports, however, was a sobering fact: more than thirty years after *Roe v. Wade* and the bishops' subsequent efforts against legalized abortion, American Catholics are indistinguishable from other Americans in their acceptance (and practice) of abortion. A May 2004 CBS News poll, for instance, reported that 73 percent of all Americans and 71 percent of American Catholics support some form of legalized abortion.[4] Even taking into account such variables as commitment, ethnicity, and Mass attendance, these statistics are depressing. How does this rupture between efforts and results affect the way that the Catholic Church hands on its faith now and in coming years?[5]

The fundamental issue is not primarily the content or the frequency of Catholic teaching on abortion, but rather its effectiveness. Clear, steadfast teaching is necessary, but not sufficient to repair the breach between the church's faith and its members' practice. The problem is deeper: it is cultural, symbolic, mythic, imaginative, and, ultimately, spiritual. To put it bluntly, very few advocates of abortion rights want to be complicit in scraping an embryo out of a uterus or stabbing a partially delivered fetus's head with a pair of surgical scissors. They instead support — or tolerate — abortions because of a seeming lack of plausible alternatives, a desire to pursue other goods that might be jeopardized by the birth of a child, or an inability to grasp the gift-character of each human life. Consider, for example, the recent name-change of America's foremost abortion-rights organization from the National Abortion Rights Action League (NARAL) to NARAL Pro-Choice America; its Web site address is even simpler: *www.prochoiceamerica.org*. NARAL Pro-Choice America's literature and lobbying speak more of "choice" and "reproductive freedom" than of "abortion." NARAL knows its audience and its culture, and so shapes its message to tap into the foundational American mythos of freedom. Details of embryology and abortion procedures are rarely — if ever — mentioned.

The church's efforts to transform Catholic and American cultural and religious life, then, will bear fruit only to the extent that they engage such culture by offering a spiritual vision that is capable of affirming its authentic desires and challenging its distorted ones. Sixty years ago, in an article calling for a renewed theological formation for the laity, John Courtney Murray put it thusly:

> [I]t is important to realize, first of all, that secularism and indifferentism are not just religious errors, but religious diseases, which have to be healed at a level deeper than that of reason. Though they have their "philosophies," they are not intellectual aberrations; their origins are not so much in reason, as in myth — the myth of the self-sufficient man in the naturalist closed universe — which then seeks to rationalize itself.
>
> Hence the appeal to reason and apologetic argument against them is of very limited efficacy; it may demolish the rationalization, but it leaves the myth untouched. Their appeal is that of a spirit, a total and generalized way of life, an all pervasive mode

of thought, affection, sentiment, action. And this appeal can only be met successfully by the creation of a counter-spirit, generated by a vision of the whole Christian truth about God, man, and the world, which in turn generates a victorious sense of the uniquely salvific value of faith. Only this vision and this inner experience can fortify the spirit against infection from our secularist environment. What it needs is solid nourishment, and exercise in the full-orbed sun of Christ, the Light of the World; medicine, minor surgery, isolation, and the careful application of little apologetic "band-aids" here and there will not suffice....

In this situation our tactics should be clear. To a radical and total challenge, one must fling a radical and total answer.[6]

Besides offering proof that there was never a golden age of moral uprightness — even for the so-called "Greatest Generation" — Murray's words remind us today that the controversy over abortion is representative of a broader concern for the education and formation of the Catholic community. The challenge of *traditio* is precisely a spiritual one, as Murray realized, and so the church's response must be equally spiritual. It must foster a spirituality of communication that can transform in Christ the reigning symbols and myths of our times.

We propose, in this paper, some signposts and suggestions for such a spirituality of communication. As we have no expertise in catechetics or communications theory, our focus will be on the theological roots of communication. We will first analyze briefly belief and unbelief in our contemporary Western culture. Second, the pivot of our argument will be an interpretation of the Apostle Paul's encounter with the Athenians, as presented in Acts 17. Paul's approach offers an enduring model for how to transform culture and form disciples of the Risen One. The writings of the Anglican bishop-exegete N. T. Wright and the Irish Jesuit Michael Paul Gallagher on this passage provide complementary insights into how to engage what we call the "New Athenians," those contemporary Catholics who fill our churches and marketplaces. Next, we propose two virtues — humility and courage — as the foundational dispositions that should guide such cultural discernment. And, last, we suggest some practices and disciplines that seem necessary today for communicating and handing on the faith: contemplation and dialogue.

II

In his 1975 apostolic exhortation, *Evangelii nuntiandi,* Pope Paul VI wrote some of his most enduring words: "The split between the Gospel and culture is without a doubt the drama of our time, just as it was of other times. Therefore every effort must be made to ensure a full evangelization of culture, or more correctly of cultures."[7] Such evangelization of cultures, he stated, must be done "not in a purely decorative way as it were by applying a thin veneer, but in a vital way, in depth and right to their very roots."[8] Recognizing this interplay of Gospel and culture is essential for any communication of the church's faith. Belief and unbelief do not develop in a cultural vacuum, and so discernment of culture is central to any attempt to hand on the faith.

In *Clashing Symbols,* Michael Paul Gallagher sees contemporary unbelief among Christians arising more from apathy than from the anger or the alienation more prevalent in decades past. Such unbelief flows from a lack of exposure to Christianity and is more a cultural by-product than something chosen: "This is no longer [Henri] de Lubac's 'drama of atheistic humanism' but rather an undramatic limbo of non-belonging."[9] Gallagher describes four main forms of cultural unbelief that affect believers and nonbelievers alike; no one is immune to their influence.[10] The first type is "religious anemia," characterized by a distance from Christian roots in which the church's language of faith is experienced as a "foreign tongue." This credibility gap is caused largely by a lack of "pastoral imagination," in which the church fails to enter into the cultural world of its intended hearers. It offers answers to unasked questions and fails to ask the right questions.[11]

The second type of unbelief is "secular marginalization." Faith is essentially private, unworthy of serious intellectual attention. It is banished from the public square and made to seem implausible, irrelevant, even dangerous. We call this the *"New York Times* phenomenon," in which columnists like Maureen Dowd and Thomas Friedman use words like "theology" and "dogma" as synonyms for blind adherence, fanatical attachment, and ignorance of reality.

"Anchorless spirituality," Gallagher's third type, can result from the excesses of the first two types. Lacking a meaningful language of faith (religious anemia) and bored by an unsatisfying materialism that privatizes faith (secular marginalization), persons and communities become susceptible to fads and even recurring heresies such as Gnosticism and pantheism. The spiritual hunger of these seekers is good, he notes, but their rootless drifting is dangerous and can lead to extremes of narcissism and fundamentalism.

Gallagher is most concerned, however, with a fourth kind of unbelief that he calls "cultural desolation." Here, cultural pressures — often unrecognized — stifle and even "kidnap" the imagination, thereby rendering people "unfree for Revelation — or more precisely, for the hearing from which faith comes (cf. Romans 10:17)." Unbelief of this sort affects one's very readiness or disposition towards faith. He quotes from Cardinal Newman's *Grammar of Assent* that "the heart is commonly reached not through the reason, but through the imagination." Imagination must therefore be the primary faculty to which communication of the faith must appeal, first by "clearing the ground" of the dehumanizing aspects of culture and then by "liberating levels of hearing and desire." The movement here is, as Gallagher puts it, from the "dia-bolic" to the "symbolic," from division to synthesis, from blockage to flow. The means by which one moves from unbelief to belief is our next topic.

III

Acts 17:16–34 is perhaps the classic scriptural account of the encounter between Christianity and culture. Its outlines are familiar: Paul arrives in Athens, the apotheosis of culture and wisdom, and is disgusted by its idolatry. After some debate with Jews in their synagogue and with Greek philosophers in the marketplace, he is led to the Areopagus to explain his teaching on the Resurrection. There, he begins by noting the Athenians' deep religiosity displayed in their many altars and temples. Alluding to Stoicism and quoting Greek poets and philosophers, he tells them that the "unknown god" worshiped at one of their altars is the God who created the world and all of its inhabitants. This same God, who transcends his creation, calls all to repentance and to faith in the Resurrection of his "appointed" one from the dead. At this point, some of his hearers scoff at this teaching, others are intrigued, and still others believe. Paul has taken the heart of the Christian faith into the heart of worldly wisdom, and the Resurrection is both stumbling block and synthesis to the cultured Athenians.

N. T. Wright and Michael Paul Gallagher offer complementary anal-
yses of Paul's evangelization. If Wright focuses more on the Athenians'
transformation, while Gallagher concentrates on Paul's own transformation as a preacher, both nonetheless see Acts 17 as offering an
enduring approach to communicating the faith. Wright proposes that
Paul's preaching follows a threefold method of affirmation, confrontation, and outflanking or transforming exposition.[12] Paul begins his
Areopagus speech by affirming all that is good or potentially good in
Athenian culture: their religious devotion, however misguided, to the
Unknown God; their philosophical and poetic heritage; their belief in
a Creator. However, Paul also confronts the Athenians' "rank idolatry": "[w]ith the Parthenon and the other wonderful temples in view,
he declare[s] that man-made temples [a]re a waste of time" (e.g., Acts
17:24–25, 29–30). Affirmation and confrontation culminate in Paul's
attempt to transform culture and communicate his faith through "outflanking exposition." Wright says that Paul deploys a thoroughly Jewish
understanding of God as Creator to transform Greek thought; by presenting God as the Creator who both dwells in, and yet is distinct from
and sovereign over, his creation, Paul outflanks the distant God of Epi-
cureanism and the pantheism of Stoicism (has contemporary idolatry
changed much from its ancient forms?!). Paul thus enters into the Athenian world in order to entirely transform it from within. He shows the
Athenians that their noblest ideals find fulfillment only in Christ and that
they should not settle for the "second-best" of worldly, Greek thought.

Like Wright, Gallagher finds in Acts 17 a threefold approach to communicating faith and transforming culture. He focuses, though, on the
transformation of the communicator. His lens is the Ignatian framework
of the discernment of spirits, of the interplay between consolation and
desolation. Gallagher, unlike Wright, begins by recounting Paul's disgust
upon entering Athens. Seeing idolatry all around him, he argues with Jew
and Greek alike, and is dismissed as a "babbler" and a "proclaimer of
false divinities" (Acts 17:18).

Unaccountably, though, Paul's approach changes when he enters the
Areopagus. Instead of immediate confrontation, he begins — as we
know — by mentioning the Athenians' evident religiosity and putting
aside explicit judgment upon it. His teaching affirms the good in their
culture and appeals to their desire for experience of God. Although Paul
is not afraid to call the Athenians to repentance, his preaching succeeds

because it enters into the culture and so can awaken its deepest desires. As Gallagher writes, Paul "identif[ied] seeds of the gospel within pagan religiousness.... Behind the frivolous appearances lay deeper spiritual hungers. Behind the games of argumentativeness lay a poetry and a spirituality that he began to appreciate in a new way."[13]

Gallagher is intrigued by Paul's change in tactics as he moves from the Agora to the Areopagus: how can one account for such a dramatic transformation? Gallagher suggests that Paul moves from a state of desolation to one of consolation. Such consolation — a state of "being-in-tune-with Christ," a "sense of expanding in harmony with what is deepest in us, the Spirit in us" — liberates Paul to embrace whatever good can be found in Athenian culture. Trusting that God is not absent even from idolatry, Paul can now discern the seeds of God's presence and activity in what is opposed to God. Where desolation is like "closed fists, ready to reject," consolation is like "open hands, ready to receive."[14]

Such consolation enables one to discern honestly and fruitfully one's cultural situation. It enables one to leave behind the tense, adversarial hostility that can see only what is evil, because it "see[s] desolation only with desolation."[15] One thinks, for instance, of what we call the " 'ism' criticism," that intellectual and spiritual laziness that avoids the hard work of discernment through the construction and demolition of such easy targets as, say, "secularism," "relativism," or "materialism." Conversely, the experience of consolation can also prevent one from settling for an unquestioning, promiscuous, or even resigned acceptance of culture. A basic disposition of consolation does not exclude denunciation, then, but rather keeps one from "rejecting entire ways of life as utterly beyond the reach of the gospel."[16]

Moreover, although Acts 17 involves an encounter of Christianity with a non-Christian culture, it can also apply today to handing on the faith in a Christian context. In this sense, the dividing line runs not simply through Christian and non-Christian, but through the heart of each Christian believer and each Christian culture — devout, indifferent, moribund, antagonistic, or some mixture thereof. How do we communicate with the "New Athenians" in our churches, our families, and our own hearts? How do we relate to their culture, their education, their achievements, their belief and unbelief? How do we find the dispositions and practices that can help transform them — mindful, of course, that our success, like Paul's, may be modest at first. For that matter, how do we foster in our communicators that same transformation from desolation to consolation undergone by Paul?

Gallagher argues that the church must cultivate a sense of "cultural agency" in both its communicators and its hearers if faith is to be communicated and culture transformed. It must not be passive, but rather a "producer of meaning" both intellectual and spiritual.[17] The church does so when it first interprets and judges its cultural situation and second fosters alternative communities and spiritualities. Transformation is possible only when a positive vision is proposed and embodied.

The church's stance on abortion is an obvious example of the deep need for such agency. Following Wright and Gallagher, the first step in such agency would be to affirm the value of freedom and of choice. In a world in which many struggle to be free, while a relative few have the opportunity to shape deliberately the course of their lives, the rhetoric of freedom is powerful and attractive. In particular, women, long subject to various forms of domination, have a rightful desire to be in possession of their bodies and lives and thereby exercise a legitimate autonomy. The church must listen to women and their experiences of oppression and of liberation. If women (and men) believe that they are not being listened to, that their interlocutor is merely waiting to speak, then church teaching will get nowhere. Relationships matter, as Cardinal McCarrick said, and true relationships are always mutual ones. These relationships, like any others, will need time to build trust.

The next step, though, must be confrontation and challenge. This can be scientific, philosophical, even autobiographical. Embryological data can be astonishing; we, for instance, were amazed during Deborah's first pregnancy when we read of the fetus's development: the liver and kidneys begin to form within a week of conception, the heart begins to beat after three weeks, brain waves can be detected at six weeks. Such easily available knowledge can counteract the tendency to depersonalize the embryo and reduce it to an abstraction.[18] Communicators should speak, too, of the logic of freedom: What is freedom for? What is the object of "freedom of choice"? Does such license liberate and empower women and men? Here, sensitive, nonmanipulative accounts of suffering, depression, and guilt from women and men who have experienced abortion can help tie together scientific and philosophical insights through the autobiographical witness so valued in our culture. Ultimately, such challenges must expose the Orwellian language and thought that mask the violence of abortion.

The final step will be that of consolation and outflanking. Intellectually, communicators need to propose a truer sense of Christian freedom, its essential bonds to truth and love; they should show that contemporary understandings of freedom as autonomy and self-expression are incomplete, "second-best" notions that find their fulfillment only in relationship to Christ. Such teaching will be effective, though, only to the extent that it becomes visible and attractive in communities that give flesh to the Gospel of life. Gallagher, in particular, argues that such alternative communities are the only effective means of resistance and formation in cultures that are indifferent or hostile to the Christian values of self-transcendence and self-giving in community. These new communities — informal or formal, small or large — will give a witness of true freedom, generosity, hospitality, and a "contemplative outlook"[19] able to perceive all life as a gift. Their consoling "open hands" will succeed far more than desolate "closed fists."

In this context, if Wright and Gallagher differ somewhat in emphasis — the former's evangelicalism may lead him to emphasize confrontation and discontinuity more than does the latter, who has a greater sense of Catholic continuity — both would agree, we think, with Pope John Paul II, who said in a 1995 homily in Baltimore that "[s]ometimes, witnessing to Christ will mean drawing out of a culture the full meaning of its noblest intentions, a fullness that is revealed in Christ. At other times, witnessing to Christ means challenging that culture, especially when the truth about the human person is under assault."[20] We turn now to the virtues that shape such effective communication of Christ.

IV

Communication — from affirmation through confrontation to transformation — depends in great measure upon the character of the communicator and the manner of his or her communication. The virtues of humility and courage seem to be particularly appropriate ones for handing on the faith in our time and place, marked as they are by the sexual-abuse crisis, religious indifference, and national political controversy. Our comments here are more suggestive than exhaustive.

Humility, a distinctively Christian attribute, is our starting point, and St. Augustine, the *doctor humilitatis,* is our guide. Augustine maintained that humility, above all other virtues, characterizes the way that God communicates with us. The humility of God is revealed in the Incarnation. God does not cling to what is properly God's own (power, splendor, majesty), but chooses to be poured out into the human: "Though he was in the form of God, he did not deem equality with God something to be grasped at..." (Phil 2:6).

God's humble approach in Christ seeks us out and meets us "where we are at." Through likeness to us, God in Christ communicates in a new way, establishing a new bond, a new meeting place, between God and humanity. By making our trials his own, Christ becomes himself the "common ground" between the divine and human. He mediates and overcomes the chasm of sin that separates God and humanity. His likeness to us opens up a new way for our return to God: "[H]e applied to us the similarity of his humanity to take away the dissimilarity of our iniquity, and becoming a partaker of our mortality he made us partakers of his divinity."[21]

Christ's humility not only draws us in through kinship, but it also disarms us through contrast and even confrontation. By not "grasping" at the loftiness of his divinity and, instead, reaching out to us in our depraved condition, Christ reveals our own desperate clinging to the claims of the ego. God's extravagant, self-emptying love contrasts with our possessiveness and desire for control. The humbling of the Word simultaneously reveals the immense worth of humanity and exposes the desperate state of humanity steeped in prideful isolation and hostility. In brief, we find our redemption in both similarity and dissimilarity with the humble God.

The full measure of Christ's humility, however, is seen in his death on a cross. The humble Christ not only does not cling to divinity; he does not cling to a humanity of honor, comfort, or enjoyment. He freely and without calculation chooses through his suffering and death to make himself accountable for our sin. Augustine stresses that Christ's humility is God's initiative given in love and generosity for our sake.

Can the way that Christ extends himself to us in humility inspire us today in our struggles with communication? In the American church, the difficulty of good conversation among "liberals" and "conservatives" can reveal an unwillingness on all sides to reach beyond the confines of one's own framework and language. In speaking about the "cup of humility," Augustine writes:

> It's easy enough to think about grandeur, easy enough to enjoy honors, easy enough to give our ears to yes-men and flatterers. To put up with abuse, to listen patiently to reproaches, to pray for the insolent, this is the Lord's cup, this is sharing the Lord's table.[22]

Is it not finally pride and despair, the illnesses cured by humility, which lead us to talk past one another and remain within our self-enclosed circle of conversation partners? We despair of thinking that we can learn from one another, that our time would be well spent trying to hammer out our differences. But how can we draw those on the margins closer to Christ, when those of us who are active in the church remain so divided and embittered? How do we come to terms with this failure to witness? Can Christ's humility inspire us to renounce pride, to take the first step, to listen, to acknowledge before our "opponent" that we don't know everything, that some of our judgments may have been hasty, and that perhaps there are facets of a given issue that we have not yet considered?[23] What might humility look like in the context of a divided and polarized church?

The life of the late Cardinal Joseph Bernardin of Chicago offers one witness. In his book, *The Gift of Peace,* he begins a chapter on being falsely accused of sexual abuse with a meditation appropriately entitled "Emptying Oneself." Faced with the accusation of sexual abuse by a former seminarian, he harbored feelings of anger and distrust towards many in the church and the media. In the midst of his humiliation, he "wondered if the voice of truth could be heard in a culture in which image making and distortion have almost completely replaced it."[24] He added, "I was being emptied of self in a way that I could never have anticipated."[25] Through prayer and the support of many friends, however, he was led to pray for his accuser, Steven Cook. Intuiting that Steven was in great pain and being used by other adversaries in the ordeal, Bernardin wrote him a letter to ask if they could meet and pray together; Steven's lawyer kept the letter from him. Several months later, after the charges were dropped, Bernardin continued to seek Steven out, and, when a meeting was arranged, he writes, "I only prayed that he would receive me."[26]

Bernardin describes the meeting as one of the most powerful man-ifestations of "God's love, forgiveness, and healing" that he ever experienced.[27] He listened to Steven's life-story, his sexual abuse by a priest "friend," his bitterness toward the church, his struggle with AIDS. The meeting was not without hard, necessary moments of confrontation. At one point, Bernardin looked directly at Steven, seated a few inches away from him and said, "You know that I never abused you." "I know," Steven answered. "Can you tell me that again?" Again, Bernardin looked directly into his eyes and said, "I have never abused you. You know that, don't you?" "Yes," Steven replied, and then offered a "simple, direct, deeply moving" apology.[28] Their reconciling, grace-filled meeting concluded, to the surprise of everyone, with the celebration of Mass. "Never," Bernardin writes, "in my entire priesthood have I witnessed a more profound reconciliation.... And I could not help but recall the work of the Good Shepherd: to seek and restore to the sheepfold the one that has been, only for a while, lost."[29]

Augustine and Cardinal Bernardin teach us that Christ's humility introduces a new strategy for communication — at once mediating, challenging, and, ultimately, transforming. His humble, healing touch is gentle or bracing, depending on our various illnesses. The radically unexpected nature of the Word's descent into the ordinary human expe-rience of weakness and frailty allows for a new vision of God and of communication. The *way* that God saves us is inseparable from salva-tion itself. So, too, does the way that we communicate Christ to others reveal who Christ is.

Humility flows into courage, particularly the courage to speak and to do the truth in love at whatever price. One of the most visible icons of courage in the church was undoubtedly Pope John Paul II. Tirelessly preaching the Gospel throughout the world, in season and out of season, "be not afraid" was his unceasing refrain. Avery Dulles, for one, sees the pope's "New Evangelization" as one of, if not *the,* keys to his ministry. In a lecture on courage delivered to the English and Welsh bishops in 2002 (as yet unpublished), Timothy Radcliffe, the former master gen-eral of the Dominicans, suggests that such evangelization is a threatened project in the Western world. The West, he notes, is at once blessed by a previously unimaginable level of security and yet perhaps the most fearful culture in the world. Such fear cripples people by inducing a sense of helplessness and defensiveness. Many in the church, he claims, are afflicted by a "dis-courage[ment]" that endangers the much-needed work of evangelization.

The good news of the Gospel, however, is that there is no need to fear anything or anyone. When angels appear in scripture, Radcliffe writes, their first words are invariably, "Do not be afraid." Fear is the death of love, for it closes us up on ourselves and isolates us from others. Courage first consists, then, in helping us to face up to our fears and to confront our vulnerability. Often seen as the antithesis of courage, vulnerability is actually its presupposition: the one who has no fear cannot be courageous.[30] Courage consists precisely in encountering one's fear and overcoming it. The central symbol of Christianity, Radcliffe says, is the naked vulnerability of the Cross.

Liberated from fear and anxiety by courage, one is then "free to do what a right perception of the situation requires," be it bold speech, great deeds, endurance in the face of suffering, or the ability to accept one's own death. In each of these challenges, Radcliffe holds that the characteristic "flavor" of courage is generosity: a freedom from the fearful self in order to lose oneself in service to others. The courageous person is not an Olympian hero, standing apart from society, but the saint who gives himself or herself to others, even to the point of death. Where the ancient god was invulnerable, the Christian God is precisely the one who is vulnerable unto death. The generosity of courage encompasses a passion for communion (and communication) with God and with humanity.

The communicator must never be afraid to confront what is distorted or evil, then, but he or she must always do so from an awareness of one's own weakness. The stridency that comes from invulnerability may appear courageous, even prophetic, but it often fails to transform others or even oneself. Radcliffe wonders whether the church's prophetic stands sometimes fail to gain a hearing because of a perception that its leaders are often invulnerable, unable to show vulnerability within the church itself:

> We do often dare to take unpopular positions on such topics as abortion, or peace, or for the poorest. We do often dare to risk ridicule and dismissal because of our convictions. We know that we are vulnerable and may be crucified by the press and be misunderstood by the young. Sometimes, and I am not altogether sure why, I have a sneaking feeling that our courageous stands do not

quite ring true, do not entirely convince. Why is this? I suspect that it is because we are not so courageous at facing our vulnerability within the Church. For [our] deepest vulnerability is to each other, and so it is here that our most profound courage is required. We are bound together within the Church by far deeper bonds of love and communion, and so it is here that we can be most hurt. It is here, with each other, that we can be most touched by the loss of face, by the destruction of reputation, by scorn or neglect. It is here where we must face the most painful forms of alienation, misrepresentation and mental exile. If we cannot be truly courageous *ad intra,* then maybe our brave stands *ad extra* will not entirely ring true.

Vulnerability is not the end of courage, but it is its beginning. Communicators in the church must keep this in mind, lest they fall into desolation when they survey an often depressing culture within the church and in the world. Courage will help them to endure so as not to let "adversity crush [their] joy."[31]

V

"Modern man listens more willingly to witnesses than to teachers, and if he does listen to teachers, it is because they are witnesses."[32] In writing these words, Paul VI knew that witness is the *conditio sine qua non* of Christian communication. And, at a time when the Catholic Church in the United States has lost many of its long-standing cultural supports (e.g., immigrant subcultures, parish-based social life, esteem in popular culture) and even much of its credibility, the witness of both communities and persons is often the only convincing means of handing on the faith. The sexual-abuse crisis and its aftermath give obvious, tragic evidence of the harm caused by corrupted witness. In this concluding section, then, we propose two dimensions of Christian witness that seem particularly apt modes of Christian communication in today's cultural context: a "contemplative outlook" and dialogue.

Christian communication finds its deepest wellspring in prayer, communication with God; one cannot give what one does not have. Karl Rahner famously said that the Christian of tomorrow will be a mystic, or he [or she] will not be at all. Even granting its rhetorical bluntness, his comment seems even more prescient today. In Western cultures, Christianity can no longer rely upon the broad cultural matrix that helped to sustain belief and practice. Formation by osmosis is no longer possible, and so religious identity must now be more intentionally chosen and intentionally formed:

> [I]t would be wrong to think that ordinary Christians can be content with a shallow prayer that is unable to fill their whole life. Especially in the face of the many trials to which today's world subjects faith, they would be not only mediocre Christians but "Christians at risk." They would run the insidious risk of seeing their faith progressively undermined, and would perhaps end up succumbing to the allure of "substitutes," accepting alternative religious proposals and even indulging in far-fetched superstitions.[33]

An autobiographical note may be helpful here. As believers and as theologians, we know how we — who have the luxury of work that allows time for reflection — both crave silence and yet flee from it; we live, for example, three blocks away from a church that has perpetual adoration, and collectively we have been there three times in two months. And, with two young children of our own, we also know how parents — worn out from work and childrearing — struggle with the temptation to have their children watch television and "educational" videos.

Moreover, as teachers, we find ourselves astonished and often frustrated by the sheer noise and activity of our students. Twenty-year-olds have rarely been temperamentally Carthusian, but we notice a change from even fifteen years ago (when we were about twenty and, of course, meditative and ascetic). Cell phones, DVDs, Wi-Fi, Instant-Messaging, PowerPoint, Friendster, student lounges filled with televisions: none of these existed in 1990. More important, most of our students have scarcely a still moment in their day; they often work twenty to forty hours a week to pay for school and for luxuries, take a full load of classes, and participate in extracurriculars and resumé-building. In these circumstances, how can evangelization and catechesis break through this "wall of sound and image," to paraphrase the music producer Phil Spector? How can we compete with the immediacy, omnipresence, and superior professionalism of mass media, particularly advertising and music videos? How can the Word of God be heard?

Simply put, the church cannot compete with such forces and will waste precious time and resources in trying to do so. Flannery O'Connor once wrote, "To the hard of hearing you shout, and for the almost-blind you draw large and startling figures." We think she was wrong: to the deaf, one shows a picture; to the blind, one speaks. Likewise, to those bombarded by sound and image, one should offer silence. A contemplative outlook is thus perhaps the best way forward. Such an outlook comprises both a worldview and a set of practices or disciplines. The shape of this worldview is sketched in the fourth, final chapter ("You Did It to Me: For a New Culture of Human Life") of Pope John Paul II's 1995 encyclical, *Evangelium vitae:*

> Because we have been sent into the world as a "people for life," our proclamation must also become a *genuine celebration of the Gospel of life*. This celebration, with the evocative power of its gestures, symbols and rites, should become a precious and significant setting in which the beauty and grandeur of this Gospel is handed on.
>
> For this to happen, we need first of all to *foster*, in ourselves and in others, *a contemplative outlook*. Such an outlook arises from faith in the God of life, who has created every individual as a "wonder" (cf. Ps 139:14). It is the outlook of those who see life in its deeper meaning, who grasp its utter gratuitousness, its beauty and its invitation to freedom and responsibility. It is the outlook of those who do not presume to take possession of reality but instead accept it as a gift, discovering in all things the reflection of the Creator and seeing in every person his living image (cf. Gen 1:27; Ps 8:5). This outlook does not give in to discouragement when confronted by those who are sick, suffering, outcast or at death's door. Instead, in all these situations it feels challenged to find meaning, and precisely in these circumstances it is open to perceiving in the face of every person a call to encounter, dialogue and solidarity (italics in original).[34]

Gratitude, beauty, wonder, communion, solidarity, and celebration are the dominant optics in this vision.[35] They can be cultivated, though, only through deliberate practices, especially those that embrace silence. A paradox emerges: the most needed dimension of a spirituality of communication is perhaps silence. Spouses and families need to be shown how to pray together, to listen to God together; the Ignatian *examen*, for one, can be easily adapted for familial use. Believers need to find in their liturgies a sense of reverence and stillness, instead of extremes of stimulation and drabness. Students and parishioners need formation in the spiritualities that have flourished through the centuries; the monastic practice of *lectio divina* is well-suited for the classroom and the prayer group. For all believers and potential believers, such disciplines of silent attentiveness can be profoundly transformative, giving them the sustenance and the space that their homes and workplaces and cultures cannot.

Furthermore, as the battle over abortion (as with other life issues such as capital punishment, reproductive technologies, and cloning) is ultimately one of imagination and heart, a contemplative outlook seems necessary if the church is to transform both itself as well as the broader culture. Only in such a worldview can human life be seen as a gift rather than as (tragically) expendable or manipulable. A people skilled in silence and attentiveness can grasp that, in the words of the poet e e cummings, "A world of made / is not a world of born."[36]

A spirituality of communication entails not only silence but speech. In a letter to the American bishops written just before his death in August 2003, the late Msgr. Philip Murnion asked, "[D]oes not the living out of such a spirituality of communion require dialogue as its very life-breath: the dialogue of prayer with Jesus Christ, the dialogue of mutual building up on the part of the members of Christ?"[37] Such dialogue is thus primarily not a matter of proper technique or courtesy, but a way of life, a personal encounter that demands conversion of its participants.

Pope John Paul II's 1995 encyclical on ecumenism, *Ut unum sint,* provides a suggestive account of dialogue, which, although pertaining directly to ecumenism, applies equally to other forms of Christian dialogue and communication. The pope notes, first of all, that dialogue engages the entire person — spiritually, intellectually, emotionally, imaginatively. This personalist vision of dialogue must not be reduced to "simply an exchange of ideas," but is an "exchange of gifts."[38] It recognizes the other party as a "partner" and begins with the presumption that "each side must presuppose in the other a desire for reconciliation, for unity in the truth" (*UUS*, #29). Genuine dialogue also calls for prayer and a searching examination of conscience. Each partner needs to acknowledge his or her own sinfulness before the other and before God. "Vertical" reconciliation with God, in fact, gives rise to "horizontal" communion: it "creates in brothers and sisters living in Communities not in full communion with one another that interior space where Christ, the source of the Church's unity, can effectively act, with all the power of his Spirit, the Paraclete" (*UUS*, #34–35).

Most promising, though, for our topic of communication is the pope's reminder that differences in theological and dogmatic language do not necessarily indicate differences in belief. Under the appearance of out-right contradiction, agreement — even substantial — may exist. It may be the case, he writes, that parties use the same words to describe different realities, or different words to describe the same reality; the pope alludes to the christological agreements of recent decades with the Assyrian and the Ancient Churches of the East that have overcome centuries of bitter theological and ecclesial estrangement. We need, it seems, to be creative with our words and humble enough not to cling to our own formulations — valid as they may be — if they distract or mislead those we seek to engage. Sometimes this may mean not inventing new words, but reappropriating older ones.

We find this distinction (not separation) between reality and language helpful in engaging our students, friends, and families in dialogue. They are often inarticulate about their deepest beliefs, and so often fall back on clichés: "It's true for me," "All religions have the same basic message," "I can't impose my beliefs on someone else." Many — probably most — of them profess some form of relativism, be it religious, epistemological, moral, or cultural. At this point during conversation, we usually have to fight the urge to throw up our hands in frustration or to mutter snide dismissals.

However, if we patiently ask them whether rape is always wrong, for instance, the limits of their relativism quickly become clear. They do, in fact, have strong, even absolute convictions, but are hamstrung by the language of relativism that surrounds them. We can then help them develop a more thoughtful, accurate language. But, we can also gain a renewed respect for how difficult faith is for so many — especially those who are earnestly if confusedly seeking transcendence and meaning; we can grow in humble gratitude for the gift of faith that has been given to us by God and the church through no merit of our own. Further dialogue can then help develop a trust and a language that find common ground in what might seem to be incommensurable positions. Such advances — however infrequent or meager — are no small achievements in a culture that, as the philosopher Charles Taylor has stressed, is frighteningly inarticulate about its beliefs and desires.[39]

VI

There is little disagreement about the importance of handing on the Catholic faith to present and future generations. We are not sure, though, that the *urgency* of this task is sufficiently grasped. The religious and cultural capital built up over decades and centuries is rapidly dwindling in American Catholicism. If faith is not deliberately proposed and fostered, it will be washed away by a culture that has distorted and stifled the religious instinct inherent in every person. We sense that the "New Athenians" — apart from cultural and intellectual elites who seek liberation everywhere but in the Judeo-Christian tradition — are not so much hostile to religion, as they are suffering from a lack of vision, meaning, and challenge. Liberal Catholics have shown themselves unable to pass on their faith to younger generations in any sustainable, attractive, intellectually coherent manner; their intra-ecclesial battles are often of little interest to the young, who wonder why the church is even necessary at all. Conservative Catholics settle for moralism, fearful cultural denunciation, and the *Catechism,* and so fail to appeal to the imaginations or hearts of the young. The "New Athenians" in our church and world need and deserve more than they are presently getting from a polarized leadership class. Handing on the faith to them will succeed only if the church has the imagination to affirm their spiritual longings, confront their contemporary idols, and transform both in a renewed preaching, celebration, and service of Christ.

When the vision of God's being and doing has become weak, theology becomes defensive — and so do Christians in general and priests in particular.... But somehow or other, we all have to undergo a fairly fundamental conversion from seeing revealed truth as a possession to be guarded to seeing it as a place to inhabit; not one bit of territory that needs protection, but the whole world renewed. We shall not proclaim Christ effectively if we are constantly reverting to what makes us anxious rather than what makes us grateful.[40]

Chapter 9

Communication in Handing on the Faith

TERRENCE W. TILLEY

Communication as Fundamental

BERNARD LONERGAN, S.J., devoted a mere fourteen pages to "communications," his eighth and last functional specialty, in his monumental *Method in Theology.* He gives each of the other seven specialties an average of over twenty-nine pages of text. Yet communications is devoted, Lonergan wrote, to "interdisciplinary relations with art, language, literature, and other religions, with the natural and the human sciences, with philosophy and history." But that is just the beginning. Communications also deals with "the transpositions that theological thought has to develop if religion is to retain its identity and yet at the same time find access into the minds and hearts of men [*sic*] of all cultures and classes." And communications also deals with "the adaptations needed to make full and proper use of the diverse media of communication that are available at any place and time."[1] Quite a lot of work to be described in a mere fourteen pages (few of which, it must be admitted, were directly devoted to communications).

As theological work has increasingly become postmodern and postliberal, the last has indeed become first. Theology in the university — now the primary academic home of theologians working in the United States — cannot but be interdisciplinary, inventive, and media-savvy. We can no longer do our research, interpretive, historical, dialectical, foundational, doctrinal, or systematic work except in interdisciplinary ways, especially in dialogue with history and the social sciences, and even with the so-called "hard sciences," that are becoming increasingly recognized as "soft." Since our primary teaching work is no longer to train future clerics, but to engage in general education courses for undergraduates and in specialized education for our majors and our predominantly lay graduate students in theology, religious education, and pastoral ministry, we must be inventive if we are to pass on the ancient creed in this new world. And in a culture dominated by information, we have not only to compete for visibility in a saturated universe by using new media from "Blackboard" to "PowerPoint" to "electronic reserves" to "web-based" or "web-augmented" pedagogy, but we also have to teach our students how to evaluate the information about the Christian tradition that they garner from a wide variety of electronic sources, most of which have an axe to grind and many of which are simply unreliable. Communications, as described by Lonergan, must be our first specialty, not our last.

However important it is for church folk in general and professional theologians to use media well, that is not my focus here. Communicating the faith is the most important task of the whole Christian community and each of its members. Theologians have role-specific responsibilities that affect communicating the faith, but as it takes a village to raise a child, it takes a church to make a Christian. Or so I will attempt to show here.

Two Presuppositions

Human Nature as Socially Constituted

I make two distinctive presuppositions about context and content. With regard to context, in 1978, Walter Ong, S.J., wrote, "new technologies of print and electronics have affected not just the external world but the interior of man's mind, the entire noetic economy in which he experiences himself and the world around him. In this sense, the technologies of writing, print and electronics are more operative within us than outside us."[2] In short, media not only *affect* us, but also, in an ontological sense, *effect* us. If the emergence of an electronic culture shifts human consciousness as profoundly and pervasively as Marshall McLuhan, Ong, and others have said it does, then we are in some ways substantially different from our forebears who lived in oral or print cultures. This has profound importance for our understanding of how to hand on the faith.

Theologians seem to presume, unwarrantedly, that these differences are accidental, not substantial. But this underestimates the power of our communities and the power of our language to shape our world. The very potentiality for the sort of social self one might actualize is not a constant in human history. The media in which and through which we communicate are constitutive of the sorts of selves we can become. This does not mean that there are no constants in human nature that transcend time. But in the concrete actuality of humanity, the essence of human nature is not and cannot be exhausted by these constants. Some constants are necessary, but not sufficient to define actual human nature.

Ong's insight is not always recognized. Each of us is a *zoon politikon;* together we are *zooi politikoi.* Each and all of us is/are *homo loquens, homo ludens, homo sapiens.* But to be each of these — political-social, speaking, playing, knowing — is to be a social self. If we, as human beings, are social by nature and if the social component of human nature shifts, then human nature itself shifts. Our *polis* today is quite different from the *polis* of yesterday. And so are we different in nature. Some strands of the rope that constitute human nature change enough to say that human nature itself changes. Or at least that is the way I understand Ong's point.

Diverse Communities Shape Our Identities Diversely

However it may have been in other times, contemporary people do not derive their identity from one community or tradition. We are formed by and participate in distinct civic, national, social, familial, religious (and other) communities. We have access to an uncountable number of images, unimaginable amounts of information, and incredibly quick communication with far-distant people. Such participation and access contribute to our identities. We are compelled, as persons, to *negotiate* our identities because of such multiple belongings and such inundation with information and communication. We did not choose to have to negotiate our identities. This is not a role we take up, but part of the situation in which we live.

I also use the term "situation" advisedly. Theologians often work with a dualistic understanding of "the church and the world" or "religion and culture." In doing so, it is easy to reify any of the terms in these dichotomies. This is a huge mistake. All participants in a religious tradition live not in a reified entity called "culture" or "the world," but in the situation in which we are shaped by multiple practices and multiple traditions. Such divisions are not necessarily external to communities. Baptist theologian James W. McClendon Jr. once wrote that "the line between the church and the world passes right through each Christian heart."[3] This sort of insight has been part of the Christian tradition at least since St. Augustine. The division is as much internal to the participants and the community as it is external to either. Nor is the division simply "dual"; rather, it is multiple. Religious practitioners engage in a wide variety of practices and have a wide variety of allegiances. They are not only Jews (or Christians or Muslims), but may be socialists (or capitalists), politically liberal (or conservative), and so on. Because these divisions are multiple and both internal and external, rather than dualist and only external as the "church and world" or "religion and culture" rubrics suggest, the division is not necessarily between "us and them." Of course, some religious rhetoric asserts otherwise, but this rhetoric is typically used in an effort to cement and ossify religious identity, often in a religious community that tends to understand itself as under siege from its enemies.

In Which Story Shall We Live?

What this means is that the Christian narrative that carries and is carried by the Christian community is not merely in external competition with other narratives, whether secular, consumerist, Americanist, or otherwise. Rather, these narratives are at battle in the hearts of those who practice Christianity as well as those who live out other traditions.

Such battles, however, may be quite subtle. Sometimes people live in multiple worlds, or perhaps, take on multiple roles not fully compatible with each other. It is not that our lives are watertight compartments. Rather, it is because the traditions in which we live are partly compatible that we can live within each of them without noticing (or at least without being troubled by) the conflicts among them. McClendon's invaluable discussion of the conflict of stories[4] is followed by his own confession of his acceptance of the pattern of racism of the culture of his youth, a pattern his understanding of Christianity as given to him by his parents and community did not confront.[5] Many of us accepted both the Christian story and the story of white superiority. Many of us accept today the Prince of Peace as we go to fight wars to establish and preserve a new world order in which our country dominates. We have come to see that we could not accept the principles of the racist tradition if we are Christian. Some of us see an incompatibility between being Christian and going to war on behalf of the state, but others would not find the principles of American patriotic and Christian religious traditions incompatible.

The point is that in our information-saturated era, we live in multiple traditions and live out multiple stories. The conflicts between them may not become evident until triggered by circumstances. And when that happens, the authority of multiple stories for us is at stake. We cannot simply appeal to one of them as authoritative. It is arbitrary to solve the problem of "multiple authorities" or "multiple traditions" by an appeal to one of them. While religious elites assume that our ultimate loyalty should be to God and the controlling story of our lives should be our religious story, in this culture, no story has *automatic* hegemony or presumed authority. We are forced to decide which story is our primary story, that is, in and by which story we shall live.

The Primacy of Practice

With regard to content, the fundamental issue is not dogma or doctrine. Among Christian theologians, the turn to "praxis" is crucial. But good practice (or praxis)[6] requires wisdom, specifically practical wisdom.[7] Theologian Edward Schillebeeckx, O.P., in my judgment, gets it exactly right when he put it this way: "Personally, I would call religions wisdom schools.... Religions are not systems of truth constructs; they try to trace a way of life, albeit not without truth and insights."[8] British Catholic theologian Nicholas Lash drew out the implications of Schillebeeckx's insight:

> A "disciple" is a learner, apprenticed to a teacher, and, in educational contexts, we still speak of particular patterns of apprenticeship, areas of study, as "disciplines." It is of paramount importance that Christians learn once again to understand Christianity to be a *school* whose pedagogy, as I have put it elsewhere, "has the twofold purpose ... of weaning us from our idolatry and purifying our desire."
>
> This is, of course, an endless task, for nothing is more difficult than learning to worship, to have one's heart set somewhere, while yet not worshiping any thing, any feature of the world, any idea,

image, person, nation, theory, dream or fact, and nothing is more difficult than learning "not to stifle or suppress desire, but to release it from the chains which bind it in egotism's nervous and oppressive grasp."

If Christianity is such a school, then the paradigm in terms of which questions of authority and governance in the Church are best understood and tackled will be educational rather than political.[9]

To communicate a tradition is more to "train" someone "how" to believe than to "indoctrinate" someone in "what" to believe. Communicating doctrinal propositions is not communicating a faith tradition. One needs to communicate how to engage in the practices that give sense to those doctrines. To communicate a faith is to teach someone how to live in and live out a tradition.[10] The doctrines can make sense only in the context of practicing the faith.

Learning How to Speak

Philosophers like Martin Heidegger, Ludwig Wittgenstein, and their followers have taught us that language does not merely describe the world, but constitutes the kind of world in which we live. "When we learn a language we learn a world." When we learn a language, we learn not merely how to describe things, but how to do things, how to live. Hence, the motto, "Don't ask for meaning, ask for use!" suggests that we shouldn't attempt to analyze what a word or sentence means, but rather we should begin by observing how people actually use language and what they use it to do. The languages in which we learn to communicate, the ways in which we learn to use what our shared tongues give us, the patterns and images we discern and create in our communications all simultaneously give us a distinctive (but not isolated, private, or impenetrable) self in a common (but not determined, final, or unchangeable) world.

By "language" I mean to invoke the whole network of communication, verbal and nonverbal, words and gestures, images and sentences, in and through which we communicate (or fail to communicate) with each other. Poststructuralist thinkers have taught us the very complex ways in which language, institutions, communities, and communication are co-constituted. We are not constituted as social selves by words alone but by the use we make of words and images.

Thus, one way to understand how to be a participant in a tradition, in a "wisdom school," is to understand how to learn a language. To become a Christian is to learn how to use Christian language. And that is not an abstract learning *what* to say, but a practical learning *how* to live and speak. To learn a language is to learn how to participate in a way of life that is constituted by a complex set of practices. And this learning shapes us. For example, when we learn *how* to say our prayers, we become pray-ers. Note that we cannot merely learn the words of a prayer; we must learn *how* to pray. The central issue is not communicating the words or propositions or doctrines, but showing someone *how to* practice the faith, including the practice of learning how to understand, articulate, and apply its "truth and insights."[11]

Faith, in this perspective, can be understood as a set of practices, even a complex virtue. Faith is not something we first believe, then practice. Rather, we practice the faith and in so doing come to understand it. God's gracious initiative makes this possible. What this means for our work in communicating the faith is the subject of the main section of this paper.

Communicating the Faith

Communicating the faith is the complex practice of empowering people, disciples, to engage in the practices that constitute the faith tradition, including practices of participating in the sacraments and worship life of the church, and in distinctively Catholic social and moral practices that fit the local community in which we live, and of believing.

"Learning How"

One has to learn how to be a Christian. And this learning is crucial. Once upon a time, my university inaugurated a "learning-teaching" center to help students. I was befuddled by the nomenclature. "How can one have learning before teaching?" I asked. "Isn't that like having a 'catching-throwing' center in baseball? Isn't teaching prior to learning as throwing is prior to catching?" That this was part of the "new" "learning-centered paradigm" that had become an educational buzzword didn't assuage my concerns. "What were we doing when we were teaching our students if not teaching them how to learn?" But, oddly enough, if one considers learning a practice, "learning" is prior. For I cannot teach you *how* to do something, be it perform a triple axel or ride a bike or sing *bel canto* arias or do calculus or write elegant prose. If and only if you are interested in learning how to ride a bicycle will you try to ride a bicycle. What I do is not to teach you how to ride. You learn that. What I do is to *show* you how it can be done. I can guide you, give you pointers, stop you from falling, and so on. But eventually I must let you go on your own. When you are more advanced, I may continue to give you pointers (and you may well return the favor), but in the end my role is not that of a teacher, but that of a coach. *If we are to pass on the faith as a practice, then, we need to have people who are interested in pursuing the practice of living in and living out the tradition, and we need to coach, not teach, the faith.*[12]

Being a faithful Christian is not merely "knowing that" some doctrines are true and some commandments are right. Being a faithful Christian is not merely "knowing Jesus" or "knowing God." Being a faithful Christian is a "know-how," specifically, knowing how to be a disciple.[13]

Communicating the faith is more like coaching someone than it is like dictating propositions to be memorized or handing over a book to be read.[14] But if faith is a practice or set of practices, then portraying and communicating the faith is *shown* in performance more than *said* in dogma, doctrine, or rules. When it is said at all, it must be in a narrative form, not a propositional one, because one cannot lay out a practice or form of life except in a narrative form. The faith is communicated not in doctrine or rule, but in showing what it means to practice the faith. Narratives which show how to practice the faith can invite one to dwell in the faith or, in other words, to enter into the discourse practice of Catholic Christianity.

My colleague Brad Kallenberg has argued that members of a faith community must be "*trainers* rather than *translaters* of the Gospel" into terms "anyone" can understand.[15] He means by this that "communication of the Gospel is a function of the sort of community out of which we speak."[16] What gives sense to the words we use are our practices. It is not only that our practices give sense to our concepts, but also that the concepts we have and use grow out of our practices. If all we do is to translate our words for another, or simply tell them what we believe (especially using their linguistic presuppositions), then we have evacuated them of sense as we have disconnected them from our practices. Kallenberg put it this way:

> Our fluency in theological terms is...bound up with our activities. If a young child is asked who God is, the response is likely to include, "He's the one we pray to before bed," "we're 'pposed [*sic*] to confess our sins to God," "We sing songs to him and visit him on Sunday," "He's the one we thank before we eat...." The richer this child's engagement with these activities, the richer will be his or her understanding of God and of how to use the concept of "God" fluently. But catch the significance for evangelistic conversations: You or I may talk with someone who neither prays to God, confesses sin to God, thanks God, worships God, sings to God, nor testifies about God. How then can we possibly assume he or she has even the slightest inkling of who we're talking about? For them, the word "god" is very nearly a null set.[17]

If we want to attract people to become interested in learning how to live as a Christian, we must practice the faith together well. Our liturgies must be joyous (*not* "good entertainment"). Our moral lives visibly satisfying (*not* fun, comfortable, easy, or scrupulous). Our communities must be places and gatherings of love, justice, and service (*not* obligatory meetings). Our gathering must be the gathering of a community whose discipleship is radiant. Our constant work must be that of reconciliation, not division. Our tradition can then be a school for recovering sinners.

Learning How to Live Out the Christian Tradition

The Christian tradition is carried and communicated in stories. The narratives show us what it means to live in and live out the faith. The Christian faith is constituted by stories of God with us and of us with God. When we learn how to live in them and live them out, we learn how to tell the stories rightly. The stories of the Christian tradition are stories of a God who creates, redeems, and sustains. Hence, they must take a triune and christological form. But these are simultaneously narratives of discipleship, because from a practical perspective, discipleship (being a follower of Jesus) and Christology (understanding who it is that we follow) are intimately linked — one of the meanings of the Pauline saying that we are the body of Christ and members thereof.

The position developed here implies that "communications" is no mere functional specialization of theology. Rather, it is what the whole Christian community does and what the local Christian community does. Our communicative practice cannot be the sharing of doctrines and morals as if theologians were the primary communicators of the faith. Rather, our communicative praxis is and must be the attempt to shape ours and others' lives and practices into the stories of being a disciple of Jesus. The praxis is not and cannot be the delivery of information but is always, wittingly or not, the shaping and reshaping of lives in communication, the involvement of people in wisdom communities, the initiation of folk into our discourse practices.

The Challenge of Consumerism

The challenge to our communicating the faith is made more difficult because we tend to resolve the fundamental strains in our identities as persons and communities by the tactics of consumerism.[18] Our culture schools us to resolve our living in many communities, with many narratives, and disparate languages by the dominant tactic of consumerism: to choose among them and to acquire as many desirable goods as possible.

Because so many of us are rather materially wealthy, we have easy access to commodities of various sorts. We learn how to choose among commodities — which brand of car, soap, diaper, beans, or computer shall be ours? This learned skill is transferred into the realm of choosing our identities. In this context many narratives and traditions appeal to us as do many brands of commodities. We choose our identities as we pick soap brands: shall I choose to be an entrepreneur, a parent, a Christian, a spiritual person? Even our religious traditions have become commodified. Religions or spiritualities are now items for consumers' choices. Marketers compete for market niche in the spirituality market. The church growth movement dominates evangelization. Megachurches provide an hour of Sunday entertainment and label it "worship" — while serving up Starbucks coffee. One pays one's spiritual guru just as one pays the trainer at the local spa or health club. It does not take much of a jaundiced eye to note that the commodification of spiritual realities has reached epic proportions when spiritual corporate entities resort to litigation to preserve their intellectual property rights — so that no "unauthorized" (that is, "non-paying") person can have the spirituality they sell.[19]

In the United States and much of Western Europe, many turn away from the demands of "institutional religion" to a "spirituality" available to them "on demand." But as Catholic theologian Vincent Miller notes, "Spirituality as the emergent form of religious life is consonant with the workings of commodification."[20] We are consumers: our desires are shaped so as to be satisfied by goods we can buy in the spiritual market-place, use, and discard when inconvenient. Our culture does not shape us to desire the Good that only can be "bought" by a life of commitment, that we give our lives to and for, and that we cannot discard without dis-carding our selves. How can modern folk live in fidelity to their religious traditions? Since our culture "trains" us to desire commodities, how can we learn how to desire the living and true God and life in God's church? The key insight here is that our goods own us as much as we own them; and the only Good worth being owned by — being a slave to — is God, whose service is perfect freedom.

The faith lived in and lived out in the church of tomorrow will not look like and cannot look like the faith that was lived in and lived out in the church of yesteryear. We have far more live options for our self-actualization than our forebears had. What we can see on television, investigate on the Internet, and explore in our home towns has exploded over the last forty years. The variety that confronts us forces us to make choices. We cannot but try to cope with a cascade of possibilities. For a largely well-to-do, educated laity in a consumerist culture, everything is a choice. How can we live in and live out the Catholic faith tradition in this consumerist culture?

Two Ways of Living Out the Tradition

Some of us appear to "pick and choose" from the goods on offer from the Catholic Church. We are "discriminating" Catholics. Many of us choose not to buy into the magisterial teaching on the "pelvic issues" regarding specific sexual acts and reproductive choices while we may applaud the basic valuing of human sexuality as sacred and share the revulsion at promiscuity. Some of us do not follow the bishops on issues of social justice (especially the death penalty) or even sacramental practice. This is not because we want to be obstinate or reject the authority of the tradition or the hierarchy. Rather, we are invited into and live in so many narratives that we cannot but pick and choose among them. We choose the best we can find and then hope to fuse it into a coherent whole. The historian William Clebsch once pithily put it about modern humanity, "This new humanity makes history; the old was made by it. The same holds for religion."[21] We make up our religious lives. We are consumers choosing from all the attractive options. We try to make choices that bring us goods that will enable us to narrate a coherent life.

Our postmodern, consumerist era intensifies the religious style of modernity. Now we each and all make our own religion, but the ingredients from which we have to choose are far broader, the mixes available to us far wilder and spicier, and the results far more individualistic and private. We are constantly forced to choose. Because there are so many narratives and because they are so attractive, we cannot but choose elements from among them.

Others of us appear to choose to commit ourselves to one narrative wholeheartedly. This is the pattern of the "evangelical Catholics." In effect, they try to give up the consumer mentality that permeates our culture. Rather than constantly remaking their choices, refashioning their religions, and renarrating their lives, they give their lives over to a tradition. Whether it is a movement like Opus Dei or the Legionaries of Christ, a religious order, or simply a commitment to a traditional devotional life and to the current authoritative hierarchical teaching in all (or most) of its aspects, evangelical Catholics give up choosing and accept the formation of their lives by a particular form of the tradition which has an authority and a community not of their own making — but of God's.

The danger for evangelical Catholics is that they become rigidly fundamentalist or that they identify Catholicism with one strand of the tradition and wind up rejecting the whole tradition if they reject the pure evangelical strand. Such participants often seem to want to find certainty by clinging to a rock of tradition. But they are consumers who choose their own tradition as much as "discriminating" Catholics choose theirs.

However, in modernity and postmodernity, nothing is certain this side of the grave. The remedy for such fundamentalist tendencies is a commitment to seeking the truth; for if you seek the truth, you cannot know that you "have" the truth. It is not merely that there is always more to learn, but that the fundamental way of practicing the faith is not merely repetitive, but creative response to God who is revealed in and through everything (in various ways, of course). And others, even those wildly different from you, may have been given insights you do not have.

The danger for "discriminating" Catholics is that they become "cafe-teria" Catholics, so flaccidly liberal that they wash out of the church without even realizing it. They are in danger of structuring their lives in ways that render the central and distinctive practices and beliefs of Catholicism minor constituents, perhaps "mere rituals," in their lives. The remedy for "discriminating" Catholics is active participation in a flourishing community that acknowledges the ways consumer culture shapes us, but that also resists that culture by showing how a narrative of a life given to and for God through others can create a unified social self beyond the assembled shards that is the consumer culture's substitute for a self. When they do pick and choose, they must not be, in the winsome image of my colleague Dennis Doyle, like people in a cafeteria loading up a tray, but like people who are given a tray that is so overloaded that they cannot keep it all and are unwilling to throw it all away (acknowledging that some items — formally called dogma — cannot be offloaded), so they respond by selectively ignoring or eliminating certain "items" that overload them. Both "evangelical" and "discriminating" Catholics need support and coaching, not mere tolerance or, worse, the disdain cap-tured in labels like "fundamentalist" or "cafeteria" Catholicism. Both patterns require practical support.

Three Kinds of Supporting Practice: Gathering, Sustaining, Evangelizing

Faith traditions are passed on through local communities embedded in enduring institutions. Participants are responsible as participants both for participating in the community, nurturing its life, and for support-ing the institutions that enable the tradition to endure in multiple times and places. A faith *tradition* requires both a *local community* and an *enduring institution.* It is important to distinguish the institutional from the communal and traditional elements of religion. However, it is dif-ficult to do so, for they are so complexly intertwined that they cannot be separated in practice, even if they can be distinguished in analysis.[22] It is unfortunate that these distinctions are so often ignored in both popular and academic writing. Making such distinctions is crucial for understanding how to communicate the faith.

An institution is an enduring communal authority structure. These authority structures function to maintain a tradition over time. It is a commonplace that institutional patterns of authority and responsibility are enormously varied and complex. There are many institutional patterns creating social locations and particular roles in the community in which authority is exercised in multiple ways in passing on a tradition.

Those with institutional authority roles are not the primary agents in communicating the faith, but play supportive roles. Community members, especially those with specific roles in the local community, are the primary agents. Institutional authorities give the community members the tools to work with, to coach them in their practices, and to discern what constitutes good practice in the school of discipleship that is the local community. As the institution is the servant of the tradition and the gathered community, so institutional authorities, especially bishops and theologians, serve the bearers of the tradition, the participants in the community. In communicating the faith, they are servants (not "servant-leaders") — both participants and coaches.

Enduring traditions have both institutional and communal elements. But the key point is that this is not a merely nominal distinction. While institutions sustain the tradition through time so there is a tradition to be handed on, communities gather together in mutual support, prayer, worship, and reconciliation in a specific place and typically at a specific time and in so doing work to hand on the tradition. Institutions are fundamentally diachronic and translocal; communities are synchronic gatherings in particular locations.

Gathering

"Gathering" marks the communal aspect of enduring faith traditions. American Protestant theologian Edward Farley has helpfully used the French philosopher Emmanuel Levinas's notion of the "community of the face" to define "community" in this sense as "a social group in which face-to-face relations are valued and pursued for their own sake. Face-to-face relations are part of the raison d'être of a village, therapy group, and some kinds of schools. Accordingly, in most instances, a small village is a community and a staff of researchers is not."[23] For Farley, Christian and Jewish communities have been prime examples of such gathered, face-to-face communities. "Face-to-face relations" are central and distinctive of communities, not institutions. (It is too soon to tell whether dispersed or virtual communities linked electronically fall more on the communal or institutional side of the distinction; can gatherings be "virtual"?)

Communities gather for a purpose. Christian communities gather for a number of purposes, such as worship, service, fellowship, and learning. The practices of this sort of "face-to-face" community shape people as members of that community. They become, to use Farley's examples, villagers, patients and therapists, teachers and learners. Members of Christian communities become Christians in learning how to live in the Christian community. One learns how to be a Christian from other Christians who gather together for their distinctive shared practices.

Sustaining

Generally speaking, a person is raised or converted, and is initiated into a religious tradition in a local community. Communal leaders and familial authorities teach a person. A tradition is learned face-to-face, in community, because a tradition is not information or even beliefs, but a pattern of practice or set of practices. When learners are tested to see if they have understood the tradition, the testing may be done by designated authorities. But the coach primarily functions "face-to-face," while the tester primarily functions as an officer empowered to decide if the learner has understood the tradition sufficiently to be a full member. Whether one is born into a religion or is converted into a religion, generally speaking, a gathered community shapes one's religious life and one's entry into the religion. As local, then, a religious community *gathers face-to-face*, and is constituted by interpersonal and social relationships.

Face-to-face religious communities form themselves when and where folk join in the practices of actualizing or realizing (making real) a religious tradition. The participants have the responsibility of creating and re-creating the gathered community. Many Christians identify a church as a place, typically one for worship. Yet a Christian can ask, "When is church?" A Jew might ask, "Do we have a *minyan* yet?" The gathering of a religious community is an event. The sense of church or worship or group meditation as an "event," more common in evangelical than in Catholic traditions, means that the participants have a responsibility for making the event happen, for making it possible and desirable for the community to gather. With regard to Christianity, Avery Dulles described this responsibility:

The idea of discipleship, as we know it from the New Testament, makes ample room for both freedom and failure. Unlike the bare notion of community, discipleship brings out the demands of membership. The Church is not a club of like-minded individuals, but a venture in which all depend on the community and are obliged to make contributions to the community and its work. The possession of the Spirit is seen as the mark of a mature disciple and as a prerequisite of responsible, creative ministry.[24]

What Dulles writes of the Catholic Church applies to all forms of vibrant religious communities. The gathering of the community for worship and prayer, for instruction and guidance, and for restoration and healing of rifts does not happen automatically. Religious participants have the role-specific responsibility of gathering for the purposes of sustaining the community in the tradition. In the Western traditions, prayer and worship is a fundamental reason for gathering.

How we live as a community communicates the faith; it shows what sense our stories have and what our doctrines mean. If our moral lives are shoddy, our gatherings tepid or rote, our communities cantankerous and our work divisive, who would want such faith thus displayed? In short, *the way we practice "communio" communicates the faith we actually have.*

Evangelizing

But communities are not only sustained and gathered, they are also "sent out." As with the patterns of sustaining and gathering in, the patterns for "going out" are as varied as are the traditions. For better and for worse, belonging to a religious tradition creates a division. In Christianity, this division has often been rendered in a dualistic way, as in the division between "church and world" noted above. The church, then, is to go out into the world. This can easily make "the world" as the realm of the enemy. This is not the sort of distinction contemporary Christianity can accept because, as noted above, divisions between church and world are not external to communities, but run through each Christian heart.

How can a religious community and its participants sort out these competing loyalties? Two patterns of practice respond to this situation. First, participants may witness to their tradition and to its primacy of place among their loyalties. Second, participants may engage the world by service, social action, and other efforts at transforming the world in which they live into something close to the way their tradition says it should be.

Witnessing

Witness is diverse. It can be simply living out in disciplined fidelity the way of life that constitutes the tradition; our gatherings are a form of witness. Avery Dulles understands this as part of the sacramental life of the church: "Authentically sent by Christ, the disciples make him present anew as they live under the direction of his Spirit. Thanks to the sacramentality of the Church...the members of the Church experience his power as they are remade in his image."[25] Protestant theologian Stanley Hauerwas put it this way: "Witnesses must exist if Christians are to be intelligible to themselves and hopefully to those who are not Christians, just as the intelligibility of science depends in the end on the success of experiments."[26] What we do says who we are and attracts others to join us in our life and work. The lives of witnesses, then, exemplify what it means to live in and live out a tradition.

The root meaning of the Greek word we transliterate as "martyr" is "witness." In the era of post-biblical expansion, the first distinctively Christian pattern of life was martyrdom. Inspired by the tales of the martyrdom of the Maccabees and of the stoning and vision of St. Stephen (Acts 7) and committed to their Lord and Savior as a martyr unjustly killed, some early Christians witnessed to the truth they found in the Christian tradition by their martyrdom (or willingness to accept martyrdom). Clebsch describes the period as one in which Christians sought "dual citizenship": to be citizens of Rome and citizens of the true eternal city. In many instances, these dual commitments could be lived out with little or no conflict. However, when the commitments became irreconcilable, e.g., when the legal authorities demanded that the Christians turn over their Scriptures and/or worship Roman divinities, the martyrs witnessed unto death their commitment to the community and its God. Ultimately, their true home was heaven.

Witness, especially in the form of martyrdom, is not "sectarian" or "withdrawn from society." Indeed, properly understood, the witness that leads to martyrdom must be a political act — for it is political authorities who kill the martyrs. To be a witness is always "transitive." One witnesses *to* another *about* something. Sometimes one's life is a witness to members of the community; other times one's life testifies to others outside of the community. Sometimes one witnesses for the tradition to the community as well as to those outside by exemplifying how to live in and live out a tradition. To live a life of witness is not to withdraw from engagement with others outside the community, or from opponents within the community, but to engage them not with force nor with political action to change structures in the society, but with confronting them with someone who does actually place the tradition to which he or she witnesses at the determining center of his or her identity.

"What would you die for?" should have the same answer as "What do you live for?" If there is nothing that we would give our lives *for,* then is there anything we should give our lives *to*? Is our church a community worth dying for? If not, how can we communicate a faith worth living for?

One increasingly persuasive account of a crucial difference between Christian and American traditions illustrates this point of the importance of witness. The question is not whether to witness, but, as McClendon put it, given the situation, how to witness:

> At least at one point, though, [the American master story] contrasts sharply with the biblical master story. . . . In the story Americans tell themselves, every great problem from independence to slavery to totalitarian threats is finally resolved by the *ultima ratio* of war. . . . Not even the best bearers of the American legend (Lincoln?) have escaped its inbuilt savagery. In surprising contrast, the biblical master story pivots upon a slave people who ran away "in urgent haste" (Deut. 16:3), upon a Savior who enters the capital city riding on a donkey and who is called the Prince of Peace; today it demands a living witness to that peace.[27]

To put it more harshly, the biblical tradition asks one to be willing to live and die as a witness to God's love and justice; the American tradition asks one to be willing to kill to get our way in the world. Our lives, then, witness to and reveal which faith tradition we truly live in and live out.

Another form of witness, not only in the Christian tradition, has been the witness of asceticism, of people's commitment to supplant the (evil) practices of the world in their own lives with the graced practices that would allow them to focus on witness to God alone. Ascetics, however, are also not withdrawn. Many Christian ascetics lived in cities. But even when some early Christian monks withdrew from the city to the desert, people flocked to them. There they showed people how to overcome the passionate vices that threatened to distort their love of God: "piggishness, lechery, greed, depression, hatred, inability to care, bragging, and egotism."[28] They served as exorcists, as arbitrators of disputes over tithes, water rights and property rights, and as physicians for ailments such as infertility.[29]

Martyrs and monks show that what is good enough to live for is good enough to die for; if one would not die for what one lives for, whatever that might be, one has failed to live one's life as one ought. Only what is great enough to die for is great enough to live for. This does not mean eschewing enjoyment or pleasure, but of unshackling one's desires from attachment to things so that one is freed to desire God. Ascetics do not snuff out desire, but channel their desire to the divine. The ascetics' witness is not a withdrawal, but precisely a witness to the rest of the members of their community and to others who sought to understand what they were doing, a witness about the practices of living in God's love, of living in the tradition. While all might not be as spiritually athletic as the ascetics, they can and should witness to one another concerning how to order one's desires to what one really desires.

Witness is not sectarian; it is one way for engaging the world. Sometimes a gathered community or sacramental church can be "inward-looking." Sometimes religious communities can withdraw, insofar as it is possible, from communication with those outside the camp. But these are not so much witness as failures to witness *to* others *about* one's ultimate commitments. The question is not whether to witness, but how to witness, given the circumstances. The question is how to witness today.

There are many who would refuse the stark opposition here portrayed. They might recognize the ultimate differences in the traditions and the lives they inspire and shape. But some would find that "witness" is not the right "tactic." They would argue that the point is not merely to witness to the world, but to engage it in order to change it and to bring it closer to the way God would want it. These folk would work to transform the world.

Transforming

Often, "witness" slides over into "transformation." The dichotomy between charity and justice popular in some intra-Christian polemics is too easy. Transformation on a small or individual level may be called charity, but it is work for justice nonetheless. Transformation on a social or structural level may be called justice, but it is intimately connected with charity nonetheless. Many religious groups operate shelters for the poor. This is typically identified as charity. This witness to hospitality comes closer to work for justice in some of the activities of the Catholic Worker movement. Dorothy Day, for example, did not merely extend hospitality, but also demonstrated against war and publicly supported striking unions in both New York and California. Such witness suggests that witness and charity are not separable from justice and transformation, but distinctive ways to seek to bring the vision and the reality of the community to those who will benefit from such work. Whether the practice is bishops' seeking to influence politicians on issues of social justice, protestors' demonstrating against human rights abuses, volunteers' giving a year of their lives to enable impoverished people to improve their plight, or parishes' founding development corporations to rehabilitate properties in degenerating inner-city neighborhoods, those engaging in these practices work to transform the world in which they live as an expression of their Christian commitments.

Social activism is distinct from, but not separable from, witness. Indeed, it is best understood as an activist form of witness. Witness of "communio" exposes others to what the good life can and should be and provides a model for the community to live in and live out. Activism seeks to transform the social structures that can deform the people of a society and make it practically impossible for them to be able to live in and live out the way of life the community valorizes. Nonetheless, some patterns of witness are "activist," and some active interventions clearly "witness" to what it means to live in and live out a tradition. Each of these, at their best, also shows that there is something quite worthwhile beyond consumer goods and a selfless whole self; beyond the postmodern jangle of the fractured self dominated by desires. Each of these provides patterns for those often elusive goals: of a religious life that integrates both mystical and political and of a theology that can be adequate to help sustain that form of life.

Conclusion

We communicate the faith by who we are and in what we do. This is a descriptive claim. Whatever our faith, whatever story or stories structure our lives we show what it is by our being and doing. Our practices give sense to our claims. Again, this is not a normative, but a descriptive claim. You will see what we mean by God when you see how we deal with God.

I have suggested that there are two emergent ways of being Catholic today, "evangelical" and "discriminating." Again, this is a descriptive claim. Both ways of being Catholic are legitimate, not because they are both "good" or "better" than other ways of being Catholic. It is just that they are inevitable patterns made possible by our late-capitalist, pluralist, affluent, consumerist, and commodified culture; our very nature as humans has been redesigned in this culture, and so have our ways of being religious. The normative, theological point is not to disown either pattern, but to help shape the practices of both so that the patterns of practice do not become so distorted as to be real degenerations of the practice of faith.

What we need to do, then, is to be a community that attracts people who then want to reach the goals we strive for. That is the only way that "coaching in the faith" becomes possible. The members of a community coach each other in how to live out the faith. Faith is communicated in this (dialectical, not sequential) two-step process of desire (to live out the faith) and training (in living out the faith). Again, I take this to be a descriptive, not a normative claim.

Elites in the community then, such as bishops and theologians, are not fundamentally governors, but servants who are coaches' coaches — scholars and teachers. We are to discover, understand, and creatively transform (when necessary) the tradition we live in and live out using those skills in which we have been specially trained. As teachers, we have an important role — but even in academia, we may function best if we understand our teaching roles as coaches, not transmitters or translators. And in so doing, we have to be interdisciplinary, inventive, and media-savvy as Lonergan suggests; these are the patterns of academic practice that must be ours. But the main task of handing on the faith is the whole community's task, carried out as members of the community gather together to sustain each other, go out and witness to, and even work to transform (when appropriate) the world in the name of Jesus, the Christ. How we witness — perhaps not as martyrs or monks, but perhaps as "evangelical" or "discriminating" Catholics — shows what it means to be women and men whose fractured lives are made whole by the grace of being "owned" by the one "Possession" worthy to possess us in a consumerist society. Such witness attracts or repels those to whom we wish to communicate the good news.

In sum, I take it to be a descriptive claim that it takes a good church to make a Christian, that is, to communicate how to be a good Christian both by attracting folk to join the community and by mutually coaching those in the community in the ways of gracious response to Grace. And thus, communication is not the last, but the first and foremost functional specialization not merely for theologians, but for all Christians.

Chapter 10

Handing on the Faith

The Need for Total Catechetical Education

THOMAS GROOME

O THER ESSAYS in this collection attend to the *where* and *what* of educating in faith — the context and content. My assigned task is to reflect on the *how,* on ways of "handing on the faith" that might be effective in our sociocultural context and true to the tenets of Catholic Christian faith. First, a comment on the subtitle of the essay; it signals a foundational conviction toward my overall proposal, so let me show my hand at the outset.

Many authors make a distinction between religious education and catechesis. They think of the former as teaching the content of religious tradition(s), as more intent on information than formation. On the other hand, they view catechesis as socializing people into Christian identity, as more formative in its dynamic and purpose. Some authors even favor "a divorce" between religious education and catechesis.[1] I reject this dichotomy as reductionist for both,[2] insisting instead that religious education and catechesis are essential to each other; in practice they must function as symbiotic.

When it helps, religious education and catechesis might be distinguished as dual emphases within "handing on the faith"; a particular context might focus on one more than the other — compare the responsibilities of formal program to family. Yet, we need religious education that lends a thorough knowledge, understanding, and conviction of Catholic faith — enhancing catechesis; and likewise catechesis that socializes and renews people in Christian identity — as well informed. To signal the necessity of both and their partnership, and to avoid awkward repetition, I favor the phrase *catechetical education* throughout this essay.

172

Then, the term "total" in my subtitle intimates a comprehensive and community-centered paradigm that forges *a coalition of parish, family, and school/program, engaging every member and all aspects of each in sharing faith together.* Here I echo a number of other essays in this collection that emphasize the need for a communal approach to catechetical education. As William Dinges proposes wisely, the task of handing on the faith "is a profoundly sociological one"; it requires "handing on the community" as well. The body of my essay will unpack *how* we might go about it.

The Ground Gained

Contemporary catechetical education has more than its share of critics and criticisms, many justified. This essay describes the inadequacy of the now dominant schooling/program paradigm and proposes that we move beyond it — though without leaving it behind — toward a thoroughly communal approach. Yet, we must retain "the ground gained" by contemporary catechesis and build upon it, rather than jettisoning its achievements. The *General Directory for Catechesis*[3] (hereafter GDC) notes that "Catechetical renewal, developed in the church over the last decades, continues to bear very welcome fruit" (#24). But many aspects of this renewal are but tender seedlings; we need to nurse them along rather than uprooting or trampling underfoot.

The modern catechetical movement might be dated from the turn of the twentieth century (circa 1900) and what was known as the "Munich Method." This movement amounted to bringing more participative and conversational styles of teaching into catechetical education,[4] attempting to learn from what was then emerging as modern pedagogy.[5] Its dynamics of preparation (getting learners interested), presentation, explanation, and application were a significant departure from rote memorization,[6] and encouraged students to integrate the content of faith with their everyday lives — a hallmark of contemporary catechetical education.[7]

With the founding of the Religious Education Association (REA) in 1903, a profession began to emerge to lend well-trained leaders to the Church's educational ministry. At first predominantly Protestant, the ecumenical movement brought many Catholics into the REA, as well as to bond in specifically Catholic organizations, like the National Conference of Catechetical Leaders. In 1971, the Association of Professors and

Researchers in Religious Education (APRRE) was founded and serves as the guild of academic scholars for the discipline in North America (some 350 members).

Religious education continues to develop as an academic discipline, offering graduate programs of study (e.g., at Boston College) and publishing scholarly research. Mediating between theology and education, the discipline also draws insights from the social sciences — the psychology of learning and human development, the sociology of knowledge and community, the anthropology of symbols and culture, and so on. And guilds of scholars have emerged in other parts of the world that work to develop the foundations of catechetical education and lend insights from and for diverse cultures.

Within pastoral practice, there has been a common charge that the textbooks which emerged in the aftermath of Vatican II fell short in presenting the content of Catholic faith. Whatever excesses or deficiencies there may have been during those experimental days, however, have been fully corrected. Anyone who claims otherwise has not reviewed the mainline catechetical curricula currently available for grades K to 8. The half dozen most widely used series may vary a little in style but all reflect a thorough catechetical education in Catholic faith, with sound theology and engaging pedagogy. All employ a scope and sequence that tells "the whole story" of Catholic faith,[8] presented according to developmental readiness and through a spiral curriculum that catechizes core themes (e.g., Eucharist) at each grade level.

All the religion curricula now used by Catholic schools and parishes have been judged "in conformity with the *Catechism of the Catholic Church*" by the committee established by the American bishops to "Oversee the Use of the Catechism." In fact, there is growing concern that in its monitoring for orthodoxy, this committee is unduly insistent upon technical formulas of faith — often language beyond the readiness of children and impeding their personal appropriation of it. Meanwhile, let us put to rest the stereotype that contemporary catechetical series do not represent Catholic faith; they do, and with an engaging pedagogy that encourages children to make it their own in their heads, hearts, and lives.

Of course, contemporary catechetical education is not limited to graded curricula. Think of all its other expressions that have emerged since Vatican II: the sacramental preparation programs that actively engage parents; the RCIA, likely the most effective innovation/revival of this era; the service component now "required" by many schools and parish programs; the initiatives in youth and young adult faith; the increase in parish faith sharing groups, usually focused on Scripture; family-centered programs that correlate catechesis with the liturgy and lectionary; the emerging "generations of faith" approach that engages the whole parish and family in catechetical education and is very resonant with the proposal I make in this essay; and more.

True, young adult Catholics today cannot recite the formulas of faith as could a previous generation. However, Tom Beaudoin, reflecting the social research on young adult Catholics, argues that though many fall short on "linguistic" literacy, they have a far higher "performative" literacy in their faith than previous generations.[9] He refers especially to their commitment to the works of justice and compassion. He may be correct. A recent survey here at Boston College indicated that 75 percent of our graduating seniors have volunteered in some kind of community service during their college years. Today's young Catholic adults might be stretched to distinguish between the Immaculate Conception and the Virgin Birth, but they likely have a keener sense than my generation had that the works of justice and compassion are constitutive to Catholic faith. Let us build on all of these accomplishments.

Turning toward my proposal, *total catechetical education* amounts to a paradigm shift *beyond* schools and formal programs to reclaim the whole Church as catechist educator. I highlight "beyond" because I don't intend to leave schooling and formal programs of instruction behind; bring them with us but do much more by intentionally engaging the whole family and parish in catechetical education.[10] But to so expand our consciousness and practice toward a communal paradigm, we must first debunk the pervasive myth that *education* is synonymous with *schooling* of some kind.

Beyond Schools to Every Christian Person, Parish, and Family

Many times I've begun a course at Boston College by asking participants how "education in faith" is typically perceived in their culture. No matter where people come from or how they name it, the reigning stereotypes are fairly universal. A sample from a recent survey: children in a classroom learning about religion; didactic instruction in religious knowledge; a teacher getting kids to memorize religious answers to questions they never ask; learning religious knowledge from a textbook; sitting at a desk being told what to believe as a Christian; or, a recent clincher, a one-hour, once-a-week drop-off that will "make y'er kids Catholic." Note that all presume some mode of schooling.

Catechist educators roundly reject such stereotypes as does the mind of the Church, and yet we should be sobered by their tenacity. Truth is that our sense of the agency of all baptized Christians to share and grow in faith, of the responsibility of parents to be "the first educators of their children in the ways of faith" (Rite of Baptism), of the community life and ministries of the parish as its most effective curriculum, has been dulled if not nullified by the schooling paradigm for catechetical education.

The notion of universal education emerged slowly in the Western world and represented a major breakthrough in social consciousness. Plato first made the philosophical argument that all citizens should be educated (though "citizen" here included less than 10 percent of the male population). The first real attempt came when the Emperor Charlemagne decreed (circa 800) that the monastic schools must open to all boys of the empire, not only to those interested in becoming monks. Note: that girls should have equal access to schooling would take another thousand years.

The watershed for schools came with the great Reformation catchcry of *sola scriptura,* calling all Christians to read the Bible, thereby encouraging universal literacy. A particular catalyst was Martin Luther's letter of 1524 to the German nobles urging them to establish and fund schools that would educate every child — boys and girls. They did, and thus began the public school system of the Western world. Note well, however, that Luther never intended schooling to replace family or community education. In fact, he advised that boys attend school for no more than two hours each day and girls for only one, lest their schooling diminish their education at home and in the community around them.[11]

Alas, Martin's caution fell on deaf ears. Before long, Western culture had bought hook, line, and sinker into the schooling paradigm, equating universal education — a fine ideal — with universal schooling. The latter became a totalizing affair in that it subsumed everything that could pass for education, with the parental role reduced to seeing to it that children attend a didactic process by professional teachers in an institution designed to "school" them. Though the professionalizing of teaching was a breakthrough, its unfortunate underside was the impression that amateurs — like parents or neighbors — have nothing to contribute to the education of children. Huckleberry Finn said that he tried not to let schooling interfere with his education; the rest of the Western world wasn't nearly so wise.

We must deeply appreciate the work done over the years by the Confraternity of Christian Doctrine (CCD) — often against great odds — and by Catholic parochial schools, whose very existence reflects heroic sacrifices on the part of many people. And indeed, schools, in general, are fine educational endeavors. However, the schooling paradigm has colonized our modern consciousness and especially regarding education in faith. When we think of "handing on the faith" we simply must stop *equating* this with a school/program project and instead reclaim the notions that all Christians are responsible to share their faith, and that catechetical education must be a communal effort that intentionally engages every Christian community — family, parish, and bonded group. Let us imagine that the whole Church *is* catechetical more than does catechesis as one thing among many others.

Everything about the Church and everything it does in the world should be intentionally crafted to nurture people in faith. The Risen Christ gave the mandate to evangelize and teach to the Christian community assembled on that hillside in Galilee, and everyone present received the same commission (see Mt 28:16–20). Catechesis cannot be delegated to a select few or to a particular agency; by baptism, every Christian person, family, and parish is responsible for it.

In particular, a Christian family cannot delegate its responsibilities to a parochial school or parish program. Vatican II reiterated that "parents must be acknowledged as the first and foremost educators of their children." Then, to drive home the point, it added, "Their role as educators is so decisive that scarcely anything can compensate for their failure in it."[12] Alas, such rhetoric can be counterproductive — only encouraging guilt — if parents hear "education" as "schooling," as demanding that they be more didactic with their children, sitting them down regularly for periods of instruction from a textbook. Rather, the parental catechetical role is much more one of attending to the socializing power of the home, intentionally crafting its common life to nurture in Christian identity.

Whole and Communal Faith Requires Total Catechetical Education

The essays in this collection on the context of catechesis make abundantly clear that our contemporary situation poses tremendous challenges to "handing on the faith." Indeed, it would seem to have been easier when most Catholics lived in "life-style enclaves" that provided the subculture socialization to initiate and sustain people in Catholic identity. Though we can never return to such "good old days," we must retain the insight reflected there — it still takes a family and a village to raise a Christian. We simply need to be much more intentional and find contemporary ways to do whole community catechesis.

In addition to the demands of our postmodern world, however, *total catechetical education* is warranted by the very nature of Christian faith itself, and particularly as it pertains to the identity of a person and community. Karl Rahner claimed that Vatican II revolutionized catechesis by redefining Christian faith as a holistic affair. His point was that when faith was defined as *belief* in stated doctrines — the dominant sentiment of the Council of Trent (1545–63) — then catechesis could be done by a catechism that summarizes the beliefs to be taught in a school by a teacher. Two great blessings of the Second Vatican Council was that it reclaimed Christian faith (1) as engaging the whole person — one's identity — and, (2) as radically communal.

Catholic Christian faith has a *cognitive* aspect in which a person needs to be informed and to reach personal conviction; an *affective* dimension that encourages prayer, worship, and a relational spirituality; and a *behavioral* requirement that demands living "the way" of Jesus as lifelong conversion into holiness of life. Thus, Christian faith should engage the whole person — head, heart, and hands — shaping our beliefs, relationships, and ethics. It should be the defining foundation of people's total "being" — as both noun and verb, who they are and how they live. Echoing the breadth of its Great Commandment, to be Christian is to invest one's whole mind, heart, and strength as a disciple of Jesus.

And to what end are Christian disciples to invest their whole person, to define their identity? Jesus summarized his own sense of purpose —

and thus of discipleship to him — as living for God's reign. To believe in the Christ of faith demands that we invest ourselves in the commitments of the historical Jesus. We must give our whole selves over to doing God's will of love and compassion, peace and justice, wholeness and fullness of life for all, "on earth as in heaven." To be Christ-centered in our catechesis is to forge our identity around commitment to the reign of God à la "the way" of Jesus. This point — the unity of being Christ-centered and committed to God's reign — is summarized well by the GDC when it refers to Jesus with the lovely title, "catechist of the Kingdom of God" (#163).

That Christian faith is so whole, so constitutive of identity, is precisely why it is deeply communal as well. The communal nature of being Christian was evident from the beginning, with roots in God's call to Abraham and Sarah to become the parents of a people. The first Christians had such a communal understanding of their identity that Paul used the rich metaphor of the human body to describe them, urging all members to work together as the Body of Christ, alive by the Spirit in the world. "In one Spirit we were all baptized into one body, whether Jew or Greek, slave or free person, and we were all given to drink of the same Spirit" (1 Cor 12:13).

Vatican II was a watershed in returning Catholics to the communal nature of Christian faith, and to the agency of each baptized member for the mission of the Church in the world. Over and over it restated in one way or another that the Church must function as a community, and that all the baptized "share in the priestly, prophetic, and royal office of Christ."[13] Thus baptism calls us to "full, conscious, and active participation" in the Church's worship[14] — to be a priestly community; to side with those "who are poor or in any way afflicted"[15] — to be a prophetic community; and "to express (our) opinion on things which concern the good of the Church"[16] — to be a co-responsible community.

These dual emphases of Christian faith — holistic and communal — make imperative the proactive participation of family and parish in catechetical education. If it amounted to no more than teaching people what Christians believe — the cognitive content — then catechetical education could be done by some kind of schooling alone. But because being Christian pertains to one's whole identity, and requires active membership in a community of disciples, a schooling model can help but will not be sufficient. Though good instruction in "the faith" is imperative, it takes something more to form the Christian being of people. To nurture Christian identity requires socialization and inculturation by Christian faith communities — and the primary candidates are family and parish, with every member accepting responsibility for the task.

On the matter of personal identity, all the social sciences agree that we become who we become — in large part — through the influence of our sociocultural contexts. We interiorize the worldview, value system, and self-image mediated to us from our communities, and nothing is more influential than the primary socialization of family and neighborhood. So, coupling this consensus of the social sciences with the holistic and communal nature of Christian faith — and stating the obvious — to raise a person with a Polish identity requires a Polish family and community, to raise a Hispanic person takes a Hispanic family and community, and to raise a Christian person requires a Christian family and community.

No "One Way" Alone but the Broadest Coalition

Christian faith as whole and communal means that there is no one program for doing catechetical education; there is no sure or easy procedure for handing on the faith. There have been a series of programmatic proposals of late that, though worthy, are piecemeal and cannot deliver the easy salvation that their proponents promise. One can even detect some naïveté in the GDC when it claims that all catechetical education should be modeled on the catechumenate — as if this is the panacea. I don't believe any one program or approach will ever again be able — if one ever was — to educate effectively in Christian faith. Instead, we need to make our best efforts on all fronts, and to weave a grand coalition of family, parish, and school/program into a seamless garment that provides total catechetical education. So:

+ *Not the "program" or "school" alone* can fulfill the Church's responsibilities for catechetical education, although a parish program or parochial school with trained catechists and good curricula are indispensable to handing on Christian faith;

+ *Not the "parish" alone* can do all catechetical education, though a vibrant local faith community is vital, and every aspect of parish life can be structured to educate in faith;

- *Not the "family" alone* can be the sole catechist, though its influence is enormous and its common life can be crafted to nurture Christian identity and commitment;

- *Not the liturgy alone* can hand on the faith, though nothing is more effective to foster people's faith than good liturgy, or more hazardous to faith than poor liturgy;

- *Not the lectionary alone* can provide the scope and sequence for "the whole Story" of Catholic faith, though lectionary-based curricula can bond liturgy and catechesis, and help to recenter the Scriptures for Catholic Christians;

- *Not the (published) curriculum alone*, though the texts and media used in schools and programs should reflect a thorough and theologically sound presentation of Catholic faith with pedagogy that actively engages participants in the teaching/learning dynamic;

- *Not catechist educators alone* can bear all responsibility for faith education, though well-informed and formed catechists who are credible witnesses to what they teach are vital agents of handing on the faith;

- *Not the catechumenate alone,* though when done well it is most effective for initiating adults into Christian community and its values can inspire all catechetical education.

Instead of any one way alone, total catechetical education demands:

- an intentional coalition of "family," "parish," and "program/school"

- involving all aspects of each — their whole communal life

- engaging all members as teachers and learners, sharing faith together

- across the life-cycle from cradle to grave — in "permanent catechesis" (GDC)

- informing and forming each other's identity in whole and communal Christian faith

- as disciples of Jesus Christ for God's reign in the world.

This shift toward total catechetical education requires us to continue doing catechesis well as a ministry of the Word, but to also recognize and harness the catechetical potential of all the Church's other ministries. And this must be effected by every Christian person and parish, family, and school/program.

Since the early days, the Church has described its core ministries as *koinonia,* requiring it to be a community that *witnesses* to Christian faith; *leitourgia* as requiring the public work of *worshiping* God together; *diakonia* which demands care for people's physical and spiritual *welfare;* and *kerygma* which is fulfilled by evangelizing, preaching, and teaching God's *word* of revelation that comes through Scripture and tradition. So, we can summarize the Church's core ministries as *witness, worship, welfare,* and *word.* I place *word* last because it is the obvious concern of programmatic education in faith, whereas we need to raise catechetical consciousness around the other three functions of the Church's ministry. Let's imagine every parish, family, and school/program as fulfilling each of the four — as appropriate to their context — and doing so *with a catechetical consciousness.*

The Whole "Family" as Catechetical Educator

Beyond the two-parent ideal, "family" must also include extended and blended families, single-, double-, and triple-parent families; in fact, *any bonded network of domestic life* can function as a family for faith education. The Second Vatican Council reclaimed an ancient image of the family as "the domestic church."[17] If we take this seriously, then, in its own way, the family should participate in all of the Church's ministries, and, I highlight here, do so with a catechetical consciousness.

Family as community of Christian witness requires that the whole life of the home be suffused with the values and perspectives of Christian faith. The members must constantly review the family's environment and atmosphere, lifestyle and priorities, relationships and gender roles, modes of discipline and accountability to each other, language patterns and conversations, work and recreation — every aspect — to monitor how well it reflects the convictions and commitments of Christian faith. If still caught in the schooling paradigm, we hear that parents are the primary catechetical educators as requiring them to become more didactic. But more important by far is their attention to the whole ethos of the home, its example, and the quality of shared family life. Everything about the Christian family should bear *witness* to its faith; this is how it educates.

Family as a place of worship calls it to integrate shared prayer, symbols, and sacred ritual into its patterns of daily life. As catechist, every

Christian family needs its home liturgy to symbolize and celebrate, nurture and sustain its faith. I once asked an observant Jewish friend how she came by her strong Jewish identity; she immediately responded, "Oh, from the rituals in my home." Surely every Christian family can create or rediscover — old Christian cultures had lots of them — sacred rituals for the home that will nurture the Christian identity of its members. Without family prayer — morning, night, grace — rituals and sacred symbols, the home is unlikely to nurture its members in faith.

Family as a place of human welfare requires it to care for the spiritual, physical, and emotional well-being of its own members, rippling outward toward others in need and serving the common good of society. Family life must reflect love and compassion toward all, promoting justice within and without. If children grow up and adults dwell within a family that tries to live the social values of God's reign, it will surely hand on this "constitutive" aspect of Christian faith effectively. A school or program can teach about justice, but people will be much more likely to live justly and commit to justice for all if they experience as much in their own families.

Family as a place of God's Word calls members to share their faith around Scripture and tradition, among themselves and in the broader community. Parishes and publishers must help parents — with resources, training, suggestions, support, encouragement, expectation — to integrate attention to God's Word into the patterns and conversations of family life. Every catechetical series or curriculum must be crafted around partnership with parents, and should lend them the resources to be actively involved in the formal catechesis of their children. Modern parents are admirably intent to teach even the youngest children their numbers, alphabet, and so on. Why not be equally proactive and from an early age to handing on the language and symbols of faith?

The Whole Parish as Catechetical Educator

Elliot Eisner has written insightfully about the explicit, implicit, and null curricula of schools — what they formally teach, what they teach more subtly through the school's environment, and what they teach by what is left out of the curriculum.[18] Eisner's schema is helpful in thinking about a parish as well; it helps us to recognize that everything about it educates, that the whole life of a parish *is* its curriculum. Indeed, ministry of *the*

Word is a parish's explicit curriculum. However, its shared life and all of its other ministries are its implicit curriculum — at least as significant as the explicit one — and a parish teaches by what it neglects to teach as well. For example, if a parish does not preach and do the works of justice, it actually teaches — by default — that justice is *not* constitutive of Christian faith. The key is for a parish to become conscious of how its whole life educates — or can miseducate — for Christian faith; it must intentionally craft all of its ministries to maximize their catechetical potential.

Parish as community of witness: A parish should reflect the Good News it proclaims, and be readily identifiable as a Christian community of faith, hope, and love. Beginning with Vatican II, official documents increasingly portray the Church as God's "universal sacrament of salvation" (GDC #45). Recall Aquinas's definition of a sacrament — a sacred symbol that causes what it symbolizes. As such, every parish should be struggling to realize and effect what it preaches. Members must constantly ask: Does the life of this parish — its worship, shared prayer, and spiritual nurture, its community ethos, modes of participation, and structures, its human services, outreach, and social values, its preaching, catechesis, and sharing faith programs — does everything about us bear credible witness to *the way* of Jesus? To the extent that a parish can say "yes," it is an effective catechetical educator.

Parish as worshiping community: Stating the obvious, every parish must assemble as a Christian people to worship God together. For the majority of Catholics, Sunday Mass is their primary participation with their faith community. Now, the social sciences teach that a community shapes its people primarily through its symbols, and a people's sacred symbols are the most formative of all because they have what anthropologist Clifford Geertz calls "an aura of ultimacy." In sum, the quality of a parish's liturgy is likely the measure of its effect as an educator in faith.

Now, the primary function of liturgy is to worship God. To cite Vatican II, "the sacred liturgy is above all things the worship of the divine Majesty." So, to use liturgy to catechize in a didactic way would be an abuse of liturgy. On the other hand, precisely because it is so symbol-laden, the liturgy contains "abundant instruction for the faithful." Referring to all the sacraments, the Council continued that "because they are signs they also instruct. They not only presuppose faith, but by words and objects they also nourish, strengthen, and express it."[19] So, likely the most effective strategy for a parish to educate well is to care for the quality of its liturgy.

Pastoral practice of late reflects growing awareness that the liturgy and catechesis of a parish should be intimately linked, and there are many creative efforts to deepen their effective partnership. Indeed, catechesis is to prepare people for "that full, conscious, and active participation in liturgical celebrations which is demanded by the very nature of the liturgy."[20] Likewise, as cited, good liturgy nourishes and strengthens faith. But beyond this formal partnership, there are many ways that liturgy, and especially Sunday Mass, can permeate the catechetical life of a parish. For example, parish meetings can begin with faith sharing around a scripture reading from the previous or upcoming Sunday; families can reflect together on what they heard from the readings or sermon; homes can have symbols or rituals that celebrate the liturgical seasons (Advent wreaths, Christmas cribs, Lenten fasts), and more.

Parish as community of welfare: Living *the way* of Jesus demands the works of compassion and mercy, of justice and peace. So, every parish must be a community that cares for human welfare — spiritual and physical, personal and social. It should offer people the inspiration and organization, the support and persuasion that prompts them to carry on this aspect of God's saving work in the world. *Diakonia* is required of Christians by their faith. My added point here, however, is that it's also required for the parish to be an effective catechetical educator. When a parish has outreach to the poor and marginalized, when it participates in the social struggles for justice and peace, then it most likely hands on the faith effectively.

Parish as community of Word: Every local Christian community — as well as the Church universal — must function with "the Scriptures together with sacred tradition as the supreme rule of faith."[21] It must constantly evangelize, preach, and teach this Word of God that is ever "expressed in human language."[22] A parish fulfills its ministry of the Word most eminently through the Sunday lectionary and preaching, and within its formal programs of catechetical education. However, the call to the Church by Vatican II that we recenter the Word of God at the core of our faith, and give all our people "easy access to sacred Scripture" is a long way from being realized. Though Catholics have made progress in becoming more familiar with the Bible, we need to redouble efforts so that people have ready access to and personally appropriate God's revelation into their everyday lives.

There is much evidence that gatherings of people to share their faith around scriptural texts have a particular power to them. Such conversations in which people bring their lives to the text and the text to their lives are more likely than purely academic study to enable people to personally appropriate the spiritual wisdom of the biblical word, encouraging ongoing conversion and growth in holiness of life. Total catechetical education requires that explicit catechesis be "permanent...for the whole of life" (GDC #56). The community should be ever teaching and learning together, from cradle to grave, around God's Word that comes through Scripture and tradition.

The Whole "School" or "Program" as Catechetical Educator

"School" includes any church-sponsored school that educates in Christian faith. By "program" I mean every other formal effort at catechetical education — the graded parish program for children and adolescents, all adult religious education, RCIA, youth and young adult programs, faith sharing groups, and so on. Thus, "school" and "program" epitomize the Church's intentional efforts to provide a formal curriculum of education in faith. The point I emphasize, however, is that formal programs of catechetical education should not limit themselves to being a ministry of the Word alone, but should integrate the other functions of ministry into their curriculum as well. The school or program should contribute to formation as well as information in faith.

Witness as an Aspect of School and Program. The whole environment of the school or program should reflect the communal values of Christian faith — respect and reverence for every person, hospitality and care toward all, and living witness to faith, hope, and love. Years ago, John Dewey argued that schools should reflect the values of a democratic society — if they intend to educate people for democracy. Surely a Christian school or parish program should be suffused with the values and commitments of Christian faith. Further, all formal catechetical education should encourage students to participate actively in their parish community, nurturing their ecclesial identity.

Worship as an Aspect of School and Program. I'm not suggesting that the Catholic school or catechetical program try to duplicate the parish in its ministry of worship. Yet, opportunities for shared prayer and liturgy, for experiences like retreats and spiritual mentoring should be integral to every formal catechetical curriculum. And the very pedagogy of a class or gathering can include moments of prayer and contemplation, of ritual and celebration. Likewise, the effectiveness of formal catechetical curricula is enhanced by correlation with the liturgical year and engagement with the local parish liturgy.

Welfare as an Aspect of School and Program. In parishes and schools, "service programs" have come to be recognized as powerfully effective in faith education. This is as it should be. We can probably do a better job in the formal curriculum, however, of giving students opportunity to name and reflect on their service experiences, and to integrate their reflections with Catholic social teachings. When corporate decisions are made, the catechetical program — within its limits — should offer students the opportunity to carry them out.

We must stop thinking of works of compassion, justice, and peace simply as an outcome of catechetical education; such praxis is a source of formation in faith as well. *Doing* Christian things is not just the consequence of knowing our faith, but a source of such "knowing." As Jesus explained, when we live according to his teachings, we become true disciples, and thereby come to "know" the kind of truth that sets us free (see Jn 8:31–32). Note the sequence he proposed here — from praxis, to relationship, to knowledge — though, of course, it can be reversed as well. My point is that when catechetical programs sponsor the works of justice and compassion, such works are not simply an "outcome" or ancillary but are integral to the curriculum.

God's Pedagogy as Our Own

Within the comprehensive umbrella of *total catechetical education,* we need an effective and appropriate pedagogy, an intentional way of structuring teaching/learning events. Such pedagogy should be capable of honoring the values of both catechesis and religious education. This means that it should nurture people's Christian identity with a thorough knowledge of and conviction about their faith, and conversely, teach the wisdom of Christian faith in ways likely to form and transform people's identity.

Regarding pedagogy, the GDC makes perhaps its most insightful proposal. It says that "the pedagogy of God," which was also reflected in "the pedagogy of Jesus," should be "the source and model of the pedagogy of faith" used by all catechetical educators (see esp. #139–147). At this point in a lengthy essay, I can only extrapolate and summarize how the GDC understands such "divine" pedagogy.

God enters into and is actively present through the events of human history. Thus, history is the locus of God's self-disclosure and saving grace; within their historical experiences, people encounter God and discern what God's revelation means for their lives. Over time, and guided by the Holy Spirit, the great Scriptures and traditions of Christian faith emerged from communities reflecting upon their experiences of God's presence and saving deeds, climaxing for Christians in the historical life of Jesus Christ. Now, people can inherit this "faith handed down" by learning the Scriptures and traditions that mediate this normative revelation. However, if people are to appropriate Christian faith as their own and be likely to live it, then our pedagogy now should be modeled on God's experiential pedagogy over time. In this light, the GDC suggests three guiding principles.

First, the teaching/learning dynamic must be an active and participative one; a docile reception of "the faith" is not sufficient. So, catechetical education should "promote active participation among those to be catechized" (#145), encourage "dialogue and sharing" (#159) among participants. Likewise, every participant "must be an active subject, conscious and co-responsible, and not merely a silent and passive recipient" (#167). And the rationale for this is both anthropological and theological: "The active participation of all the catechized in their formative process is completely in harmony, not only with genuine human communication, but specifically with the economy of Revelation and salvation" (#157).

Second, the teaching dynamic must draw upon and engage the lives of participants as integral to the curriculum. The GDC reiterates this point repeatedly. For example: "Catechesis is . . . realized in the encounter of the word of God with the experience of the person" (#150); "Experience is a necessary medium for exploring and assimilating the truths which constitute the objective content of Revelation" (#152 b); "The catechist must teach the person to read his [and her] own lived experience" because experience is "the locus" of "the pedagogy of the Incarnation" (#152 c).

Third and following on, the core dynamic of catechetical pedagogy should teach the faith tradition *through* and *for* people's lives. This means bringing together and integrating people's lives with the faith handed down, merging "life" and "Christian faith" into lived and living Christian faith. Thus, catechetical pedagogy should encourage "a correlation and interaction between profound human experiences and the revealed message" (#153). Again, "Catechesis... bridges the gap between belief and life, between the Christian message and the cultural context" (#205); it ever intends "to link orthodoxy and orthopraxis" (#237), intentionally "correlating faith and life" (#207).

Over many years, my own work has attempted to articulate a "shared Christian praxis approach" to catechesis and religious education. The ideal context of this approach is a community of conversation and active participation by all in sharing and learning faith together. It typically unfolds as a process of "bringing life to Faith" and "bringing Faith to life." It invites people to look at and reflect critically on their lives in the world. It encourages them to bring their own praxis to encounter, reflect upon and learn the wisdom of Christian Story and Vision. Then, more than correlation,[23] it invites people to integrate the Faith into their own lives, to personally appropriate it, and to choose to live it as "faith alive" in the world.[24]

Such a pedagogy bonds catechesis and religious education, and as a communal process is eminently appropriate to *total catechetical education*. By God's grace working through some such overarching paradigm and participative pedagogy, I'm confident that we can effectively hand on the faith in our time and place.

Faith and Culture

Following the Boston College conference that gave rise to these papers, I'm prompted to add a reflection on the relationship between "faith and culture." I promised at the beginning of this essay to propose a way to hand on the faith that might be effective in our sociocultural context as well as true to the tenets of Catholic faith. But have I offered as much and what is the relationship between "faith" and "culture" that total catechetical education both presumes and promotes? (Of course, "culture" and "faith" are ever intertwined but let us set them out as distinct in order to imagine their most fruitful relationship by way of handing on the faith.)

Some colleagues at the conference and their papers here reflect a pessimistic assessment of contemporary culture, as if the "cultural catechesis" (Griffiths) is entirely negative and only to be resisted by people of Christian faith. Accompanying this bleak sentiment and by contrast, there was a very positive assessment of traditional formulas of Christian faith, presuming them to reflect "the Lord's style of language" (Wilken), and certainly not to be adapted to a cultural context. I find that neither position reflects a distinctly Catholic attitude.

Similar to its anthropology that the person, though capable of sin, is not inherently or inevitably sinful, Catholicism's cosmology sees what people create — their cultures — as most likely both graced and sinful. Though we and our cultures are "originally" capable of sin, we are also originally graced, and more prone, by God's grace, toward good than evil. So, we can expect every culture to have both positive and negative aspects, things that Christian faith can build upon and aspects that Christians should resist and work to change.

In the phrase of Justin Martyr, writing circa A.D. 150, every culture has "seeds of the Word" already present within it; these can be brought to fruition by encounter with the explicit Word of God through Scripture and tradition. Indeed, every culture will have "weeds to the Word" as well, for which Christians must be critically alert and determined to resist. Yet, a guiding principle might be that there is never a (totally) Godless culture; God's revealing presence and saving grace can be recognized and encountered within every cultural situation.

If there is never a Godless culture, likewise, there is never a cultureless Christianity — as if we have some ahistorical expression that comes immediately from God, instead of being mediated through human language and its cultural context. From the beginning, Jesus Christ, the Son of God, was "made flesh" at a particular time and place; both he and the Gospel he preached reflected the culture and mores of his context. Since then, and instead of standing over against or above the world, the wiser attitude has been that this Christian faith must become incarnate in every time and place. The faith must become as indigenous to every culture, while remaining true to its core tenets and convictions. This requires constant "inculturation" of the Gospel that it might be heard — according to the mode of the receiver — in new times and places.

Vatican II called for such a "living exchange" between faith and culture.[25] Pope John Paul II said that "the synthesis between culture and faith is not just a demand of culture, but also of faith. A faith which does not become culture is a faith which has not been thoroughly received, not fully lived out."[26] So, inculturation might be understood as *an "exchange of gifts"* (John Paul II) *between faith and culture, whereby Christian faith, remaining true to its core, becomes native within each culture, thereby enhancing both the local culture* and *the mosaic of Christian faith with a unique expression.*

All catechetical education is faced with the task of inculturating Christian faith in its particular time and place. To this end, catechetical educators must encourage what I understand as a dialectical exchange between faith and culture. By dialectic here I don't mean Marx's misinterpretation of Hegel as thesis, antithesis, and synthesis; rather I intend dialectic in the sense that Plato imagined it as the give and take of good conversation, as mutual affirming, questioning, and moving on to new possibilities.

So, as Christian faith encounters a culture, there will be aspects of the culture that Christianity will affirm, aspects that it will challenge and may even condemn, and ways that it will bring reform and new life to the culture. Likewise, as a receiving culture appropriates a cultural expression of Christian faith, there will be aspects that the receiving culture will readily affirm, aspects within the culture-laden expression of faith that the receiving culture may challenge or renew, and ways that the receiving culture will forge its own unique Christian expression, enriching the universal mosaic of the Church.

One need only note the rich diversity of cultural faith expressions within Catholicism — Italian, Polish, French, Hispanic, African, Asian, American, to name a few — to recognize that integrating faith and culture, to the enhancement of both, has been a rich aspect of the Catholic charism throughout history. And it has managed to welcome such diversity while maintaining a deep bond of communion and unity in faith. Inculturation can work!

Reflecting further on the two-way dialectic, we can readily presume that Christian faith can contribute to every culture, but may be more reluctant to recognize how a cultural context can enhance the cultural expression of Catholicism that it receives. At the Boston College conference, Bishop Cupich had a helpful way of explaining how a culture can enhance "the faith" — not in the latter's essence but rather by bringing out something that had remained latent. In his phrase, a culture can bring out something of Christian faith that had been a "recessive gene." Let me give one of my favorite examples.

Catholicism's encounter with modernity helped to bring forth its recessive gene about human rights. The grand listing by Pope John XXIII in *Pacem in terris* and the championing of human rights that we find in Vatican II's *Gaudium et spes* was initially brought to the fore of Christian faith when the Church was confronted by the French Revolution and the modern quest for liberty, fraternity, and equality. In fact, throughout much of its prior history, the Church preached and practiced to the contrary. But modernity forced the Church to return to its sources and to see, as if for the first time, that indeed all people are created in the divine image, entitling all to equal rights and dignity, that the prophets had championed as much, that Jesus had amplified such social teaching, and so on. Of course, it was "all there already," but it took modernity to bring it to the fore.

When Catholics bring a dialectical attitude to American society, we will indeed find aspects to be condemned — its materialism, militarism, racism, lack of respect for the rights of the unborn and the elderly, and more. But there will also be aspects of American culture from which Catholics and our Church can learn — structures of oversight and accountability, an appreciation for public discourse that especially concerns unsettled issues, the practice of consultation with all members of a community, and so on.

Total catechetical education as I've briefly outlined it here has the potential to "hand on the faith" in our postmodern culture, doing so in ways "according to the mode of the receiver." By God's grace, it seems to be our best hope to promote lived and living Catholic faith.

Chapter 11

Handing on the Faith through Community-Based Faith Formation
Our Common Challenge and Shared Privilege
BISHOP BLASE CUPICH

T HE SHADOWS inched longer over the narrow streets of the small port city I was visiting last fall. I knew it was time to head back to my hotel. Sunset would soon turn into nightfall. It was then that one of the street vendors caught my eye. He had wrapped up his wares early and was joking with the others as he said farewell for the day. Many youths like him from North Africa are attracted to tourist towns along the southern Italian coast. They make enough to get by and hope to make enough to get ahead by hawking their hand-carved wares, knock-off watches, and clever street toys for visitors.

As he left his friends, the young tall black man walked with purpose along the same street leading to my hotel. Curious, I held back a bit to see where he was heading. Suddenly, he made a sharp left down an alleyway. Reaching the same corner, I spotted him about fifty yards ahead at a spigot. He had turned it on and was washing his hands, face and feet. He then pulled out of his sack a tightly knitted carpet. Placing it on the pavement, he faced eastward, bent down on all fours and began to pray. I understood. The setting sun was calling him to join his distant Muslim family in prayer to Allah, the One God.

Later that evening I recounted this scenario for my travel companions. They shared my admiration for the young man's faith and how his relationship with God obviously centered his life. One woman remarked that the practice of his Muslim faith was all the more remarkable given that he was living in an alien land and culture. In all likelihood there was little in his new surroundings that supported the traditions of his family and faith and probably a lot to undermine them.

Seamlessly our conversation turned to the situation many of these Catholic parents and their peers are facing with their children and grand-children. For some reason, the story of this young man's witness in practicing his Islamic faith hit a sensitive nerve. It touched a commonly felt anxiety about the faith lives of their own children and grandchildren, and the decreasing participation in the life of the Church by these later generations. Admittedly, their children and grandchildren are growing up in a more secular world than they did. The influence of Catholicism in the culture and family is much less evident today. But, this only made these veteran Catholics all the more curious — or should I say — more envious of the young Muslim. He deliberately stepped away from the crowd in an alien land and culture to make time for prayer according to his tradition. Was that too much to expect of the Catholics of his generation?

◆ ◆ ◆

The anxieties these parents expressed are not new to me. I heard similar comments during our diocesan synod consultations. Over a two-year period we gathered in a series of parish "speak-up" sessions, regional meetings, and a final general assembly, to identify our most pressing challenges and to adopt strategies and goals to address them. Quickly a consensus emerged about the top priority. People insisted that we do a better job in passing on the faith to the next generations. What we were doing was not working.

In what follows I will describe the steps our small rural diocese and our parishes are taking to improve the way we pass on the faith. Simply put, we are moving away from a model of catechesis as schooling, which places the responsibility solely on a few and tends to create false expec-tations about the nature of faith formation. In its place we are adopting an inter-generational/ecclesial approach done in the context of the faith life of the community, involving every member of the parish.

By way of introduction, I will first recount in greater detail the con-cerns people expressed during our synodal consultation. Their critique of our catechetical efforts was important in our attempt to identify what specifically was not working. The significant changes we decided to make in our catechetical approach are a direct response to the insights and suggestions people offered. With that background in mind, I will then provide a brief overview of the inter-generational/ecclesial model. I will also comment on how it differs from the schooling model, and thereby addresses the concerns expressed in our diocesan consultation.

Developing a process to bring about such a dramatic shift from a model of catechesis as schooling to an inter-generational/ecclesial approach to ongoing formation is key. It requires a great deal of thought and sensitivity to each particular situation. As a result each parish has been given the freedom to develop its own process and timeline for implementation. With a view to all the parishes I will give a composite summary of best practices that are being used by our parishes.

Finally, I will offer a preliminary evaluation of the faith formation model we are using, both its gains and challenges. I will conclude with some observations on this new approach as it relates to the Church's great tradition of handing on the faith. In doing so, I hope to offer some suggestions as to how to keep our focus as we take up this task anew in our time.

What We Are Doing Is Not Working

Many people came to this conclusion about the general status of our religious education programs, but for varying reasons. Parishioners pointed to dwindling and aging populations to conclude that our efforts were not inspiring children to make a lifelong commitment to the faith. Parents referred to the minimal grasp that their children had of the basics of Catholic teaching and tradition. Teachers and catechists expressed concern that the present system of religious education was creating false expectations about the nature of faith formation and how it takes place.

The Absence of a Lifelong Commitment

The aging population of our Sunday congregations was evidence enough for the average parishioner that we are failing to pass on the faith to our youth. While most people were not sure what could be done about this, there was a general sense that any new approach should aim at inspiring our young people to continue in the practice of the faith. It was obvious that our youth were not active once they left high school or when religious education classes ended. One mother starkly described the crisis we are facing at this moment in the life of the Church and crystallized what is at stake. After describing her disappointment that none of her children practices the faith, she mused that she and her husband could most likely be the last generation of Catholics in their family.

Religious Illiteracy

After years of CCD classes many children seem not to know the basics about what Catholics believe or the essentials of our tradition, e.g., how many Gospels are in the Bible, when Jesus lived, and the meaning of words like "Incarnation," "Exodus," "Real Presence," and "sacrament."

Young people were some of the first to express concern in this regard during our consultation. They complained about being ill-equipped to respond to the challenging comments and questions about Catholicism posed by classmates of other faith traditions. A teen expressed her frustration: "I feel cheated that my non-Catholic friends know more about the Bible and their religion than I know about my faith. I really do not know what it means to be a Catholic."

Some parents noted that the extent of this illiteracy is much more significant than failing to master a few facts, dates, or definitions. John Cavadini recently echoed these sentiments: "This vast ignorance is not just a question of missing bits of information, retinal holes marring an otherwise excellent field of vision. It is something more like a retinal detachment, a whole field of vision pulling inexorably away toward blindness. Not only are the words gone, the bits of information, but the system in which the words made sense is fading."[1]

Our parents expressed this same frustration and asked for a new approach that would relate the content of our faith to the context of their children's lives. Failure to do so has created a moral vacuum in the lives of their children. In the place of a religious field of vision, their children are opting for other "value systems" to shape their view of the world and their attitudes about important issues such as human dignity, sexual mores, and social justice.

False Expectations

Teachers, catechists, and pastors also weighed in, agreeing that change was needed. It is true that our present system is leaving children religiously illiterate and only superficially connected to the faith life of the

Church. However, the main problem with the system was not poor text-books, unprepared or indifferent catechists, or bad children. Rather, according to them the model of schooling as catechesis creates false expectations on a number of levels.

First, catechesis as schooling done in a classroom gives the impression that faith formation is no different from learning math, science, or history or any other school subject. Learning these subjects requires no personal commitment. Children's interest in any of them is often tied to their natural aptitude. We should not be surprised that children are leaving our programs with little commitment. According to some of our teachers, the schooling model unwittingly subverts the goal of catechesis, namely, to initiate young people into a life of ongoing faith formation.

The schooling model also affects the attitudes of parents. When teaching religion becomes just another subject to learn, it is viewed as the responsibility of the "experts," i.e., the teachers or the pastor. As this mind-set takes hold, parents tend to be less involved — and eventually less supportive — of their children's faith formation. One educator offered this apt description of the false expectation I am speaking about: "I am afraid we have led parents to believe that it is possible to drop their child at the church for religious education, run to the dry cleaners, the bank, and the grocery store, then come back an hour later and pick up a Catholic!"

Again, when religion becomes just another subject to teach to children, and not a matter of faith formation, parents lose sight of the value of their own practice of the faith. "The real issue here is one of witness and how it is at the heart of the faith formation of our children," according to one parish priest. A more recent trend confirms the impact of reducing religion to just another school subject and removing the value of witness. More and more we are seeing families suspend their Sunday Mass attendance during the summer months when classes are not offered.

The trend of waning parental support for religious education and formation is being mirrored in the broader community. The practice of leaving one night a week open for religious education has been abandoned even in rural communities in favor of sporting events and school activities. This only puts more pressure on already crowded family schedules and makes it easier for parents to justify giving a lower priority to religion.

In sum, there was a growing consensus that the very design of the schooling model is the heart of the problem. It has created a false understanding of what it means to pass on the faith by undervaluing the importance of witness. It also has created the illusion that the responsibility of faith formation belongs to just a few and requires little parental or community involvement and support. The general sentiment was that a totally new approach would be needed if we are going to be serious about handing on the faith to the next generations.

Designing a New Direction

From these diocesanwide discussions it was clear that the design of a fresh approach to catechesis had to address three issues: (1) We need to pass on the faith in a way that creates a thirst for God and the Church in the lives of young people. Childhood catechesis then becomes the beginning of one's long and ongoing faith formation. (2) Consideration has to be given to the context of Church life and practice when it comes to sharing the content of our faith and tradition. (3) The participation and witness of everyone is needed. Everyone is responsible and has to be involved. We found such a design in the inter-generational/ecclesial models that many dioceses were beginning to use.

From a Catechesis of Schooling to an Inter-Generational/ Ecclesial Approach

The problems and challenges of passing on the faith which we identified through our synod process have been brewing for a long time. This is true not only in western South Dakota, but throughout the nation as Cavadini highlights. As a result we were interested in learning more about how other dioceses and parishes around the country were responding to this crisis. Many were finding success in shifting from a catechesis of schooling to a new model of catechesis, commonly called inter-generational or church-based faith formation.[2]

These new approaches have a common starting point in the vision of catechesis offered in the General Catechetical Directory of 1999:

> Catechetical pedagogy will be effective to the extent that the Christian community becomes a point of concrete reference for the faith

journey of individuals. This happens when the community is proposed as a *source, locus,* and *means,* of catechesis. Concretely, the community becomes a visible place of faith-witness. It provides for the formation of its members. It receives them as a family of God. It constitutes itself as the living and permanent environment of growth in faith.[3]

Shifting from a model of catechesis as schooling to a catechesis as community-based faith formation has enormous consequences and implications. It redefines who is responsible for passing on the faith, it forces a reconsideration of how content relates to the context of learning, and it reinforces the role of the family.

First, with the inter-generational approach, everyone is responsible. The responsibility for passing on the faith does not belong exclusively to a few, whether that is the pastor, the religious education coordinator, the teachers, or the parents. Whether one is actually involved in the programs or just someone who witnesses by the practice of the faith, all take responsibility for creating the circumstances for handing on the faith to all. That means that faith formation is not just for the young. It is inter-generational because faith formation is a matter of lifelong learning.

Second, the context for learning the content of faith is the events in the life of the Church. This means that the parish must begin thinking about its keeping of feasts and seasons, its social justice and spiritual renewal efforts and its fellowship gatherings as "teachable moments." Each of these is the context for learning the content of our faith and for creating a corporate Catholic identity in the parish.

As a result, this events-centered and lifelong learning approach has an impact on the design of the curriculum, requiring it to be both systematic and cyclical. Typically, this means a six-year rotation of the major content areas found in the *Catechism of the Catholic Church*.[4] The four pillars of the *Catechism* (profession of faith, celebration of the Christian mysteries, life in Christ, and Christian prayer) are covered over a six-year period: (1) Church Year feasts and seasons, (2) sacraments and Church rituals, (3) justice and service, (4) Creed, (5) morality, and (6) prayer and spirituality. The six-year curriculum makes it possible to explore the Catholic faith with breadth and depth. As a spiral curriculum, the six themes are explored more deeply when the six-year cycle begins with year one again.

More specifically, it should be noted that each year's curriculum is divided into monthly segments during which time there are both age-appropriate and inter-generational gatherings. Nonetheless, there is a multigenerational experience of the theme which is tied to specific events of the Church's life. In the Year of the Sacraments, for instance, the entire community prepares for the celebration of Pentecost by learning about Confirmation. Marriage is covered during December as the community prepares to celebrate Holy Family Sunday, the Wedding Feast of Cana, and "World Marriage Day."

Finally, what happens at home and in the family reinforces what takes place in the community as it learns and develops a corporate Catholic identity. The parish helps the parents do this not by teaching them all they need to know about the faith so that they can in turn teach their children. Rather, the parish has the responsibility of assisting families, especially parents, to create a pattern of family faith sharing which involves learning, praying, serving, and celebrating with the Church. This means providing them with home materials that are designed to expand on the event learning that is taking place in the entire parish during a given month. These event-specific home materials help families to celebrate traditions and rituals, continue their learning, pray together, and reach out in service to others.

In sum, this model invites all generations in the parish to respect their own and each other's baptism as a source of mutual spiritual growth and lifelong formation. Sharing the content of the Catholic faith takes place in a systematic and cyclic way as it is tied to the celebration of the events in the life of the Church. Teaching takes place in the home, at age-specific sessions, and at inter-generational gatherings, as all ages in the parish participate in these ecclesial events.

The Implementation Process Is Key

Change does not come easily for any of us. The changes involved in this shift to an inter-generational model involve more than religious education. It also means rethinking the way parishes operate and function. Both individual parishes and the diocese have a role in this process.

Those parishes that have been most successful in bringing about this shift from catechesis as schooling to catechesis as inter-generational/ecclesial faith formation have invested a great deal of effort in the process both in terms of decision making and communication.

The idea is that if we are serious about asking parishioners to assume responsibility for the faith formation of all members, then they have to be involved in the decision making through ongoing communication. Such a change can not be a top-down decision made by the pastor or just a few people mandating a new approach and placing a new obligation on parents and the people of the parish. The message of mutual responsibility has to be matched by a corresponding form of involvement and decision making. Without this starting point, there is little chance of getting people to rethink their approach to parish life and of convincing them that they have a common responsibility for passing on the faith. In this instance, how things are done is as important as what is said.

By way of example, one pastor began with his parish leadership. They spent some weeks evaluating the religious education program, and came to a consensus that the Synod's call for a change had to be made in their parish. Not only did they approve going forward with the inter-generational approach, they also worked on a strategy to implement it. The first step was to host a parish picnic, at which families were introduced to the new approach. By scheduling a noneducational event for families to gather in a relaxed atmosphere, they immediately conveyed that the new approach had a wider aim than schooling children. The goal of the new effort is to include everyone and to build up the parish community and families.

At the picnic and in the weeks that followed, various small gifts such as bookmarks, yo-yos, key chains, and holy cards were distributed with the logo of the inter-generational program, GIFT (growing in faith together). This allowed people to take something home with them that would keep the conversation about this new program alive in their homes.

The parish leadership used every opportunity on the weekend and in mailings to inform people of the new effort, realizing that people need to hear something new a number of times. Information was designed to anticipate possible misconceptions and questions. The parish developed a team of families strategically located in the various neighborhoods. These parents served as a core group prepared to address concerns and encourage participation.

One expected objection was that parents were once again being stretched to do something that institutions had failed to do. Could not the priest be more available to teach the kids in Confraternity of Christian Doctrine (CCD)? Why isn't the diocese doing something to better train and retain teachers? In response, every effort was made to be clear about what parents were being asked to do and what the parish would do to support them. Additionally, the parish leaders took the occasion to speak about the issues raised in the synod process. If parents are really concerned about their children making a lifelong commitment to the faith, then their involvement, the involvement of the whole adult faith community was necessary.

It was also important to avoid any misunderstanding that parents were being threatened or forced to cooperate lest their children be unable to participate. The leadership stayed on message: the parish was not threatening but enabling parents, especially those who had doubts that they had something to offer for the faith formation of their children and others in the parish. One parent put it succinctly in a discussion with a neighbor: "This new program is about preparing our kids for life and eternal life. What better description is there for a Catholic parent?"

The diocese also makes two important contributions in the process of implementing this new approach in the parish. The first is to provide outside resources to train parish leaders, facilitators, and other personnel in developing a curriculum and providing the organizational framework. During initial workshops pastors and other parish leaders had an opportunity to learn more about an inter-generational approach. Follow-up sessions with consultants were also sponsored and coordinated by the diocese.

Secondly, the diocese can support the parishes in setting standards and policies. Early on pastors noticed that those parents not wanting to participate in this new approach were transferring their membership to other parishes that maintained the schooling model. After consulting with the presbyteral council and the diocesan pastoral council, a decision was made to craft new education standards and policies that would reflect the need for parental involvement and a parish commitment to ongoing faith formation.

These reformulated policies did not mandate a particular program, and parishes were allowed a grace period of three years to meet the standards. Pastors and parish leaders were asked to make a commitment to redesign their programs, and they were given the leeway to make the decisions on how they will comply with the new standards. The aim is to instill in parishioners a sense of mutual responsibility for religious education. Forcing implementation along a narrow framework and timeline was seen as counterproductive to this eventual goal. As one of our pastors told me, "We need to adopt polices that nudge not shove if we are going to be credible about parishes taking responsibility."

A Preliminary Assessment

Gains

Most parishes report that the response on the part of parishioners and families has been almost overwhelming. Parents welcome the chance to be better connected with their children's learning, and they find support through the interaction with other parents. Pastors also report that participation in their parishes on weekends and at monthly meetings is up significantly. Many parishes are providing an evening meal at the monthly inter-generational gatherings. This makes it easier for working mothers and fathers to participate, but it also has spawned a new group of volunteers to prepare the meals.

Since the parishwide gatherings are less frequent, smaller parishes seem more willing to twin with each other in sharing their otherwise sparse teaching resources. Pastors are also reporting that a parishwide faith formation program impacts the way families deal with issues and problems. One father spoke of now having a "neutral corner" to talk to his children about serious matters. While this new approach places more demands on the time of parents who already suffer from time-poverty, the benefits to their family life have made it easier for them to take up the needed task of reevaluating and adjusting their priorities.

When parishes decided on this new model, there was a concern about the impact on single-parent families. A special effort was made to support them by arranging for two-parent families to partner with them if needed. These partnerships have developed into a much larger network of support for family living than was anticipated. Likewise, the monthly inter-generational gatherings have provided a context for people of different ages and family situations to meet.

Finally, the rapid spread of the inter-generational model of catechesis has caught publishers unprepared. Only now are some beginning to close the gap and design resource materials and textbooks for the specific needs of this new approach. While there is a downside to this present gap between program and texts, it has created a unique opportunity for dialogue between publishers and those working on the grassroots level.

Challenges

The gains have outweighed the challenges, but the challenges are not insignificant and deserve attention. The first is the loss of families who have not been able or willing to make a change. Some parishes estimate that up to 20 percent of the families formerly enrolled in religious education have dropped out or transferred to parishes offering the schooling model. This loss is disappointing to pastors and parish leaders but must be placed in context. As one Director of Religious Education noted, these families participated infrequently in the program and in Sunday Mass. They were not supportive of the teachers and demonstrated little if any commitment to taking responsibility for the formation of the children's faith lives. This does not mean that we write them off. The parishes will have to develop a special outreach to these families. At the same time, there is a general consensus that the program is much healthier without the burden of trying to form children of parents uninterested and uncommitted to faith formation.

More also needs to be done to train facilitators of age-specific and inter-generational parish gatherings. The content and curriculum provided by the centers offering these programs are very well done but require greater attention to pedagogy. Smaller dioceses like our own and many of our rural parishes lack the necessary personnel to lead the gatherings and fashion the material so that they are age-specific. The new model of relating content to the context of living and celebrating our faith in worship demands new skills and a different kind of preparation.

As a result, two things should be kept in mind. First, we must recognize that this is a time of transition. A full inter-generational approach may need to be phased in over a number of years. Even the authors of such programs recognize that they are in the very early stages of introducing this new model of faith formation. As one of them told me, "it will take at least four to six years in a parish community for this new approach to become anchored in the practice of the whole parish community." As noted above, publishers are also behind the curve and have not yet caught up to the new and specific needs of this model.

Consequently, we have to remember, especially in this time of transition, that the faith formation of our children is our priority. That most likely may mean that we will have to schedule age-specific gatherings with greater frequency and continue using familiar texts for the time being, so that children receive a full and systemic catechesis. Children should not fall through the cracks as the adults attempt to make a very revolutionary change, albeit with the great promise it holds.

Secondly, the diocese has to step in and help parishes evaluate their programs. Dioceses also should provide ongoing training of leaders and facilitators lest the burnout of catechists experienced in the former model be replicated in those introducing this new approach.

Keeping Our Focus: A Concluding Observation

G. K. Chesterton once said that discouragement is the most diabolical of all temptations. Discouragement convinces us that we are alone, adrift, and on our own as we face life and the future. Many people today are discouraged about the future of the Church and the faith lives of their children because they feel that we are adrift in uncharted waters. They feel somewhat homeless after going through the seismic shifts in the Church, society, and our culture these past years. The support systems and points of reference they counted on in the past seemingly have evaporated. The question that one mother asked is on all of their minds: "Will they be the last Catholics in their families?"

But if we are honest about it, Christians have asked this question since the earliest days of the Church. Those living in the final days of the age of the apostles no doubt wondered about the future. How would the Church continue after the death of the last person who knew the Lord as Jesus of Nazareth? We should remember that it was out of this context that the New Testament, especially the Gospels, were born. The Evangelists, especially John (20:31) and Luke (1:1–4), make a point of saying that they are writing not just to recount the life of Jesus, even if it is a recounting through their communities' experience of the Risen Lord. Rather, they claim that their retelling the events of Christ from their experience has the power to create the very same experience whenever this retelling is proclaimed to future generations. "This is written that you may come to believe that Jesus is the Messiah, the Son of God, and that through this belief you may have life in his name" (Jn 20:31).

I believe that these early Christian communities, which faced challenges not unlike our own, have something to teach us by the approach they took in passing on the faith. Three things are noteworthy. First, they were faithful to the past. Second, they knew the importance of their own witness. Finally, they took up this challenge with a deep faith that the generations following them would be gifted with the Spirit to respond to the perennial truth of the Gospel and be able to make it their own for their time.

These three attributes should mark our efforts as we take up the task of passing on the faith in our time. We should never underestimate the importance of having a firm grasp of our tradition and the basics of our faith. If we do not want our youth to be theologically illiterate, then the adult community must prize and value its own ongoing learning. Also, the adult community must be able to demonstrate to young people not only that they have a grasp of the faith but that they are grasped by it. This means giving witness to our youth that our faith is the point of reference for the decisions we make and the kind of life we live.

Finally, we need to take up the work of forming young people in the faith with the confidence that God's grace is active in them calling for a response. Practically, that means teaching in a way that shows that we value them as partners in passing on the faith in our time. In sum, they both receive and have something to offer.

I wish that I would have had a chance to tell that young Muslim man how much my friends and I admired him for the witness he gave by practicing his faith in an alien land and culture. I even think it may have encouraged him. While that opportunity has passed, it does prompt me to suggest that all of us involved in passing on the faith should not overlook the importance of letting our youth know that their own practice of the faith is inspiring to their elders. By letting them know that they have much to offer as well as to receive, we plant a seed in their hearts about their future responsibility in handing on the faith. We create in them a thirst for Christ that can only be satisfied by doing the same for others. That seems to me to be at the heart of an inter-generational approach to faith formation and the hope it offers all of us in a moment of great challenge.

Afterword

Continuing the Conversation

John C. Cavadini

I T IS DIFFICULT to find oneself in the position of commenting on such
a distinguished set of papers and on the learned and truly clarifying discussion among all of the participants — leaders in scholarship,
education, and publishing. I learned so much from listening to the reflections of fellow members of our symposium that it seems otiose to add
anything further! I will begin, then, by naming two areas of major contribution — areas of such strong agreement among participants that they
seem to offer recommendations for the future. I will then turn to one
area where I believe the conference participants did not fully address all
that is implied in the topic "Handing on Catholic Faith." I will conclude
with some observations on the role of beauty in the practice of handing
on the faith.

In Handing on the Faith,
What Is Primary Is *Practice*

The "catechumenate of culture," as Paul Griffiths puts it, is really a catechumenate of particular practices more than anything else. The culture
of commodification inculcates a way of being, a *habitus* that can only be
countered by a set of practices which proceed from an essentially different inspiration from that of the culture at large. William Dinges's paper
specifies one dimension of this cultural catechumenate as a formation in
"individualism" and recommends the primacy of the practice of Church,
one might say, as the only suitable principle of formation to the contrary.
Mary Johnson's paper demonstrates the extent to which a certain kind
of practice of the faith has been eroded. The case seems effectively made

that handing on the faith means first and foremost handing on the practice of the faith in its sacramental and liturgical dimensions and in the virtues that they form. In other words, the "context" is such that only the primacy of a different "practice" as a way of life will offer an alternative catechesis to the one culture offers now.

Terrence Tilley, in a particularly attractive way of putting it, suggests the category of "witness" as the primary category for "communication" of the faith. "Witness" is essentially a set of practices drawing its inspiration from faith and from commitment to living out one's faith in communion with the Church. It shows the world a different way of constructing the self, in a way, a different "self" altogether, than the self defined by the consumerist economy of choice (echoing Griffith's way of putting it here). Thomas Groome reminds us that it is time to "reclaim the whole Church as catechist educator": "Let us imagine that the whole Church *is* catechetical more than does catechesis as one thing among many." This is very much the sort of holistic counterpractice, if I may put it that way, which Griffiths and Tilley and others are calling for as primary in the face of a culture that does not share the Church's primary assumptions about God and human beings. The essential in communicating the faith is ultimately the communication of an attitude, the humility of Christ, and the struggle is essentially "one of imagination and heart," as the Ruddys say of the controversy over abortion. Michael Himes's emphasis on *hilaritas* or "joy" as the "absolutely necessary requirement for all successful preaching and teaching" reaffirms the idea that what is essential is the passing on of an attitude or, broadly speaking, a "way of being."

The papers on "content" support this basic insight. Robert Wilken's persuasive essay on the primacy of the language of faith is another way of putting the primacy of practice. "The faith . . . is handed on embedded in language. It is not a set of abstract beliefs or ideas, but a world of shared associations and allusions. . . . The Church's way of speaking is a map of the experience of those who have known God and the beliefs it carries cannot be abstracted from the words, nor the words uprooted from the persons that used them." The Church's language broadly conceived comprises in itself a "culture," the practice and propagation of which is the primary means of handing on the faith. Luke Timothy Johnson's essay on the Creed can be easily related to Wilken's observations. The

Creed is, one might say, a speech-act. When recited liturgically, John-son says, it constitutes a "countercultural act." The Creed can "shape Christian communities in accordance with the truth of revelation," that is, in accordance with what Johnson calls "the Christian myth." Robert Barron's paper provides a sense of what one might call the proper intel-lectual attitude which should inform any articulations of the content of faith, namely, an ontology that does not construe God as a competitor with human goods, and which therefore provides adequate basis for a self-correcting intellectual principle within Christianity, an intellectual space from which to judge our own conformity to the Christ of Chal-cedonian orthodoxy, who embodies the principle of God's noncompeting status in the hypostatic union. Strictly speaking such an attitude is not a "practice," but it takes the same starting point as the other papers. What we are handing on is something at least logically and conceptually not dependent on the non-Christian cultures around us, not dependent, that is, upon their fundamental attitudes as these find embodiment in speech and practice.

Relation of Church and "World"

Within this broad area of agreement, there was some disagreement on what the Church, as a community of practice, itself a culture or at least formative of cultures, can learn from the "world." Some of the papers present such a negative picture of the "world" surrounding the Church that it seems that there would be very little good influence. Other papers (in addition to comments made orally) were more positive.

Paul Griffiths suggested in the discussion that the ancient trope of taking the "gold of the Egyptians" was the proper way for the Church to appropriate elements of truth in the surrounding culture. Does this include anything that can be thought of as a practice, determinative of identity? Bishop Cupich suggested that in the sex-abuse scandal, part of what we had learned, or should have learned, was that the Church had not caught up to the culture at large in certain attitudes or prac-tices, one of them being accountability. It was precisely the wrong move, he suggested, for Catholics, and especially the hierarchy, to retreat into the Church conceived as a self-contained culture that had the ability of self-correction apart from any contribution, as it were, from the sur-rounding culture. In reply to the observation that the problem is that the

Church did not retreat far enough into its own tradition, where it would have found the humility for self-correction, Bishop Cupich noted that indeed the Church's resources for self-correction are always there, but sometimes on "genes" which have become, for one reason or another, "recessive" — they need some prodding from without to become operative — some good example from the outside, non-Christian perhaps, to provoke the humility that already resides within the tradition.

This insight struck me as the sort of thing Augustine had in mind in Book 5 of the *City of God* when he drew the attention of Christians to the achievements of the Roman heroes, whose deeds of virtue, while not enough to save them, are enough to shame Christians who may have become smug over their practice of the evangelical counsels. Those who want to think of the Church as a culture of its own or at least (as I would put it) formative of cultures, have to have a way of combating the vice that such a culture is prey to in its deformations, namely, pride and its derivatives — triumphalism, clericalism, smugness — all of which threaten to destroy the good of the original culture. This requires genuine humility before the goodness that we find in the world, even if, as in the case of Augustine's virtuous pagans, that goodness is flawed.

Here, the category of "witness," as Tilley elaborates it, seems to help. "Witness" combines elements of language and ritual practice with the attitudes of love and compassion this language and practice are meant to form. Luke Timothy Johnson's suggestion that we "must find some way of witnessing to the faith that combines deep piety, social passion, and intellectual openness" seems to articulate the balance that the discussion was tending towards.

For the future, then, the symposium seems to offer as a primary recommendation the primacy of practice where that most usefully means the primacy of Christian witness. Formed by the practice of the sacraments, with imaginations contoured by the distinctive language of the Bible and the liturgy, we bring to the world our incorporation into Christ *as* a loving and living solidarity with all of our neighbors, the poor and the inquiring especially. This means strength in the conviction of the distinctiveness of the Christian message. The very strength of that conviction, though, should also open us to the "witness" to the truth that any person of goodwill presents, as John Paul II recommends in *Veritatis splendor*.[1]

A Recommendation

From the foregoing reflections one might suggest that the first step in handing on the faith is to strengthen the distinctive practices, liturgies, and language that create Christian identity *and* the virtues these practices are meant to form. One should do so remembering that those virtues are susceptible to good example from anyone, including non-Christians, even if their definitive value and meaning are established by the Christian story. Formation in Christian virtue means attentiveness both to the distinctive Christian witness in revelation and example, as well as humility before the virtue of any person of goodwill.

Intellectual Trends and Practical Consequences

A second, though perhaps less explicit, area of agreement is that what happens in the "elite" element in Christian culture eventually affects all levels. Strong intellectual trends, no matter how seemingly limited to educated elites at first, can ultimately become formative of Christian practice and belief on every level. Wilken's paper alerts us to the example of translations, based on various intellectual agendas, which caused the English text of the Bible to lose concreteness and distinctiveness. Luke Johnson's paper shows that the loss of ontology and the consequent ascendancy of Christologies from below have resulted in an impoverished sense of the central truths proclaimed by the Creed, including the Resurrection of Jesus.

However, if the culture teaches a "meta-narrative" of choice as absolute, then even the Church itself comes to be understood against a voluntarist paradigm that makes it essentially a function of mutually elected association (a Lockean understanding of church). Put this way, the issue seems to be the loss of a meta-narrative of the Church's own, the loss of an integrated view of knowledge in which the Church makes sense not as a voluntary association or club, but as the ongoing presence of Christ in the world. The loss of the overarching intellectual integration of faith and reason that Neo-Thomism represented resulted in default to the prevailing cultural paradigm, such that the Church and all its practice and teaching is understood against a Lockean epistemology which in effect secularizes even the Church itself by making all meaning and association a function of arbitrary choice. This is not really integration but the aggressive refusal of it.

Loss of the Neo-Thomist Synthesis

Within this broader consensus about the role of intellectual trends, there was also some disagreement. It seemed true to most present that with the loss of the Neo-Thomist synthesis, Catholic education on all levels seems to have lost its balance, because it lost a unity of discourse that had penetrated all educational levels and made them cohere. As some participants noted, as times and cultures change, this loss was inevitable, and theological renewal will not come about by trying to revive something anachronistic. Nor will it come about, other participants reminded us, by forgetting the achievements of the past or the ideals which inspired the syntheses of the past.

I wonder whether, in abandoning the Neo-Thomist synthesis, we also abandoned the ideal of integration of knowledge and the dialectic between faith and reason it presupposes because we had a hard time thinking of that ideal of integration separately from the Neo-Thomist example of it. Bishop Kicanas, for one, commented on the pessimistic tone of some of the observations regarding the contemporary fragmentation of knowledge. Perhaps we have projected some of the pessimism out of our own lack of imagination. We imagine a situation in which it is all or nothing — an effective, presently accomplished integration or nothing.

But that is not the standard that John Paul II holds us to, for example, in *Ex Corde Ecclesiae*. No one argues more strongly than John Paul II for the integration of knowledge:

> It is necessary *to work towards a higher synthesis* of knowledge, in which alone lies the possibility of satisfying that thirst for truth which is profoundly inscribed on the heart of the human person. Aided by the specific contributions of philosophy and theology, university scholars will be engaged in a constant effort to determine the relative place and meaning of each of the various disciplines within the context of a vision of the human person and the world that is enlightened by the Gospel, and therefore by a faith in Christ, the *Logos,* as the center of creation and of human history.

And yet he points out that this integration is never fully and finally realizable:

> *Integration of knowledge* is a process, one which will always remain incomplete.[2]

Ex Corde presents an ideal best characterized as one of seeking and partial attainment. I think it is easier to go forward if we realize that it is this *quest* for integration that is the standard, not necessarily an already fully accomplished integration. Holding out for the latter as a *sine qua non* for progress is bound to make the situation in which we find ourselves bleaker than it really is (admitting that it is in many ways bleak). But engaging in the quest for integration, and in some ways thinking of that quest *as* integrating, is already to offer a great witness in the midst of a secular intellectual culture that has aggressively abandoned this ideal altogether.

The Quest for an Integral Vision

One implication of Robert Wilken's paper is that the Christian language embodies within it an implicit integration or synthetic view of all of reality. Our job is to use this language and actualize its implicit capacities and potentials for integration and for serving as the basis for integrative reflection. The "speaking" that results should have the "openness" that Luke Johnson's paper enjoins, for the dialectic between faith and reason is a search for integration in the face of, and *because of,* constant questioning from "reason" or the disciplines. We have to relearn the reflex of using the language of revelation, i.e., of Scripture and Tradition, in a confident way, and yet in a way that is nevertheless open to dialogue and discussion of what that language implies in answer to questions from the secular disciplines. If we set this tone at the highest levels of education, it will ultimately promote its use at all other levels.

I think that people are not confident using the language of the tradition because they are afraid they will be perceived as too closed, too narrow, not open. And, if in fact we use this language thinking that by using it we will be resuscitating anachronistically an integration from the past, we will continue to feel this lack of confidence. But if we learn to use Scriptural and Traditional language in an intellectually open way, challenging others by our use of it but also open to feeling the challenge their intellectual questions and moral example may bring, we will infuse life into the whole fabric of Catholic intellectual culture. Then, it will be able to offer an alternative between what seems like the only two options available: the ugly polarity between aggressive secularization and anti-intellectual fideism. Handing on the faith means recovering the quest for integration at the highest levels of education.

A Further Recommendation

In light of the above analysis one hazards a recommendation to those charged with leading Catholic universities and colleges. Promote the language of *integration of knowledge*. The language of integration has been largely eclipsed by the language of "interdisciplinarity," a kind of secularized version of the true ideal. Re-energize the vocabulary of "integration" based on the dialectic between faith and reason and encourage creative work flowing from the commitment to integration of knowledge.

A Crucial Concern

I found myself worrying throughout the conference about one fairly consistent omission. Virtually absent from the papers and the discussions, apart from a few comments made by a couple of the participants, was any consideration of "Handing on Catholic Faith" as handing on *the* faith, that is the *teachings* of the faith, the doctrines which express and elaborate the mysteries of the faith as summarized in the Creed. All present seemed to agree on the primacy of language and practice as the most essential element in handing on the faith, and disagreements centered on how corrosive the ambient culture has been toward the practice of the faith, how much Catholics themselves had permitted their own language and practice to be eroded, and how optimistic one might be about contemporary pedagogies of language and practice. But only Bishop Cupich's paper (prepared after the conference) made more than glancing reference to the *Catechism of the Catholic Church* or its emphasis on "the exposition of doctrine" intended "to help deepen understanding of the faith."[3]

If we were to judge from these papers, which represent a good range of liberal to conservative opinion, one might conclude that we have discovered an unexpected consensus among liberals and conservatives, namely, that doctrinal catechesis is of such little importance or significance in the life of the Church that it is not even worthy of mention in papers considering how Catholic faith is to be handed on in the twenty-first century. Yet, Mary Johnson's paper indicates that the younger people in her study are interested in more substantial catechesis. Why didn't even one of the scholars assembled here mention it as a desideratum in their papers — an omission noted by John Garvey in his comments as facilitator, seconded by Scott Appleby in response?

My worry is that this omission may reflect a pessimism about what is possible in the Church and possibly even what is ultimately possible for human nature, in particular its capacity for understanding. Moreover, if my intuition is correct, such pessimism would stand in stark contrast to the spirit of the *Catechism of the Catholic Church* and of papal documents on catechesis such as John Paul II's *Catechesi Tradendae*.[4] It is certainly contrary to the spirit of St. Augustine, whose preaching was strongly fixed on the one idea of bringing his congregation to "understanding" of the difficult *quaestiones* which Scripture raises for us. One of Augustine's most persistent homiletic themes is that of leading his listeners to an understanding of the mysteries of faith and his preaching, while not indulging in technical jargon or allusions, was not "dumbed down" in the way that homiletic rhetoric often is today.[5] The attitude that understanding is not important seems more a concession to the background culture of dumbing down political and other forms of rhetoric, and to the consumerist culture that gives rise to this cynical treatment of the public.

I believe that we need to recover a sense of the organic connection between doctrinal catechesis and formation in the Mysteries the doctrines represent in order to recover the confidence necessary for "handing on the faith" in a way which encourages a culture of "understanding." Such understanding, always derivative from practice, is also almost always fragmentary and in need of continual revision. But that does not mean there is not a thirst for it. People are always wanting to know from us why disasters happen, why bother praying, why bother remaining faithful in marriage, why Catholics venerate Mary, why we are not in favor of "choice" when it comes to abortion, and so forth.

Practice may, indeed, be primary, but it is a very short distance from a particular practice (e.g., receiving Communion) and being asked by someone to explain what it means. Language may be primary, but again it is a very short step from use of language to the need to answer questions about that language. To separate practice from understanding too easily is to forget, as Robert Imbelli pointed out in conversation, that practices are "theory laden," and, as Michael Himes pointed out, that people are genuinely moved when they have a sense that what they believe (or are asked to believe) all fits together into a harmonious whole. To construe language as primary and doctrine as secondary is to forget, too, that doctrine represents a rule for speaking. In worrying about how to pass on that rule for speaking, how to hand on doctrine, we are at the same time worrying about how to pass on a way of understanding, a way of naming and articulating teachings which are ultimately mysteries.[6]

Support for Catechesis and Catechists

Hand-in-hand with the omission of any mention of doctrinal catechesis, there was also no mention of the fact that the Church supports parish catechesis so poorly and erratically in terms of funding qualified catechetical leaders. The Church does not have a culture that supports informed catechesis at the parish level. Does the lack of mention of this mean we have given up on fixing that? Is handing on the faith so difficult, and the results so minimal, that we should just not bother? Again, there is a streak of pessimism here that does not correspond with the message of John Paul II, who says that the office of catechist is of primary importance in the Church and deserves the utmost support:

> As the twentieth century draws to a close, the Church is bidden by God and by events — each of them a call from him — to renew her trust in catechetical activity as a prime aspect of her mission. She is bidden to offer catechesis her best resources in people and energy, without sparing efforts or material means, in order to organize it better and to train qualified personnel. This is no mere human calculation; it is an attitude of faith.[7]

It may be true that our understanding is mostly woefully lacking, that our teaching may fall on mostly deaf ears, but it is not our job to assume it will or it will not — "this is no mere human calculation; it is an attitude of faith." Effectiveness is ultimately the job of God's grace, and we have no right to second-guess God's grace by a pessimism that leads us not even to try. And, in any event, as Augustine points out in the prologue to the *De Doctrina Christiana,* God wants human beings to have the honor of teaching other human beings about divine matters, and such teaching and learning engenders the bond of charity whether or not it is successful in increasing understanding. The primacy of practice and language does not mean the abandonment of teaching and learning derivative from that practice and language.

Proclamation

I would propose, then, that just as "witness" seemed to be an appropriate category for understanding how "practice" hands on the faith, so "proclamation" is an appropriate category for understanding the way in which handing on the teachings of the faith is itself a kind of practice and witness. Engendering understanding is an element of proclamation. Good preaching aims at understanding, and so does good teaching. The good teaching of the doctrines of the faith is not one that understands itself simply to be handing on mere information, but rather a continuing proclamation of the Good News in the very depths of its mysterious enactment.

Why do we believe that there are two natures in one person in Christ? Not because we are worried to get our "facts" right, just as we want to be accurate about how many molecules of hydrogen are in a water molecule, but rather because this doctrine carries within it the proclamation of the unfathomable mystery of the love of God who declared utter solidarity with us in our suffering and even — without himself being sinful — in our sin, to the extent of living under the consequences of our sin. If we think of handing on the faith under the category of "proclamation," we will include a focus at once on better preaching and on better teaching of the doctrines of the faith, even as we look as well at fostering parish structures and support that make this more effective. In so doing, we will nurture not only a culture of understanding, but that culture of charity that resists the paralysis engendered by pessimism, lest pessimism shade ever so imperceptibly into its closely neighboring attitude, despair.

The Importance of Beauty

Many of the papers emphasized the role of the beautiful in handing on the faith, and this point was taken up even more forcefully in discussion, including the beauty of the language of the Bible and the Church, of religious art, of a system of doctrine in which everything fits together, the beauty of literature carrying religious themes, of religious music, and so forth. As Christopher Ruddy pointed out to the agreement of most in the group, religious themes evoked in film can provide excellent access to themes presented more conceptually in other sources. Awakening people to the beauty of the tradition, a beauty they had not expected to find, is a way of inculcating warmth towards Catholic tradition, a receptiveness that entails, among other things, a new appreciation for mystery that cannot ever fully be put into words. Simone Weil once characterized the beauty of religious ceremony as one of the "implicit forms of the love of God."[8]

In connection with this insight, I would mention Bishop Ramírez's proposal, in discussion, of one ceremony in particular, the religious procession, as exemplifying the appeal of the beautiful in handing on the faith. In its beauty, a religious procession invites participation and reflection. A procession puts our faith on display, and in a festive, proclamatory way. It begins and ends with the language of the Church. But it takes it out to where anyone can watch. One doesn't have to enter the nave of the Church to see it. Anyone can watch, anyone can wonder, anyone can ask whatever question comes to them, Catholic or not, and can begin to seek the sort of understanding which will enable them to draw nearer. The procession implies both a confidence in our way of speaking, and an openness which will permit us to try to "give an account of the hope that is in us" to any person of goodwill who asks. The beauty of the religious procession invites a deeper look, without a hard sell or even, at first, much explanation. Whatever explanation follows will always have as its first reference point the procession itself and its beauty, which, like the mystery it celebrates, cannot be exhausted by words even as the words can afford some access to its inner reality and as such offer understanding.

The Witness and Practice of St. Augustine

If we are now willing to relocate temporarily to sometime after 396, at an Easter Vigil celebration, perhaps in a rural area near Hippo, we will find another example — and further specification — of the value of beauty in handing on the faith, and it will also help us tie together these reflections as a whole. We find Bishop Augustine preaching at the Vigil. As he seems to have done every Easter Vigil he preached (if the surviving sermons are any indication), he finds himself exhorting the faithful, and perhaps himself, to stay awake.[9] Instead of sleeping, Augustine advises his listeners to imitate inwardly the action they have liturgically enacted outwardly:

> And so may God, who *commanded the light to shine out of the darkness, shine in our hearts* (2 Cor. 4.6), so that within ourselves we may do something similar to what we have done in this house of prayer by lighting all these lamps. Let us adorn God's true dwelling place, our consciences, with the lights of justice. Or rather not us, but God's grace with us, of which we have the promise in the words of the prophet, *He will bring forth your justice like the light* (Ps. 37.6). And keeping watch in this way, we shall not be afraid of *the fear by night, and the busy thing prowling in the dark* (Ps. 91.5–6).[10]

In this passage, Augustine uses three scriptural texts to articulate some spiritual advice. More precisely, he has picked scriptural texts because of the images of light and darkness and night they carry, and he has picked these texts, in turn, because of the actions of the liturgy. Augustine is commenting not only on the scriptural text, but on the beautiful images evoked by Scripture as those images are vividly presented in the actions and circumstances of the Easter Vigil. The "darkness" of Psalm 91:6, and whatever may be prowling in it, are all around the watchers, gathered in the reassuring space of the house of prayer. The "light" shining in the darkness of 2 Corinthians 4:6 is also all around them, in the lamps they have lit and are holding. Each person has literally become a "light," has become, in their own person, the scriptural image.

"And so," Augustine advises in another sermon, "with the aid of all these lamps shining during this night, let us stave off the sleep of the body in this solemn vigil; but against the sleep of the heart, we ourselves ought to be lamps shining in this age of the world as in a night."[11] Augustine had explained in another sermon[12] that the sleep of the heart is the darkness of the heart bereft of charity. Augustine compares love or charity to the watchful sleeplessness of the vigil of the Resurrection. The life of charity is a life of watchful mindfulness of the Resurrection of Christ and as such a life of hope for our own resurrection. At the Easter

Vigil our flesh is awake, bearing lights to commemorate the solemnity of Easter, so we have in that wakefulness an image of what charity is. The believer whose life is lived in love is a watchful witness to hope, enlightening the world with its witness. The dramatic images in the liturgy capture and embody scriptural images. The catechist, in this case the preacher, unfolds the teachings of Scripture by knitting them together in accordance with the Rule of Faith, which teaches the resurrection of the flesh, but does so as an explanation and elaboration of the beautiful liturgical ceremony that he is celebrating with the faithful. In the end, the beauty of the textual and liturgical imagery is meant to be relocated, so to speak, transferred, one might say, to the life of the Christian believer.

Notes

Foreword / Robert P. Imbelli

1. The Initiative, originally planned as a two-year response to the crisis afflicting the Catholic Church in Boston, has recently been established as a permanent Center at Boston College. Information about its activities may be found at *www.bc.edu/church21*.

2. For the centrality of doxology in Catholic life and theology, see Frans Jozef van Beeck, *God Encountered*, vol. 1: Understanding the Christian Faith (Collegeville, Minn.: 1988). See especially chapter 7, "Doxology: the Mystery of Intimacy and Awe," 145–77.

3. Archbishop Sean O'Malley, O.F.M. Cap., "Handing on the Faith." The Archbishop's talk may be viewed at *www.bc.edu/church21/resources/webcast*. A print copy may also be obtained from the Church in the 21st Century at Boston College.

Introduction / Robert P. Imbelli

1. Biblical quotations are taken from the New American Bible (New York: Oxford University Press, 1995).

2. Brian E. Daley, S.J., "Response to Cardinal Hume," in *One in Christ: Unity and Diversity in the Church Today* (New York: National Pastoral Life Center, 1999), 22.

For a rich study of the central importance of discernment in the Christian theological and spiritual tradition, see Mark A. McIntosh, *Discernment and Truth: The Spirituality and Theology of Knowledge* (New York: Crossroad, 2004).

3. For a probing analysis see Stanley Hauerwas, "Self-Deception and Autobiography: Reflections on Speer's *Inside the Third Reich*," in Hauerwas, *Truthfulness and Tragedy* (Notre Dame, Ind.: University of Notre Dame Press, 1977), 82–98. For the prominence of the theme in the work of Flannery O'Connor, see Kim Paffenroth, "Deadly Self-Deception and Life-Giving Revelation in Flannery O'Connor," *Communio* 32, no. 1 (Spring 2005): 152–71.

4. For a fine development of this theme, deftly employing both theological and literary resources, see Robert Barron, *And Now I See: A Theology of Transformation* (New York: Crossroad, 1998).

5. Cardinal Joseph Bernardin and Archbishop Oscar Lipscomb, *Catholic Common Ground Initiative: Foundational Documents* (New York: Crossroad, 1997), 40.

6. Irenaeus of Lyons, *Against the Heresies*, IV, 34, 1: *omnem novitatem attulit semetipsum afferens.* Critical edition in the Collection *Sources Chrétiennes,* vol. 100 (Paris: Cerf, 1965).

7. Pope John Paul II, *Novo Millennio Ineunte* (Boston: Pauline Books, 2001), #29.

8. Ronald Rolheiser, *The Holy Longing: The Search for a Christian Spirituality* (New York: Doubleday, 1999), 74.

9. I am playing here on the double meaning in the title of Luke Timothy Johnson's fine book, *Living Jesus: Learning the Heart of the Gospel* (San Francisco: Harper, 1999).

10. For a profound study of the intimacy and incommensurability of the relation between Christ and the Church, see Jean-Marie Tillard, O.P., *Flesh of the Church, Flesh of Christ* (Collegeville, Minn.: Liturgical Press, 2001).

11. Pope John Paul II, *Ecclesia de Eucharistia* (Boston: Pauline Books, 2003).

12. Aidan Kavanagh, O.S.B., "Christian Initiation: Tactics and Strategy," in *Made, Not Born: New Perspectives on Christian Initiation and the Catechumenate* (Notre Dame, Ind.: University of Notre Dame Press, 1976), 1–6.

13. I have emended the translation of this dense passage in light of the exegesis of Heinrich Schlier, *Lettera agli Efesini* (Brescia: Paideia, 1965), 250–52.

14. For the crucial importance of imagination in the thought of John Henry Newman, see John Coulson, *Religion and Imagination: "In Aid of a Grammar of Assent"* (Oxford: Clarendon Press, 1981).

Chapter 1 / Religious Education, Mary Johnson, SNDdeN

1. See U.S. Census Bureau, *www.census.gov.*

2. Dean R. Hoge, William D. Dinges, Mary Johnson SNDdeN, and Juan L. Gonzales Jr., *Young Adult Catholics: Religion in the Culture of Choice* (Notre Dame, Ind.: University of Notre Dame Press, 2001).

Chapter 2 / Faith, Hope, and (Excessive) Individualism, William D. Dinges

1. Robert Bellah, "Religion and the Shape of National Culture," *America* 181, no. 3 (1999): 9–14.

2. Anthony Giddens, *Modernity and Self-Identity* (Stanford: Stanford University Press, 1991), 32–33; 195–201.

3. Charles Taylor, *Varieties of Religion Today: William James Revisited* (Cambridge, Mass.: Harvard University Press, 2002), 80, 95, 101.

4. Wade C. Roof, *A Generation of Seekers* (San Francisco: HarperCollins, 1993), 246.

5. Thomas Luckmann, *The Invisible Religion* (New York: Macmillan, 1967), 97, 105.

6. Giddens, *Modernity and Self-Identity,* 195; also Paul Heelas, Scott Lash, and Paul Morris, eds., *Detraditionalization: Critical Reflections on Authority and Identity* (Oxford: Blackwell, 1995); Lawrence M. Friedman, *The Horizontal Society* (New Haven: Yale University Press, 2003).

7. I am indebted to Vincent Miller's thorough and perceptive analysis of these trends and their impact on American culture and religious life in general, and on Catholicism in America in particular. See Vincent Miller, *Consuming Religion: Christian Faith and Practice in Consumer Culture* (New York: Continuum, 2004).

8. Mike Featherstone, *Consumer Culture and Postmodernism* (London: Sage, 1991), 118–19.

9. William D. Dinges, "Postmodernism and Religious Institutions," *The Way: A Review of Christian Spirituality* 36, no. 3 (1996): 215–24.

10. Joseph B. Tamney, *The Resilience of Christianity in the Modern World* (Albany: State University of New York Press, 1992), 80–81; G. Ritzer, "The 'New' Means of Consumption: A Postmodern Analysis," in *Illuminating Social Life,* 2nd ed., ed. Peter Kivisto (Thousand Oaks, Calif.: Pine Forge Press, 2001), 337–60.

11. Miller, *Consuming Religion,* 54.

12. Tom Beaudoin, *Virtual Faith: The Irreverent Spiritual Quest of Generation X* (San Francisco: Jossey-Bass Publishers, 1998).

13. Miller, *Consuming Religion,* 58, 72.

14. Miller, *Consuming Religion,* 91; also Philip Rieff, *The Triumph of the Therapeutic* (Harmondsworth: Penguin, 1966).

15. Robert Wuthnow, *After Heaven: Spirituality in America since the 1950s* (Berkeley: University of California Press, 1998), 165. Consider, for example, our material girl "Ester's" (nee Madonna) latest spiritual feeding on Kabala and her techno display of that tradition in her current "Reinvention Tour." See David Segal, "Prime Madonna," *Washington Post,* June 15, 2004.

16. Wade C. Roof and William McKinney, *American Mainline Religion: Its Changing Shape and Future* (New Brunswick, N.J.: Rutgers University Press, 1987); Phillip E. Hammond, *Religion and Personal Autonomy: The Third Disestablishment in America* (Columbia: University of South Carolina Press, 1992); Don Miller, *Reinventing American Protestantism: Christianity in the New Millennium* (Berkeley: University of California Press, 1997).

17. Robert Wuthnow, *Sharing the Journey: Support Groups and America's New Quest for Community* (New York: Free Press, 1994), and *"I Come Away Stronger": How Small Groups Are Shaping American Religion* (Grand Rapids, Mich.: Eerdmans, 1994).

18. Robert D. Putnam, "Bowling Alone: America's Declining Social Capital," *Journal of Democracy* 6 (January 1995): 65–78, and *Bowling Alone: The Collapse and Revival of American Community* (New York: Simon & Schuster, 2000).

19. Robert N. Bellah et al., *Habits of the Heart: Individualism and Commitment in American Life* (Berkeley: University of California Press, 1996); Roof and McKinney, *American Mainline;* Roof, *A Generation;* Wade C. Roof, "Modernity, The Religious, and The Spiritual," *The Annals of the American Academy of Political and Social Science* 558 (1998): 211–24, and *Spiritual Marketplace: Baby Boomers and the Remaking of American Religion* (Princeton: Princeton University Press, 1999); also, Wuthnow, *After Heaven.* "Hard" reads of secularization theory interpret this contraction of religion to the private sphere as one of the paramount signs of secularization. See Steve Bruce, *Religion and Modernization* (Oxford: Clarendon Press, 1992).

20. Wuthnow, *"I Come Away Stronger,"* 356. The emphasis on religious individualism receives academic legitimation via the current hegemony of rational choice theory as a conceptual tool for analyzing religious behavior. At the core of the rational choice paradigm is the assumption that *homo religiosus* is a rational *individual* making a series of calculated life-style "choices" about religious wares.

21. Roger Finke and Rodney Stark, *The Churching of America, 1776–1990: Winners and Losers in Our Religious Economy* (New Brunswick, N.J.: Rutgers University Press, 1992), 16.

22. Helen R. Ebaugh and Janet S. Chafetz, *Religion and the New Immigrants: Continuities and Adaptations in Immigrant Congregations* (New York: Alta Mira Press, 2001), and Paul Wilkes, *Excellent Catholic Parishes* (New York: Paulist Press, 2001).

23. Roof, *Spiritual Marketplace,* 121.

24. Wuthnow, *Loose Connections: Joining Together in America's Fragmented Communities* (Cambridge, Mass.: Harvard University Press, 1998).

25. The weakening commitment to institutional religion is not, therefore, unique to Catholicism, nor is it exclusively a failure of church leadership — although the problem has been tragically exacerbated by failed leadership in the current sex abuse scandal. The crisis of hierarchical malfeasance in the Church today came at a time of widespread scandals in other institutional sectors of American life, notably the corporate ones. While there are obvious and important differences in these domains, malfeasance in both contexts involved the abuse of authority and the exercise of deception (whatever the motive or rationale). Both, in turn, have fed the loss of confidence in institutional structures. Catholics can readily draw analogues of executive malfeasance from the corporate world to highlight what has happened in the ecclesiastical one — and vice versa.

26. See report on Barry A. Kosmin, Egon Mayer, and Ariela Keysar, American Religious Identification Survey 2001, *www.newsaic.com/mwamericanid.html;* also Michael Hout and Claud Fisher, "Explaining the Rise of Americans with No Religious Preference: Politics and Generations," *American Sociological Review* 67 (April 2002): 165–90.

27. In Richard Cimino and Don Lattin, *Shopping for Faith: American Religion in the New Millennium* (San Francisco: Jossey-Bass Publishers, 1998), 11.

28. Bruce A. Greer and Wade C. Roof, "Desperately Seeking Sheila: Locating Religious Privatism in American Society," *Journal for the Scientific Study of Religion* 31 (1992): 346–52.

29. Robert C. Fuller, *Spiritual but Not Religious: Understanding Unchurched America* (Oxford: Oxford University Press, 2001), 1.

30. Fuller, *Spiritual;* Cimino and Lattin, *Shopping;* Roof, "Modernity"; Roof and McKinney, *American Mainline;* Bellah et al., *Habits,* 1984; and Amanda Porterfield, *The Transformation of American Religion* (New York and Oxford: Oxford University Press, 2001), esp. 40–41.

31. Wuthnow, *After Heaven.*

32. Miller, *Consuming Religion,* 82; Roof, *Spiritual Marketplace;* Fuller, *Spiritual but Not;* Wuthnow, *After Heaven.* It should be noted that the relationship between "being religious" and "being spiritual" is not a zero-sum game. Marler and Hadaway, after reviewing the literature, argue that "being religious" and "being spiritual" are interdependent concepts. Most Americans see themselves as both. However, the overall pattern is toward less religiousness *and* less spirituality, especially among the younger and more religiously marginal. See Penny L. Marler and Kirk Hadaway, " 'Being Religious' or 'Being Spiritual' in America: A Zero-Sum Proposition?" *Journal for the Scientific Study of Religion* 41 (2002): 289–300.

33. While some Catholics may take solace in this phenomenon out of the conviction that God reaches for humans at all times and in all ways, there is a disquieting and not-so-subtle message here that institutional religion is not essential to this encounter — a view seriously at variance with Catholicism's communal sensibilities.

34. Hal Hinson, "Is That You, God, or Am I Nuts? The Supernatural in Prime Time," *New York Times,* March 28, 2004, 12.

35. Albert J. Bergesen and Andrew M. Greeley, *God in the Movies* (New Brunswick, N.J.: Transaction Publishers, 2000); Tom Beaudoin, *Virtual Faith.*

36. Kimon H. Sargeant, *Seeker Churches: Promoting Traditional Religion in a Non-Traditional Way* (New Brunswick, N.J.: Rutgers University Press, 2000); Don Miller, *Reinventing American Protestantism.*

37. Christian Smith, *American Evangelicals: Embattled and Thriving* (Chicago: University of Chicago Press, 1998), 103.

38. Dean R. Hoge, Benton Johnson and Don Luiden, *Vanishing Boundaries: The Religion of Mainline Protestant Babyboomers* (Louisville: Westminster/John Knox Press, 1994), 13; Putnam, *Bowling Alone.*

39. George Barna, *The Index of Leading Spiritual Indicators* (Dallas, Tex.: Word Publishing), 38.

40. Charles Lippy, *Pluralism Comes of Age: American Religious Culture in the Twentieth Century* (Armonk, N.Y.: M. E. Sharp, 2000), 160.

41. Alan Wolfe, *The Transformation of American Religion: How We Actually Live Our Faith* (New York: Free Press, 2003). Not all commentators see religious individualism as threatening, lacking the capacity to influence modern culture, or devoid of communal involvement or social responsibility. Wade C. Roof's research on baby boomers accentuates a "reflexive spirituality" whereby self-growth actually enhances a sense of connectiveness. According to Roof, spiritual individualism does not necessarily threaten communal involvement. See Roof, *Spiritual Marketplace,* 163–269.

Likewise, Dillon et al. observe that the expectation that spirituality should lead to an increase in generative interests (an individual's concern with the goal of providing for the next generation) fits well with diverse psychological and adult development theories that link spiritual growth to higher levels of cognitive development and/or self-actualization associated with the maturational processes. Their study rejected the idea that institutionally autonomous spirituality exacerbates the increased cultural tendency toward social withdrawal or indifference toward the welfare of others. See Dillon et al., "Is Spirituality Detrimental to Generativity?" *Journal for the Scientific Study of Religion* 42 (2003): 427–42.

Besecke also argues that Roof's individualized "reflective spirituality" is positive as a type of cultural resource that Americans use to create guiding transcendent meanings for a rationalized society. See Kelly Besecke, "Speaking of Meaning in Modernity: Reflexive Spirituality as a Cultural Resource," *Sociology of Religion* 62 (2001): 365–81.

42. William V. D'Antonio et al., *American Catholics: Gender, Generation, and Commitment* (Walnut Creek, Calif.: Alta Mira Press, 2001), 28.

43. Dean R. Hoge, William D. Dinges, Mary Johnson, SNDdeN, and Juan L. Gonzales Jr., *Young Adult Catholics: Religion in the Culture of Choice* (Notre Dame, Ind.: University of Notre Dame Press, 2001), 226.

44. See, for example, James D. Davidson, et al., *The Search for Common Ground: What Unites and Divides Catholic Americans* (Huntington, Ind.: Our Sunday Visitor, 1997); William V. D'Antonio et al., *Laity: American and Catholic* (Kansas City, Mo.: Sheed & Ward, 1996); D'Antonio et al., *American Catholics;* Hoge et al., *Young Adult;* Robert Ludwig, *Reconstructing Catholicism for a New Generation* (New York: Crossroad, 1996); and Patrick H. McNamara, *Conscience First: Tradition Second* (Albany: State University of New York Press, 1992).

45. See, for example, the comments by Dr. Carol Guardo, president of the College of St. Benedict in St. Joseph, Minn., in "Crisis' Complexities Explored at Saint Mary's Dialogue," *Initiative Report* 8, no. 1 (April 2004): 2.

46. C. Kirk Hadaway, Penny Long Marler, and Mark Chaves, "What the Polls Don't Show: A Closer Look at U.S. Church Attendance," *American Sociological Review* 58 (December 1993): 741–52; Mark Chaves and J. C. Cavendish, "More Evidence on U.S. Catholic Church Attendance," *Journal for the Scientific Study of Religion* 33, no. 4 (1994): 376–81.

47. Hoge et al., *Young Adult,* 54.

48. Colleen Carroll, *The New Faithful: Why Young Adults Are Embracing Christian Orthodoxy* (Chicago: Loyola Press, 2002).

49. Davidson, *The Search;* Hoge et al., *Young Adult.*

50. D'Antonio, *American Catholics,* 22, 28, 36.

51. Hoge et al., *Young Adult,* 156; Davidson, *The Search,* 219; D'Antonio, *American Catholics,* 2001; S. R. Raferty and David C. Leege, "Catechesis, Religious Education and Parish," *Rpt. #14, Notre Dame Study of Catholics Parish Life* (Notre Dame, Ind.: University of Notre Dame Press, 1989).

52. Hoge et al., *Young Adult,* 51. Thirty-one percent were not registered in Davidson's study, *The Search,* 178–80.

53. D'Antonio et al., *American Catholics,* 47.

54. Only 15 percent of Catholic children attend Catholic elementary schools (see M. T. Reidy, "Needed: The Vision Thing — Rethinking the Mission of Catholic Primary Schools," *Commonweal* 131, no. 7 [April 9, 2004]: 15–18), and approximately two out of every three Catholics attending college are at a non-Catholic institution. See Bryan T. Froehle and Mary L. Gautier, *A Portrait of the Catholic Church in the United States* (Maryknoll, N.Y.: Orbis Books, 2000), 85.

55. Hoge et al., *Young Adult,* 42–43.

56. James D. Davidson, "Outside the Church: Whom Catholics Marry and Where," *Commonweal* 10 (September 1999): 14–16.

57. John T. McGreevy, *Parish Boundaries: The Catholic Encounter with Race in the Twentieth-Century Urban North* (Chicago: University of Chicago Press, 1996).

58. In the case of Latinos, however, research has shown that with each passing generation, Latinos are leaving the Catholic Church for Protestant denominations and other religions, even where many retain a Catholic sensibility in regard to moral and social issues (death penalty, abortion, immigration) and Democratic Party affiliation. See Ariela Keysar, Barry A. Kosmin, and Egon Mayer, *The PARAL Study: Religious Identification among Hispanics in the United States* (New York: Graduate Center for the City University of New York and Brooklyn College, 2001). In addition, the number of Latinos who now self-identify as professing no religion, or as atheist, agnostic, or secular, has doubled (from 6 to 13 percent [see Keysar, 5]) over the last decade. The sons and daughters of many Latino immigrants consider

themselves less religious than their parents and children. See also "Latinos Slip Away from Catholicism," *Washington Post*, May 12, 2001.

59. Egon Mayer, Barry Kosmin, and Ariela Keysar, *AJIS Report: American Jewish Identity Survey* (New York: The Center for Cultural Judaism, 2003), 30.

60. J. Korkin and T. Tseng, "Happy to Mix It All Up," *Washington Post*, June 8, 2003, B.

Even here, however, there are hints of changing religiosity in the face of ethnic assimilation. For example, our study of young adult Catholics indicates that, national origin variations notwithstanding, Latino Catholics in the United States tend to become like other Catholics in the belief and practice of their Catholicism over time. See Hoge, et al. *Young Adult*, 113–31. Arlene M. Sanchez Walsh's recent study also shows how evangelical groups encourage the severing of ethnic ties in favor of spiritual community. See Arlene M. Sanchez Walsh, *Latino Pentecostal Identity* (New York: Columbia University Press, 2004).

61. David J. O'Brien, *Public Catholicism* (New York: Macmillan, 1989).

62. William Portier, "Here Come the Evangelical Catholics," *Communio* 31 (Spring 2004): 35–65. See also Rausch, 2000.

63. Portier, "Here Come," 46.

64. Portier, "Here Come," 56.

65. Don Miller, *Reinventing American Protestantism*, 30.

66. Stephen Prothero, *American Jesus: How the Son of Man Became an American Icon* (Farrar, Straus & Giroux, 2004).

67. Vincent J. Miller, *Consuming Religion*, 213.

68. As noted, more positive assessments of religious individualism (or "reflexive spirituality") can be found in Roof, *Spiritual Marketplace* (1999); Dillon, Wink, and Fay, "Is Spirituality Detrimental?"; Fuller, *Spiritual but Not Religious;* and Besecke, "Speaking of," 365–81.

69. Michele Dillon, *Catholic Identity: Balancing Reason, Faith, and Power* (New York: Cambridge University Press, 1999), and Paul Lakeland, *The Liberation of the Laity: In Search of an Accountable Church* (New York: Continuum, 2003). Most of these points are made by Michele Dillon in her analysis of lay Catholic groups in opposition to official church teaching. The difficulty with Dillon's position from my point of view — following a critique by John Coleman, S.J. (see John Coleman, "Dissenting in Place," *America* [May 6, 2000]: 18–20) — is that Catholicism is not just a "culture system," a definition Dillon emphasizes as a way of accentuating the pliability and socially constructed nature of its symbol system. Catholicism is also a set of beliefs and doctrines that are bounded and, from the perspective of faith, rooted in revelation. As Coleman points out, there is a long history of rejecting as inimical to the received faith individuals and groups who held beliefs that overlapped with core ones, but who also held beliefs that were eventually deemed deviant by the Church's duly constituted authority. While Catholicism cannot be reduced solely to official Magisterial teachings, neither can it be divorced — implicitly or otherwise — from that teaching office as though "doctrinal engagement means that one reasoned opinion about the tradition is essentially as good as another" (Dillon). As Coleman notes, the historical conditioning of religious language, symbolism and meaning notwithstanding, "doctrinal engagement" is not an unbounded process.

70. David Gibson, *The Coming Catholic Church: How the Faithful Are Shaping a New American Catholicism* (San Francisco: HarperSanFrancisco, 2003), 65.

Chapter 3 / Culture's Catechumens and the Church's Task, Paul J. Griffiths

1. Augustine, De doctrina Christiana, 1.55. Compare Augustine, In epistulam Ioannis, 7.10.

2. The scriptural basis for this typology of malformed desire is 1 John 2:16. For an interesting — indeed, riveting — analysis of the three kinds of malformed desire, see Augustine, Confessions, Book 10, which is largely structured around them.

3. I discuss this theme of overwriting and erasure in "Christians and the Church," forthcoming in Gilbert Meilaender and William Werpehowski, eds., The Oxford Handbook of Christian Ethics (New York: Oxford University Press, 2006).

4. On the transition from a literate to a pre-literate culture and its meaning see, e.g., Ivan Illich, In the Vineyard of the Text: A Commentary to Hugh's Didascalicon (Chicago: University of Chicago Press, 1993); Barry Sanders, A is for Ox: Violence, Electronic Media, and the Silencing of the Written Word (New York: Pantheon, 1994); Sven Birkerts, The Gutenberg Elegies: The Fate of Reading in an Electronic Culture (Winchester, Mass.: Faber & Faber, 1994); Sven Birkerts, My Sky Blue Trades: Growing Up Counter in a Contrary Time (New York: Viking, 2002).

5. On late capitalism's fundamental logic see Fredric Jameson, Postmodernism, or, The Cultural Logic of Late Capitalism (Durham, N.C.: Duke University Press, 1991). On late capitalism's effects upon identity-formation, see Thomas Frank, The Conquest of Cool: Business Culture, Counterculture, and the Rise of Hip Consumerism (Chicago: University of Chicago Press, 1997). (Frank is also editor of the Chicago magazine The Baffler, much of which is devoted to this theme.) And on late capitalism and identitarianism, see Walter Benn Michaels, The Shape of the Signifier: 1967 to the End of History (Princeton: Princeton University Press, 2004).

6. On branding and Generation Y see Alissa Quant, Branded: The Buying and Selling of Teenagers (New York: Basic Books, 2003).

7. The distinctively American form of this drive for remaking has recently (and too sympathetically) been depicted by David Brooks in On Paradise Drive: How We Live Now (And Always Have) in the Future Tense (New York: Simon & Schuster, 2004). But it is no new theme in descriptions of America, surfacing as early as Tocqueville.

8. On consumerism, choice, and plasticity, see Terri Kapsalis, "Making Babies the American Girl® Way," The Baffler 15 (2002): 29–33. This essay is a classic of analytical anthropology and deserves to be much better known.

9. On the stimulus of desire, the niche market, and Lacan's analysis of "objects" which stimulate desire but are incapable of proving satisfaction and thus provoke further desire, see the many works of Slavoj Žižek, especially (with regard to the connections with Christianity) The Fragile Absolute — Or, Why Is the Christian Legacy Worth Fighting For? (London: Verso, 2000), and The Puppet and the Dwarf: The Perverse Core of Christianity (Cambridge, Mass.: M.I.T. Press, 2003).

10. John Locke, A Letter Concerning Toleration (1685), in Political Writings of John Locke, ed. David Wootton (New York: Mentor, 1993), 396.

11. 1 Corinthians 2:9: "...no eye has seen, nor ear heard, nor the heart of man conceived, what God has prepared for those who love him..." (Revised Standard Version); see also Isaiah 64:4.

Chapter 4 / On Taking the Creed Seriously, Luke Timothy Johnson

1. These opening remarks recast the classic distinction between *fides qua* and *fides quae*.

2. See L. T. Johnson, *The Creed: What Christians Believe and Why It Matters* (New York: Doubleday, 2004).

3. See L. T. Johnson, "The New Gnosticism: An Old Threat to the Church," *Commonweal* 131, no. 19 (2004): 29–31.

4. On both sides we see the signs of the loss of critical thinking, in the best sense of that term. The refusal to acknowledge the hierarchy of truths is the surest sign that theology has devolved to a form of ideology.

5. Johnson, *The Creed*, 40–41.

6. I have recently tried to think through such a connection in L. T. Johnson, "Caring for the Earth: Why Environmentalism Needs Theology," *Commonweal* 132, no. 13 (July 15, 2005): 16–20.

7. G. Gutiérrez, *A Theology of Liberation: History, Politics, and Salvation*, trans. and ed. Sister Caridad Inda and John Eagleson (Maryknoll, N.Y.: Orbis Books, 1971), 225–32; J. H. Yoder, *The Politics of Jesus: Vicit Agnus Noster* (Grand Rapids, Mich.: Eerdmans, 1972).

8. See J. S. Spong, *Born of a Woman: A Bishop Rethinks the Birth of Jesus* (San Francisco: HarperSanFrancisco, 1992); and J. S. Spong, *Resurrection: Myth or Reality?* (San Francisco: HarperSanFrancisco, 1994).

9. J. Hick, *The Myth of God Incarnate* (London: SCM Press, 1977); see my review in *Religious Education* 73 (1978): 253–54.

10. See A. Schweitzer, *The Quest of the Historical Jesus: From Reimarus to Wrede* (Baltimore: Johns Hopkins University Press, 1998 [1910]).

11. For a review of their works, see L. T. Johnson, *The Real Jesus: The Misguided Quest for the Historical Jesus and the Truth of the Traditional Gospels* (San Francisco: HarperSanFrancisco, 1996), 1–27, 39–50.

12. N. T. Wright, *Jesus and the Victory of God* (Minneapolis: Fortress Press, 1996); for my review of Wright, see L. T. Johnson, "A Historiographical Response to Wright's Jesus," in *Jesus and the Restoration of Israel: A Critical Assessment of N. T. Wright's Jesus and the Victory of God*, ed. C. N. Newman (Downers Grove, Ill.: InterVarsity Press, 1999), 206–24.

13. R. W. Funk, *Honest to Jesus: Jesus for a New Millennium* (San Francisco: HarperSanFrancisco, 1996); for my review, see *Society of Biblical Literature* 117 (1998): 740–42.

14. See M. Borg and N. T. Wright, *The Meaning of Jesus: Two Visions* (San Francisco: HarperSanFrancisco, 1999).

15. See W. C. Placher, *The Domestication of Transcendence: How Modern Thinking about God Went Wrong* (Louisville: Westminster John Knox, 1996); E. Brooks Holifield, *Theology in America: Christian Thought from the Age of the Puritans to the Civil War* (New Haven: Yale University Press, 2003).

16. J. P. Meier, *A Marginal Jew: Rethinking the Historical Jesus* (New York: Doubleday, 1991); see my remarks in Johnson, *The Real Jesus*, 126–33.

17. From among a vast literature, a few important works: E. Cassirer, *An Essay on Man* (New Haven: Yale University Press, 1944); M. Eliade, *Myth and Reality*,

trans. W. R. Trask (New York: Harper & Row, 1963); P. Ricoeur, *The Symbolism of Evil,* trans. E. Buchanan (Boston: Beacon Press, 1967), 161–357.

18. See D. F. Strauss, *The Life of Jesus Critically Examined,* ed. with an introduction by P. C. Hodgson, trans. G. Eliot (Philadelphia: Fortress Press, 1973 [1835]).

19. See L. T. Johnson, *Living Jesus: Learning the Heart of the Gospel* (San Francisco: HarperSanFrancisco, 1998).

20. Most recently, *Beyond Belief: The Secret Gospel of Thomas* (New York: Random House, 2003); for my review, see *Commonweal* 130 (May 23, 2003): 24–26.

21. *The Da Vinci Code: A Novel* (New York: Doubleday, 2003) has gone from being a publishing phenomenon to becoming a significant cultural indicator.

22. Indeed, there has been relatively little real opposition to forms of historical Jesus research and revisionist accounts of early Christianity from scholars, either, perhaps because so much of it appeared in popular rather than academic publications.

23. See L. T. Johnson, *The Living Gospel* (London: Continuum, 2004), 37–42.

24. I have tried to express the classical Christian understanding of salvation, and therefore of spirituality, in L. T. Johnson, *Faith's Freedom: A Classic Spirituality for Contemporary Christians* (Minneapolis: Fortress Press, 1990).

25. I have made an initial effort in this direction in my paper "The Revelatory Body: Notes toward a Somatic Theology," in *The Phenomenology of the Body,* ed. D. Martino (Pittsburgh: Simon Silverman Phenomenology Center at Duquesne University, 2003), 69–85.

26. See L. T. Johnson and W. S. Kurz, *The Future of Catholic Biblical Scholarship: A Constructive Conversation* (Grand Rapids, Mich.: Eerdmans, 2002).

Chapter 5 / The Metaphysics of Co-Inherence, Robert Barron

1. Peter Brown, *The Rise of Western Christendom* (Oxford: Blackwell Publishing, 2003), 372–73.

2. Charles Williams, *Essential Writings in Spirituality and Theology,* ed. Charles Hefling (Cambridge: Cowley Publications, 1993), 146–50.

3. Robert Barron, *The Strangest Way: Walking the Christian Path* (Maryknoll, N.Y.: Orbis Books, 2002), 36–40.

4. G. K. Chesterton, *The Everlasting Man,* in *G. K. Chesterton: Collected Works,* vol. 2 (San Francisco: Ignatius Press, 1986), 302.

5. Robert Sokolowski, *The God of Faith and Reason: Foundations of Christian Theology* (Notre Dame, Ind.: University of Notre Dame Press, 1982), 35–37.

6. Kathryn Tanner, *Jesus, Humanity, and the Trinity* (Minneapolis: Fortress Press, 2001), 12.

7. *Hic solus verus Deus bonitate sua et omnipotenti virtute non ad augendam suam beatitudinem, nec ad acquirendam, sed ad manifestandam perfectionem suam per bona...liberrimo consilio...de nihilo condidit creaturam...* Decretals of the First Vatican Council *Dei Filius,* chapter 1, in *Decrees of the Ecumenical Councils* vol. 2, ed. Norman Tanner, S.J. (Georgetown: Sheed and Ward, 1990), 805.

8. Robert Louis Wilken, *The Spirit of Early Christian Thought: Seeking the Face of God* (New Haven: Yale University Press, 2003), 146–50.

9. Thomas Aquinas, *De Potentia Dei,* q. 3, art. 3, ad 3, in *Quaestiones disputatae,* vol. 2 (Turino: Marietti, 1965), 43.

10. Aquinas, *De Potentia Dei,* q. 3, art. 3, ad 3.

11. John Milbank, *Theology and Social Theory: Beyond Secular Reason* (Oxford: Blackwell Publishers, 1990), 391.

12. James Alison, *The Joy of Being Wrong: Original Sin through Easter Eyes* (New York: Crossroad, 1998), 190.

13. Thomas Merton, *Conjectures of a Guilty Bystander* (New York: Doubleday, 1989), 156–57.

14. Merton, *Conjectures of a Guilty Bystander,* 157.

15. Joseph Ratzinger, *Introduction to Christianity* (San Francisco: Ignatius Press, 1990), 106.

16. John Polkinghorne, *Faith, Science, and Understanding* (New Haven: Yale University Press, 2000), 46–47.

17. Bernard Lonergan, *Method in Theology* (Toronto: University of Toronto Press, 1971), 42–44.

18. John Henry Newman, *Development of Christian Doctrine* (Westminster, Md.: Christian Classics, 1968), 33–38.

19. Karl Rahner, *Hearers of the Word* (New York: Herder and Herder, 1969), 42.

20. See Fergus Kerr, *After Aquinas: Versions of Thomism* (Oxford: Blackwell Publishing, 2002), 30.

21. James William McClendon, *Systematic Theology,* vol. 1, *Ethics* (Nashville: Abingdon Press, 1986), 43.

22. Pierre Hadot, *What Is Ancient Philosophy?* (Cambridge: Harvard University Press, 2002), 55–56.

23. Stanley Hauerwas, *Sanctify Them in the Truth: Holiness Exemplified* (Nashville: Abingdon Press, 1998), 26.

24. Colin E. Gunton, *The One, the Three, and the Many: God, Creation, and the Culture of Modernity* (Cambridge: Cambridge University Press, 1993), 28–35.

25. Jean-Paul Sartre, *Existentialisme est un humanisme* (Paris: Editions de Nagel, 1970), 21.

26. *Casey v. Planned Parenthood of Southeastern Pennsylvania,* 112 Sup. Ct. 2791 at 2807.

27. See Servais Pinckaers, O.P., *The Sources of Christian Ethics* (Washington, D.C.: Catholic University of America Press, 1995), 229.

Chapter 6 / The Church's Way of Speaking, Robert Louis Wilken

1. See 9.5.13, Augustine, *Confessions,* trans. Henry Chadwick (Oxford and New York: Oxford University Press, 1992), 163.

2. On the centrality of the Scriptures in shaping Christian thinking, see Robert Louis Wilken, *The Spirit of Early Christian Thought* (New Haven: Yale University Press, 2003).

3. Augustine, *City of God,* 10.21.

4. See *Sermon* 310.1, Augustine, *The Works of Saint Augustine,* part 3, vol. 9, trans. Edmund Hill (Hyde Park, N.Y.: New City Press, 1994), 68.

5. See *Enarrationes in Psalmos* 93.3, trans. Maria Boulding in Augustine, *Works,* part 3, vol. 18, 375–76.

6. Augustine, *Sermon*, 25.1.

7. For the examples I draw on Lauren Pristas, "Theological Principles That Guided the Redaction of the Roman Missal (1970)," *The Thomist* 67 (2003): 157–95.

8. Antoine Dumas, a member of the Sacred Congregation for Divine Worship, cited by Pristas.

9. Anscar Chapungco, "A Definition of Liturgical Inculturation," *Ecclesia Orans* 5 (1988): 19.

10. Romano Guardini, *The Spirit of the Liturgy* (New York: Crossroad, 1998), 66–67.

11. Augustine, *Confessions*, 9.4.8.

12. Paul J. Griffiths, "Christ and Critical Theory," *First Things* 145 (August–September 2004): 46.

13. See 1.2, Origen, *Contra Celsum*, trans. Henry Chadwick (Cambridge: Cambridge University Press, 1965), 8.

Chapter 7 / Communicating the Faith, Michael J. Himes

1. See St. Thomas Aquinas, *Summa theologiae* (Madrid: Biblioteca de Autores Cristianos, 1962–65), II-II, q. 6, a. 1.

2. Aquinas, *Summa*, II-II, q. 6, a. 1: *Et ideo fides quantum ad assensum, qui est principalis actus fidei, est a Deo interius movente per gratiam.*

3. Aquinas, *Summa*, I, q. 1, a. 1, ad 2: *Unde theologia quae ad sacram doctrinam pertinet, differt secundum genus ab illa theologia quae pars philosophiae ponitur.*

4. Yves Congar, "Tradition et sacra doctrina chez saint Thomas d'Aquin," in J. Betz and H. Fries, *Église et Tradition* (Paris: Le Puy, 1963), 157–94.

5. See St. Thomas Aquinas, *Compendium theologiae*, trans. Ross J. Dunn (Toronto: St. Michael's College, 1934), 1.

6. See St. Augustine, *De catechizandis rudibus*, trans. Joseph P. Christopher (Westminster, Md.: The Newman Bookshop, 1946), 4–5.

7. Nicholas Lash, *Believing Three Ways in One God: A Reading of the Apostles' Creed* (Notre Dame, Ind.: University of Notre Dame Press, 1992), 8.

8. Augustine, *De catechizandis rudibus* 6.

9. Augustine, *De catechizandis rudibus* 8. Since the best date for *De catechizandis rudibus* is around 400, it should be noted that questions which the older Augustine, embroiled in his anti-Pelagian struggle, would have certainly raised in describing the work of the teacher of faith, e.g., the gratuity of the grace of faith, go unmentioned.

10. Augustine, *Retractationes* 2, 4, 1, quoted in Mario Naldini, "Structure and Pastoral Theology of *Teaching Christianity*," in *Teaching Christianity: De doctrina christiana*, trans. by Edmund Hill, O.P., *The Works of Saint Augustine* part 1, vol. 11 (Hyde Park, N.Y.: New City Press, 1996), 11.

11. Augustine, *De doctrina christiana* 4, 27; in Hill's excellent translation, *Teaching Christianity*, 215. The reference is to Cicero's *De oratore* 21, 69.

12. Augustine, *De doctrina Christiana* 4, 29; *Teaching Christianity*, 217.

13. John Henry Newman, "The Tamworth Reading Room," in *Discussions and Arguments on Various Subjects* (London: Longmans, Green, and Company, 1872), 254–305. The seven essays were originally published as letters to *The Times* in 1841.

14. John Henry Newman, *The Idea of a University*, ed. Frank M. Turner (New Haven: Yale University Press, 1996), 61.

15. Newman, *The Idea of a University*, 62.

16. Newman, *The Idea of a University*, 99.

17. Newman, *The Idea of a University*, 99.

18. Among many places in Tillich's writing where this idea may be found, see Paul Tillich, *Dynamics of Faith* (New York: Harper & Row, 1957), 1.

19. John Henry Newman, "Implicit and Explicit Reason," in *Newman's University Sermons: Fifteen Sermons Preached before the University of Oxford, 1826–1843*, introduction by D. M. MacKinnon and J. D. Holmes (London: SPCK, 1970), 256.

20. Newman, "Implicit and Explicit Reason," 257.

21. Newman, "Implicit and Explicit Reason," 256f.

22. John Henry Newman, *An Essay in Aid of a Grammar of Assent* (Notre Dame, Ind.: University of Notre Dame Press, 1979), 49–52.

23. Karl Rahner, "The Word and the Eucharist," *Theological Investigations* 4 (London: Darton, Longman and Todd, 1966), 259.

24. Rahner, "The Word and the Eucharist," 259.

25. Rahner, "The Word and the Eucharist," 259.

26. Aquinas, *Summa*, II-II, q. 6, a. 1: *quod requiritur ad hoc quod homo aliquid explicite credat.*

27. Rahner, "The Word and the Eucharist," 259.

28. Karl Rahner, *Foundations of Christian Faith: An Introduction to the Idea of Christianity* (New York: Crossroad, 1978), 9.

29. Rahner, *Foundations of Christian Faith*, 11f.

30. G. K. Chesterton, "The Ethics of Elfland," *Heretics/Orthodoxy* (Nashville: Thomas Nelson, 2000), 207.

31. William Wordsworth, *The Prelude*, ed. Jonathan Wordsworth (London: Penguin, 1995), Bk. 14, 11, 446–47.

Chapter 8 / Handing on the Faith to the "New Athenians," Christopher and Deborah Ruddy

1. United States Conference of Catholic Bishops, "Catholics in Political Life," *www.usccb.org/bishops/catholicsinpoliticallife.shtml.*

2. The papers were: Archbishop William J. Levada, "Reflections on Catholics in Political Life and the Reception of Holy Communion"; Cardinal William H. Keeler, "Summary of Consultations"; and Cardinal Theodore McCarrick, "Interim Reflections: Task Force on Catholic Bishops and Catholic Politicians." They can be found at *www.usccb.org/bishops/taskforce.htm.*

3. Quoted in Peter Steinfels, "Beliefs: Documents Add to Abortion Debate," *New York Times*, June 26, 2004.

4. CBS News Poll, May 20–23, 2004. N=923 registered voters nationwide. MoE±3 (total sample).

"Which of these comes closest to your view? Abortion should be generally available to those who want it. Abortion should be available, but under stricter limits than it is now. OR, Abortion should not be permitted."

	Generally Available	Stricter Limits	Not Permitted	Unsure
	%	%	%	%
ALL	36	37	25	2
Catholics	34	37	28	1

Poll results are available at *www.pollingreport.com/abortion.*

5. See the contrast, for example, between the two following quotes:

"Perhaps there is no single teaching position articulated by the bishops that is better known throughout our country than this one: 'The Catholic Church opposes abortion.'" See Donald W. Wuerl, "Faith, Personal Conviction and Political Life," Loebig Lecture, May 25, 2004, *www.diopitt.org/addresses_loebig.pdf.*

And, "Catholics, by contrast [to evangelical white Protestants], look like the public at large in their views on abortion, despite the opposition from their church. Fifty-five percent of Catholics say abortion should be generally legal, and 28 percent say their religion is the main factor in their opinion on the subject—in both cases about the same as the population at large." — 2001 ABCNEWS/Beliefnet poll in Gary Langer, "Support for Legal Abortion Wobbles," July 2, 2001, *abcnews.go.com/sections/us/DailyNews/poll010702.html.*

6. John Courtney Murray, "Towards a Theology for the Layman: The Pedagogical Problem," *Theological Studies* 5 (1944): 349–52; see also 340–76.

7. See Pope Paul VI, *Evangelii nuntiandi* (Washington, D.C.: United States Catholic Conference, 1975), 20.

8. Pope Paul VI, *Evangelii nuntiandi,* 20.

9. Michael Paul Gallagher, *Clashing Symbols: An Introduction to Faith and Culture* (New York and Mahwah, N.J.: Paulist, 1998).

10. These four types are presented in Gallagher, *Clashing Symbols,* 113–16; all quotes in the remainder of this section are drawn from these pages.

11. It should be noted, though, that what Johann Baptist Metz has called — in a phrase that could come only from a German theologian — "productive noncontemporaneity" remains essential if the church is not to be wholly assimilated by its age. He sees such noncontemporaneity positively as (1) resistance to what is deformed in one's time and place, and (2) trust in one's heritage. J. Matthew Ashley writes, "As much as [Metz] criticizes nineteenth-century Catholic theology for sealing itself off from the intellectual and cultural debates raging in Europe, it is not because it failed to 'keep up with the times,' but because it demonstrated a failure of nerve, a failure to trust that that the substance of tradition was up to a thorough confrontation with modernity." See J. Matthew Ashley, "Introduction: Reading Metz," in Johann Baptist Metz, *A Passion for God: The Mystical-Political Dimension of Christianity,* ed. and trans. J. Matthew Ashley (New York and Mahwah, N.J.: Paulist, 1998), 10.

12. N. T. Wright, "Transforming the Culture: Main Address at the AFFIRM conference at Waikanae [New Zealand] in July 1999," online at *www.latimer.org.nz/morecomment.asp?CoID=85.* All subsequent quotations from Wright will come from this article.

13. Gallagher, *Clashing Symbols,* 121.

14. Gallagher, *Clashing Symbols,* 122.

15. Gallagher, *Clashing Symbols,* 123.

16. Gallagher, *Clashing Symbols,* 122.

17. Gallagher, *Clashing Symbols,* 130.

18. See, for instance, "The Hidden Wonder of New Life: *The Tablet,* interview with Professor Stuart Campbell," *The Tablet* 259 (July 10, 2004).

19. This phrase is from #83, Pope John Paul II, *Evangelium vitae* (Boston: Pauline Books, 1995).

20. Pope John Paul II, "Homily in Orioles Park at Camden Yards," online at *www.ewtn.com/library/papaldoc/jp2us95k.htm.*

21. See 4.4, Augustine, *The Trinity,* in St. Augustine, *The Works of Saint Augustine: A Translation for the 21st Century* I/9, trans. Edmund Hill, ed. John E. Rotelle (Brooklyn: New City Press, 1990), 155.

22. See *Sermon* 340A in *Works of St. Augustine* III/9, 299.

23. See also Anthony Kenny, "The Quiet Virtue," *The Tablet* 258 (January 3, 2004), 12, especially the following: "Humility is the virtue that counteracts this prejudice [of self-love]. It does so, by making the *presumption* that others' talents are greater, others' opinions more likely to be right. But only by approaching each conflict of interest and opinion with this presumption can one hope to escape the myopia that magnifies everything to do with oneself by comparison with everything to do with others."

24. Joseph Cardinal Bernardin, *The Gift of Peace* (Chicago: Loyola Press, 1997), 23.

25. Bernardin, *Gift of Peace,* 27.

26. Bernardin, *Gift of Peace,* 34.

27. Bernardin, *Gift of Peace,* 39.

28. Bernardin, *Gift of Peace,* 37–38.

29. Bernardin, *Gift of Peace,* 39–40.

30. Radcliffe takes this insight from Joseph Pieper, who writes: "Fortitude presupposes vulnerability; without vulnerability there is no possibility of fortitude. An angel cannot be brave, because he is not vulnerable. To be brave means actually to be able to suffer injury." See Joseph Pieper, *The Four Cardinal Virtues* (Notre Dame, Ind.: University of Notre Dame Press, 1966), 117. Radcliffe takes Pieper a step further when he then comments that it is easy for angels to say, "Do not be afraid," since they cannot be hurt themselves!

31. Radcliffe refers here to II-II q. 136, a. 4 of St. Thomas Aquinas, *Summa Theologiae.*

32. Paul VI, *Evangelii nuntiandi,* #41. See also #21: "Above all the Gospel must be proclaimed by witness. Take a Christian or a handful of Christians who, in the midst of their own community, show their capacity for understanding and acceptance, their sharing of life and destiny with other people, their solidarity with the efforts of all for whatever is noble and good. Let us suppose that, in addition, they radiate in an altogether simple and unaffected way their faith in values that go beyond current values, and their hope in something that is not seen and that one would not dare to imagine. Through this wordless witness these Christians stir up irresistible questions in the hearts of those who see how they live: Why are they like this? Why do they live in this way? What or who is it that inspires them? Why are they in our midst? Such a witness is already a silent proclamation of the Good News and a very powerful and effective one. Here we have an initial act of evangelization."

33. See Pope John Paul II, *Novo millennio ineunte* (Boston: Pauline Books, 2001), #33–34.

34. Pope John Paul II, *Evangelium vitae* #83.

35. See also Louis Dupré, "The Joys and Responsibilities of Being a Catholic Teacher," in *Faith and the Intellectual Life: Marianist Award Lectures,* ed. James L. Heft (Notre Dame, Ind.: University of Notre Dame Press, 1996), 67–68: "Indeed, religion ought to teach the student to raise questions before it presents definite answers. In no case should it remain satisfied with providing 'information' about sacred history, theology, or morals, without rendering that information meaningful, that is, fit to order the theory as well as practice of one's life and to expand their limits. In presenting the human encounter with transcendence, the educator must evoke the fundamental wonder that hides behind all reality, before attempting to define mystery in doctrine (which he also *must* do, and with all the rigor demanded by an academic discipline!).

"But religious education will not succeed in its task, neither the general nor the specific, unless it lays in the student the foundations of an interior life, the beginnings of a contemplative attitude. For this purpose some appreciation of silence appears indispensable. Without it the student will be incapable of creating the emptiness needed to be open to faith or, for that matter, to wonder. In silence we learn to take our distance from our surroundings, temporarily suspending the constant summons of the immediate. Perhaps the most valuable contribution of Quaker schools consists in the few minutes of silence that inaugurate each day. Only in silence does genuine prayer originate. I harbor no illusions about the use to which the child or adolescent puts this silence. As one pupil of a Quaker school whom I questioned about the matter, candidly informed me: 'We just look around and wait for it to stop.' Quite so, but during that short period of mostly boring emptiness everyday meanings cease to be taken for granted. That is why the student feels slightly embarrassed and resists this sudden leave-taking from the familiar world. In silence the student becomes capable of surprise and thus acquires a fundamental openness toward all aspects of life. And, to repeat it, creating such an *openness* should, I believe, be our most immediate objective in Catholic education. Without it we must abandon all hope of establishing any authentically religious or selflessly moral attitude."

36. e e cummings, "Pity this Busy Monster, Manunkind." This poem can be found at *www.americanpoems.com/poets/eecummings/328.*

37. Philip Murnion, "Letter to the Bishops," August 17, 2003, *www.nplc.org/murnion/letter.htm.*

38. See Pope John Paul II, *Ut unum sint* (Washington D.C.: United States Catholic Conference, 1995), #28.

39. See Charles Taylor, *Sources of the Self: The Making of the Modern Identity* (Cambridge, Mass.: Harvard, 1989).

40. Rowan Williams, "The Christian Priest Today: Lecture on the Occasion of the 150th Anniversary of Ripon College, Cuddesdon," *www.archbishopofcanterbury.org/sermons_speeches/040528.html.*

Chapter 9 / Communicating in Handing on the Faith, Terrence W. Tilley

In writing this essay, I depend on ideas (and occasionally adapt some prose) from some of my other work, including *The Evils of Theodicy* (Washington, D.C.: Georgetown University Press, 1991; chapters 1–3 on language); *Inventing Catholic Tradition* (Maryknoll, N.Y.: Orbis Books, 2000; the central notion of a religious tradition as a practice or set of practices); *History, Theology, and Faith: Dissolving the Modern Problematic* (Maryknoll, N.Y.: Orbis Books, 2004; the practices of communicating the faith); *Story Theology* (Wilmington, Del.: Michael Glazier, Inc., 1985; narrative as central and doctrine as derivative), and "Narrative and Communication Theology in a Postliterate Culture" (with Angela Ann Zukowski, M.H.S.H), *Catholic International* 12, no. 4 (November 2001): 5–11 (the effects of media). Thanks to Maureen Tilley, Dennis Doyle and Dermot Lane who read an early version of this essay and helped make it clearer and to my colleagues in the "Handing on the Faith Conference" who offered useful comments and criticism in a supportive atmosphere.

1. Bernard J. F. Lonergan, S.J., *Method in Theology* (New York: Herder and Herder, 1972), 132–33.

2. Walter J. Ong, S.J., *Faith and Contexts*, vol. 1, ed. Thomas J. Farrell and Paul A. Soukup, with an introduction by Thomas J. Farrell (Atlanta: Scholars Press, 1992), 199.

3. James Wm. McClendon Jr., *Systematic Theology*, vol. 1, *Ethics* (Nashville: Abingdon Press, 1986), 17.

4. James W. McClendon Jr., *Systematic Theology*, vol. 2, *Doctrine* (Nashville: Abingdon Press, 2000), 358–70.

5. McClendon, *Doctrine*, 370–72.

6. For my understanding of the relationship of *praxis* and practice, see Tilley, *Inventing Catholic Tradition*, 61–65.

7. This wisdom is the sort of virtue or ability that the Greek philosopher Aristotle called *phronesis*, St. Thomas Aquinas named *prudentia*, and John Henry Newman called the *illative sense*. See Terrence W. Tilley, *The Wisdom of Religious Commitment* (Washington, D.C.: Georgetown University Press, 1995), especially chapter 4.

8. Edward Schillebeeckx, O.P., "Prologue: Human God-Talk and God's Silence," *The Praxis of the Reign of God: An Introduction to the Theology of Edward Schillebeeckx*, ed. Mary Catherine Hilkert, O.P., and Robert Schreiter, C.P.P.S. (New York: Fordham University Press, 2002), ix.

9. Nicholas Lash, "Authors, Authority and Authorization," in *Authority in the Roman Catholic Church: Theory and Practice*, ed. Bernard Hoose (Aldershot: Ashgate, 2002), 60–61. One of Lash's points is to reject the equation of "authority" with "governance" in the Church. Governance is an aspect of teaching authority. And when authorities do not teach people how to live in and live out the tradition, but use their governing power to impose certain beliefs and practices on the community, they fail to educate the community in how to live as Christians in holiness and friendship.

10. I do not intend to ignore the concern for truth here or to support solipsistic or fideist positions. My own view on this is that "true" is properly an appraisal

term, a position developed in Tilley, *Story Theology,* 187–211, and Tilley, *Inventing Catholic Tradition,* 156–70.

11. I have argued elsewhere that doctrines are best understood as rules *derivative* from practice that serve to guide the continuation of the practice; see Tilley, *Inventing Catholic Tradition,* 106–10; also see Tilley, *Story Theology,* 1–17.

12. This seems to be especially apt if "faith" is construed as a supernaturally infused virtue. Avery Dulles, S.J., makes a similar point. He describes evangelization as follows: "Evangelization . . . should not be seen primarily as the communication of doctrine or even of a 'message.' It means introducing people to a blessed and liberating union with the Lord Jesus, who lives on in the community that cherishes his memory and invokes his Spirit. To evangelize . . . is never a matter of mere words. It is an invitation to others to enter the community of the disciples and to participate in the new consciousness that discipleship alone can bring. Evangelization is too often seen by Catholics as the responsibility of a small body of 'professionals,' who alone are presumed to be competent to unravel the complexities of 'Catholic doctrine. . . .' [E]very Christian can be called in some way to become a missionary. . . . Wherever they go, convinced Christians will seek to extend the way of life revealed by God in Jesus and thus to gain new disciples for the Lord." See Avery Dulles, *A Church to Believe In: Discipleship and the Dynamics of Freedom* (New York: Crossroad, 1982), 17.

13. This "know-how" is not merely technical knowledge, but wisdom or *phronesis. Phronesis* without technical ability may be merely dreaming rather than real wisdom, but the burden of chapter 4 of *Inventing Catholic Tradition* was to show that such knowing how to live in and live out a tradition cannot be rote skill or mere technique.

14. I do not mean to say that we do not teach. Certainly theologians' tasks include teaching, as the first two paragraphs of this essay suggested. However, when the knowledge to be communicated is fundamentally "know how" rather than "know that," coaching should be the primary pattern in which other forms of teaching are subsumed.

15. Brad Kallenberg, "The Gospel We Proclaim" (paper presented to the Billy Graham Center 2004 Evangelism Roundtable, April 22–24, 2004), 13. This is, of course, not merely technical training, but training meant to develop Christian wisdom, i.e., *phronesis,* having God's ways in mind/practice, rather than humans'.

16. Kallenberg, "The Gospel We Proclaim," 14.

17. Kallenberg, "The Gospel We Proclaim," 9–10.

18. I rely here on the important work of Vincent Miller, *Consuming Religion* (New York: Continuum Publishing, 2004).

19. See Walter A. Effross, "Owning Enlightenment: Proprietary Spirituality in the 'New Age' Marketplace," *Buffalo Law Review* 51, no. 3 (2003): 483–678.

20. Miller, *Consuming Religion,* 106.

21. William A. Clebsch, *Christianity in European History* (New York: Oxford, 1979), 233. Clebsch's provocative work focuses on Christian lifestyles in some sense typical of various eras. Clebsch's work suggests that in every era, the multiple patterns of being Christian fall into two distinct categories: those that seek more to redeem the good in the ambient culture and those that seek to oppose what is evil

in the culture. Both patterns are good ways to be Christian, even if they are not perfectly congruent with each other. This duality of pattern types also can be discerned in our consumer culture as well, as the next paragraphs seek to show.

22. For elaboration of the relations between institutions, traditions, beliefs, and communities, see Tilley, *The Wisdom of Religious Commitment,* chapter 2.

23. Edward Farley, *Good and Evil: Interpreting a Human Condition* (Minneapolis: Fortress, 1990), 290.

24. Avery Dulles, *A Church to Believe In,* 15.

25. Dulles, *A Church to Believe In,* 16.

26. Stanley Hauerwas, *With the Grain of the Universe* (Grand Rapids, Mich.: Brazos Press, 2001), 212.

27. McClendon, *Doctrine,* 361–62.

28. Clebsch, *Christianity in European History,* 76.

29. See Peter Brown, "The Rise and the Function of the Holy Man in Late Antiquity," *Journal of Roman Studies* 61, no. 1 (1971): 80–101.

Chapter 10 / Handing on the Faith, Thomas Groome

1. See Graham Rossiter, "The Need for a Creative Divorce Between Catechesis and Religious Education," *Religious Education* 77, no. 1 (January–February 1982).

2. For further elaboration see my essay, "Religious Education and Catechesis: No Divorce for the Children's Sake," *The Furrow* 53, no. 11 (November 2002).

3. In 1997, the Vatican issued a new *General Directory for Catechesis.* The GDC replaces even as it builds upon the *General Catechetical Directory* of 1971. Like its predecessor, it is likely to set the tone and tenor of catechetical education for the coming era in the Catholic Church. See Congregation for the Clergy, *General Directory for Catechesis* (Washington, D.C.: USCCB, 1998).

4. Robert Barron's essay in this collection offers a powerful argument that a "communitarian manner of knowing" that is "thoroughly participative" is demanded by the classic Catholic sense of God's relationality and ours.

5. The participative pedagogy proposed by Johann Herbart (1776–1841) was a particular influence on the Munich Method, and likewise the insights of emerging child psychology. Most of the architects of modern education — Dewey, Montessori, Piaget — reflect the influence of Herbart. For some brief readings in Herbart, and a bibliography, see *Basic Writings in Christian Education,* ed. Kendig B. Cully (Philadelphia: Westminster Press, 1950), 265–74.

6. For an overview see G. Emmett Carter, *The Modern Challenge to Religious Education* (New York: W. H. Sadlier, 1961), esp. chapter 15.

7. As Luke Timothy Johnson writes in this collection, "if faith is not a faithful life, then it is nothing." See also Terrence Tilley's essay for this emphasis on faith as its practices, including the "practice of believing."

8. Luke Timothy Johnson's essay is refreshing about the centrality of the Creed. However, since the patristic era, the Church has had a strong sense that the "content" of its faith is a tripod of creed, cult, and code — its central beliefs and convictions, its sacraments and worship, and its morality and virtues. This threefold mosaic of "the content" of Christian faith has been reflected in all the great catechisms over the Church's history, including the most recent *Catechism of the Catholic Church* (1994).

9. See Tom Beaudoin, "In Praise of Young Adult Faith: Post-Vatican II Formation Produced Strong Performative Literacy," *Celebration,* 33, no. 6 (June 2004).

10. Here I touch on one of my reservations about the "generations of faith" approach as I understand it; it tends to downplay the need for formal programs of instruction, and ties its scope and sequence unduly to the liturgical season and the Sunday lectionary. Lectionary-based catechesis can be a great complement to catechetical education but is not likely to give access to "the whole Christian Story."

11. See Martin Luther, "To the Councilmen of All Cities in Germany That They Establish and Maintain Christian Schools," in *Basic Writings in Christian Education,* ed. Kendig Cully (Philadelphia: Westminster Press, 1960), 135–49.

12. "Decree on Education," #3, in *The Documents of Vatican II,* ed. Walter Abbott (New York: America Press, 1966), 641.

13. "Decree on Laity," #2, in *Documents,* Abbott, 491.

14. "Constitution on the Liturgy," #14, in *Documents,* Abbott, 144.

15. "Church in Modern World," #1, in *Documents,* Abbott, 199–200.

16. "Constitution on the Church," #37, in *Documents,* Abbott, 64

17. "Constitution on the Church," #11, in *Documents,* Abbott, 29.

18. See Elliot Eisner, *The Educational Imagination* (New York: Macmillan, 1979).

19. "Constitution on the Sacred Liturgy," #33 and 59, in *Documents,* Abbott, 149 and 158.

20. "Constitution on the Sacred Liturgy," #14, in *Documents,* Abbott, 144.

21. "Constitution on Revelation," #21, in *Documents,* Abbott, 125.

22. "Constitution on Revelation," #13, in *Documents,* Abbott, 121.

23. Though the GDC uses the language of "correlation" between "life" and "the Faith," I prefer "integration" as a stronger and more adequate term for what is needed.

24. For a complete statement of a "shared praxis approach," see Groome, *Sharing Faith* (Portland, Ore.: Wipf and Stock edition, 1998), esp. chapters 4–10.

25. "Constitution on the Church in the Modern World," #44, in *Documents,* Abbott, 246.

26. Quoted in Robert Schreiter, "Faith and Cultures: Challenges to a World Church," *Theological Studies* 50, no. 4 (December 1989): 752. The essay by Christopher and Deborah Ruddy in this collection has a similar quote from Pope John Paul II and his homily at Baltimore, 1995.

Chapter 11 / Handing on the Faith through Community-Based Faith Formation, Bishop Blase Cupich

1. John C. Cavadini, "Ignorant Catholics: The Alarming Void in Religious Education," *Commonweal* (April 9, 2004): 12–14.

2. As our diocese opted for Generations of Faith authored by the *Center for Ministry Development,* my description of an inter-generational model will be based on the materials they provided me in preparing my text. See "Generations of Faith," Center for Ministry Development, *www.cmdnet.org.*

3. See number 158, Congregation for the Clergy, *General Directory for Catechesis* (Washington, D.C.: USCCB, 1998).

4. See *Catechism of the Catholic Church,* 2nd ed. (Washington, D.C.: United States Catholic Conference, 2000).

Afterword / John C. Cavadini

1. Martyrdom is, of course, the supreme witness, and provides the extreme example of where Christians can be edified from persons of other cultures: "Martyrs and in general all saints light up every period of human history by reawakening its moral sense. Martyrdom represents the high point of the witness all Christians must daily be ready to give. Faced with the many difficulties that fidelity to the moral order can demand even in the most ordinary circumstances, the Christian is called, with the grace of God invoked in prayer, to a sometimes heroic commitment. Christians are not alone in this. They are supported by the moral sense in peoples and the great religious and sapiential traditions of East and West, from which the mysterious workings of the Holy Spirit are not absent." See John Paul II, *Veritatis Splendor* 93–94, from John Paul II, *The Encyclicals in Everyday Language,* ed. by Joseph G. Donders (Maryknoll, N.Y.: Orbis, 2001), 234–35.

2. See John Paul II, *Ex Corde Ecclesiae* (Washington, D.C.: United States Catholic Conference, 1990), 16, emphasis original.

3. See *Catechism of the Catholic Church* (Mahwah, N.J.: Paulist Press, 1994), 11,.

4. "Catechesis aims . . . at developing understanding of the mystery of Christ in the light of God's word, so that the whole of a person's humanity is impregnated by that word." See John Paul II, *Catechesi Tradendae* 20, from John Paul II, *On Catechesis in Our Time* (Washington, D.C.: United States Catholic Conference, 1979), 29. On the balance between practice and understanding, see, for example, in section 23: " . . . sacramental life is impoverished and very soon turns into hollow ritualism if it is not based on serious knowledge of the meaning of the sacraments, and catechesis becomes intellectualized if it fails to come alive in sacramental practice" (33). Also, at section 19, "The specific character of catechesis, as distinct from the initial conversion-bringing proclamation of the Gospel, has the twofold objective of maturing the initial faith and of educating the true disciple of Christ by means of a deeper and more systematic knowledge of the person and the message of our Lord Jesus Christ" (27). Again, at section 25, "Thus through catechesis the Gospel kerygma . . . is gradually deepened, developed in its implicit consequences, explained in language that includes an appeal to reason, and channeled towards Christian practice in the Church and the world" (34).

5. "The sermons [of Augustine] consistently present faith as the *sine qua non* for understanding, but even more importantly they style the faith of the hearers as a posture of inquiry or seeking. Not everyone may understand at present, but the sermons direct everyone's faith, preacher as well as hearers, toward understanding." I am quoting myself here, from an article that treats this topic in Augustine's sermons in more detail: John C. Cavadini, "Simplifying Augustine," in *Educating People of Faith,* ed. John Van Engen, (Grand Rapids, Mich.: Eerdmans, 2004).

6. From this point of view, I cannot accept Luke Timothy Johnson's call to recover the category of "myth" as in the phrase, "the Christian myth," referring to such central stories as the Incarnation and Resurrection of Christ. For one thing, it would be difficult to disentangle Johnson's understanding of the word "myth" in this context from that represented by those who have spoken of the "myth of God Incarnate" precisely in order to promote christologies from below as based on the "historical" Jesus free of mythological language, and those who use the word "myth"

with reference to Christian doctrines in order to separate the essential meaning of the doctrines from their supposed mythological form.

Further, one should reflect on how much the Old Testament is invested in distinguishing its teaching from what is commonly called myth. Are we to speak of Genesis 1:1–2:3 as a "creation myth" when it seems so heavily invested in polemic against a Babylonian mythic epic of the origin of the world? Not only the Bible but the Church Fathers engage in critique both of classical Greek and Roman myths as well as of philosophical readings of those myths. Christian and Jewish discourse does not seem to present an alternative myth so much as to be seeking another kind of narrative, related to history in an interesting and complex way, admittedly, but not a-historical. This is also what Johnson is after, and I am not sure why the traditional language of "mystery" and "doctrine" is not adequate instead of "myth." "Handing on the Christian myth" leaves one with an agenda of endless qualification over the term "myth" before any actual handing on can occur.

Finally, distinguishing Christian doctrine from "myth" might be an especially important task in places such as Africa where Christianity is experiencing massive growth and where the relationship between Christianity and native religions is recognized as an interestingly complex challenge.

7. See John Paul II, *Catechesi Tradendae* 15.

8. See Simone Weil, "Implicit Forms of the Love of God," in *Waiting for God,* trans. Emma Craufurd (New York: Harper & Row, 1973).

9. See Augustine, *Sermon* 223D.3, but this is a frequent admonition in his Easter Vigil sermons: see also *Sermons* 223B.2, 223F.3, 223G.2, 223J, 223K, etc. St. Augustine, *The Works of St. Augustine: A Translation for the 21st Century* III/6, trans. Edmund Hill, O.P. (New Rochelle, N.Y.: New City Press, 1993).

10. Augustine, *Sermon* 223I.

11. Augustine, *Sermon* 223K.

12. Augustine, *Sermon* 223J.

Index

Of Related Interest

Ronald Rolheiser

SECULARITY AND THE GOSPEL
Being Missionaries to Our Children

Holy Longing author Ronald Rolheiser has brought together an international group of the best writers on Catholic spirituality, theology, and pastoral work to reflect on secularity, the #1 challenge of our day. In the recent past, "missionary work" meant bringing the familiar Gospel to faraway places and foreign peoples. In secular America today, even our own children know little about the Gospel. In this major volume, Rolheiser offers original chapters on the question, then introduces the leading voices in Catholic thought to show how Christian faith can thrive in a secular world. Themes include: the history of secularism and enlightenment; secular cultures around the world; rediscovering prophetic Christianity; Christ-centered life; living for others; true service to the poor. Contributors include Gilles Routhier, Michael Downey, Robert Schreiter, Robert Barron, Mary Jo Leddy, Reginald Bibby, and Ronald Young.

0-8245-2412-8, paperback

Check your local bookstore for availability.
To order directly from the publisher,
please call 1-800-707-0670 for Customer Service
or visit our Web site at *www.cpcbooks.com*.
For catalog orders, please send your request to the address below.

THE CROSSROAD PUBLISHING COMPANY
16 Penn Plaza, Suite 1550
New York, NY 10001

All prices subject to change.

crossroad